the Dark Night
of the Soul

The Soul's Journey to Sacred Love

Acclaim for
YOGA AND THE DARK
NIGHT OF THE SOUL

"What do Arjuna (of *Bhagavad Gita* fame) and St. John of the Cross have in common? Among other things, both experience a 'dark night of the soul'—that is to say, they undergo necessary purgations on the path to transcendence. But do these two luminaries have a monopoly on this proverbial dark night? No. We are all privy to such existential tribulation, sooner or later, and Simon Haas makes careful record of this. In his stimulating and informative work, *Yoga and the Dark Night of the Soul*, Haas uses Arjuna's dark night to explore his own, thereby lending a hand to his own healing and, by extension, to ours. His focus, in particular, is the yoga tradition and India's ancient *bhakti* texts, primarily the *Bhagavad Gita*. Drawing on his own realization and that of the sages, he brings readers into the 'light' of enlightenment, showing us that the dark night is not so dark after all, but is, rather, a catalyst to illumination. This is an authoritative, metaphysical book on yoga that takes one beyond the needs of the body and mind and situates one in spiritual luminescence. What more can a discerning reader ask for?"

—STEVEN J. ROSEN (SATYARAJA DASA), author of some thirty books on Vaishnavism and related subjects; senior editor of the *Journal of Vaishnava Studies*; and associate editor of *Back to Godhead* magazine

"A true delight and pleasure to read, which I hope to share with young people across the world who wish to deepen their understanding of the true, majestic science of yoga."

—CHARLOTTA MARTINUS, founder of TeenYoga and Director at Universal Yoga Ltd

"Simon Haas has done it again. With the clear perception of a sage, he has retold this ancient classic, the *Bhagavad Gita*, in a way everyone can understand. ... I have used Haas's *The Book of Dharma: Making Enlightened Choices* as a course book for our students in yoga teacher training. This too will become part of our curriculum."

—DR RICHARD A. MASLA, founder of Ayurveda Health Retreat and of YogaVeda School of Yoga & Ayurveda

"Haas draws generously from the *Bhagavad Gita* and other classical yoga texts, alongside colourful narratives from his own spiritual journey and travels. From a little girl at Heathrow airport and a dog on the Yorkshire Moors, to holy men in crematoriums and Indian monkeys, we hear inspiring stories sure to open our hearts and minds in learning to appreciate the potential power in darkness to rewrite our own life stories from ones of fear and confusion into those of love and compassion."

—CATHERINE L. SCHWEIG, chief editor of *Goddess: When She Rules* (Golden Dragonfly Press, 2017) and author of over fifty articles on yoga and the *Bhagavad Gita*

"*Yoga and the Dark Night of the Soul* is by far one of the best books I've read. It's an eye-opening and heart-touching, beautifully crafted tapestry on the nature of difficult life experiences, and on how best to navigate through them. ... Every page and chapter has an uplifting message and delivers immense value for the well-being of the body, mind and self. I highly recommend it."

—ARIADNA LANDMAN, Ayurvedic medicine teacher and practitioner; founder of VitalVeda

"The writing is beautifully balanced, simple yet profound and poetic, eloquent yet direct and accessible. Simon's insights, guidance and stories warm the heart and mind."

—DYLAN HENDRIX, teacher of yoga and author of *Art of the Storm* (Balboa Press, 2017)

"A timely yoga read and ideal travel companion. I highly recommend this yoga book to anyone on a yoga journey, especially yoga teachers and students; it is a must."

—TWANNA DOHERTY, CEO at Yogamatters

"As an accomplished representative of an authentic spiritual tradition that has taught the *Bhagavad Gita* for millennia, Simon Haas guides us on a mystical journey within ourselves that leads to realms of everlasting, transcendent happiness. *Yoga and the Dark Night of the Soul* makes for compelling reading and is sure to become a classic in its genre."

—KRISHNA DHARMA, author of the world's bestselling retellings of the great Indian epics *Mahabharata* and *Ramayana*

"Simon Haas elegantly sheds light on the ancient text *Bhagavad Gita*, revealing its profound relevance to daily life. Haas weaves beautiful real-life stories into the context of this ancient wisdom, making it accessible at a time when it is so needed, in a way that perhaps has never been done before."

—JONATHAN GLASS, M.AC., C.A.T., Ayurveda practitioner and author of *Total Life Cleanse: A 28-Day Program to Detoxify and Nourish the Body, Mind, and Soul* (Healing Arts Press, 2018)

ALSO BY SIMON HAAS:

The Book of Dharma: Making Enlightened Choices

SIMON HAAS

Yoga and the Dark Night of the Soul

The Soul's Journey to Sacred Love

VEDA WISDOM BOOKS

Readers interested in the subject matter of this book are invited
to correspond with the author at **simon@simonhaas.com**

Published by Veda Wisdom Books
an imprint of The English Word Factory
www.englishwordfactory.com

Veda Wisdom Books is committed to a sustainable future.
All our books are printed on at least partly recycled or
sustainable paper.

VEDA WISDOM BOOKS

First published in Great Britain
First edition, 2018

ISBN 978-0-9575185-2-0

To my younger brother David,
who fought cancer
and survived

Contents

SET OUT ON THE JOURNEY OF THE SOUL.

LET EVERY STEP BE ITS OWN REWARD.

LET DISCERNMENT BE THE WARRIOR'S SWORD.

LET SACRED LOVE BE YOUR ONLY GOAL.

Prologue

The Journey

Homo sapiens sapiens, "human, the extremely wise". That's the name we've given our species.[1]

Today, we have access to more information than ever before, yet it struck me (even at a young age) that we're still far from wise. The name we've given humankind is more of an aspiration, an aim. Given the destruction of our planet and our capacity for greed, suffering and irrational delusions, we might, perhaps more truthfully, have named our species *Homo avarus*, "human, the greedy", *Homo vastans*, "human, the destroyer" or *Homo patiens*, "suffering human".

As a young teen, I wondered why so many of us live in a state of restless dissatisfaction with life. I hoped I might find a mentor, an example to follow; but wherever I looked, I saw people struggling with the same basic challenges: jealousy, anger, frustration, boredom, dissatisfaction. I was no exception, of course. A witness to the difficulties experienced by loved ones, I questioned Western culture's response to crises and where our perspectives might be failing us.

I began searching for answers in the world's wisdom traditions. Without knowing it, I was embarking on an inner voyage of discovery, the start of my own journey of the soul.

My search led me to the ancient yoga texts of India. One of these is the *Bhagavad Gita*, a classic on yoga wisdom.[2] In the *Bhagavad Gita* (or *Gita* for short), Arjuna, the greatest warrior of his time, falls into a deep existential crisis, a dark night of the soul, in the middle of two opposing armies facing off for battle. Krishna, his dear friend and charioteer, then imparts to him the transformative yoga teachings of the *Gita* to help him through his crisis.[3]

The *Gita* teaches us how to make daily life our yoga practice. It offers practical methods to shift our perception of the world and of ourselves, so we may become more effective in our everyday life. The aim is not *information*, but *transformation*.

In search of a wisdom capable of directing safe passage through life's tempests and of eliciting our highest potential, I had accidentally stumbled upon the ancient lessons that make such transcendence possible. Mastery of these yoga teachings awakens our innate power, allowing us to inhabit "a state of wholeness, even though your body may be broken; a state of riches, even though you may have no earthly possessions; a state of imperturbable peace and quietude, even though the world around you may go up in flames."[4]

As I was about to discover, the *Gita* contains all the wisdom of India's forgotten civilization, in just 700 short verses.[5]

If I could truly comprehend the *Gita's* teachings, I might be able to understand the essence of all of India's sacred lore. What better place to start in the discovery of self. I longed to learn more.

However, I oddly found myself unable to enter the *Gita's* yoga teachings with the depth I desired. Regardless of how hard I tried, I couldn't unlock their secrets. The reason was simple: in ancient India, the "self-help" genre simply didn't exist. The *Gita* is, therefore, more of a teacher's manual. Every verse, even every line, contains a "universe" of meaning that can transform the way we live, if we can but shift our perception to receive what it expresses.

But how was I to make that transition from intellectual learning—what the ancients describe as "mere weariness of the tongue"—to yogic perception?[6] I noticed that the *Gita* itself reveals that these age-old yoga teachings have been passed down from master to student for generations in ancient lineages (called *parampara*).[7] I decided to seek out a teacher in one of these sacred lineages.

I reduced all my worldly possessions to a single suitcase and travelled to India, making my way to the ancient town of Mathura and surrounding land of Braj, where Krishna, the speaker of the *Gita*, was born. I yearned for an understanding of yoga's deeper meanings from within one of India's authentic living traditions. I was 16 years old.

But how would I find the perfect teacher, one whom the

Gita describes as a "truth seer"?[8] In India, I encountered many with great knowledge, but I was determined to find someone who truly *lived* what they knew. If my teacher wasn't living these teachings, how would he or she be able to show me how to live them?

Wherever I went, I prayed quietly with all my heart: "Let me find a teacher, a real 'truth seer'. Where can I find you? Please reveal yourself to me."

−2−

The heavy wooden doors of the ashram, or guesthouse, were bolted shut for the night. I called out, but there was no reply. It was past 11pm.

What was I to do now? I could hammer on the doorframe with a large rock and start yelling loudly—but I hesitated. This was the sacred town of Vrindavan in the heart of Braj. I was a guest here, and I didn't want to disturb anyone. I preferred simply to wait for the doors to open again at about 4am. At that time, ringing bells and Sanskrit prayers resound from homes and temples as the town rises prior to the sun.

To pass the time, I wandered the dark, empty streets of Vrindavan, looking for somewhere to sit or lay down. A dog howled in the distance.

On one street, I found a wooden platform against a wall, just outside an old temple. During the day, it was used by street vendors to sell flowers. How different everything looked in the lonely, solemn stillness of the night. I lay down on the platform and covered myself with a thin woollen cloth, called a chaddar.

There are sadhus, or shamans of the heart, who come to Braj to perfect their spiritual practice. In doing so, they are granted access to a subtle side of Braj, a mystical, non-physical realm, invisible to the common eye, in which the truth of the land is revealed through their yoga meditation.

That arcane land of Braj is protected on all sides by a powerful guardian named Mahadeva. He is its gatekeeper. Those who are merely tourists, rather than pilgrims of the heart, cannot gain entrance: all they see is the dust, bustle and noise of a small town in North India.

Desiring to enter that sacred side of Braj, pilgrims first seek the blessings of Mahadeva. I had neglected to do this. I simply didn't know. But it so happened that the spot I had picked to rest that night was just outside an old temple dedicated to him.

That night, Mahadeva came into my dreams, his figure filling the sky. He was a dark bluish colour, and his eyes were beautiful, like lotus petals. The waters of the Ganges cascaded out of his matted hair. To my surprise, I saw the crescent moon adorning his head. It was difficult to divert my eyes from his captivating face.

"I am the gatekeeper of this land," Mahadeva said, his voice deep like a thunderous sky. "What do you want? Are you lost?"

"I've come to find a teacher," I replied, with folded hands.

Mahadeva smiled. "But there are so many; just look around you and pick one."

"I would like a teacher of the highest level, one who will teach me the yoga of loving service and help me dedicate my life to Shri Radha, the Goddess of Devotion, who rules this land."

"You are asking too much," Mahadeva replied.

"Then I will simply stay here and wait," I said. "You're the gatekeeper of this land. Surely you must know what I can do."

Mahadeva relented: "On Ekadashi, the eleventh day of the moon, make a *sankalpa* and do *parikrama*."

–3–

Thousands of pilgrims were walking barefoot on the pathway towards the River Yamuna. There were families with children; businessmen from New Delhi, their toes poking out beneath their suit trousers; young girls holding hands; and even elderly pilgrims with canes. I learned that these pilgrims were performing a sacred ritual capable of fulfilling all desires. Vrindavan, Krishna's homeland, is encircled by a dust path. For centuries, pilgrims have walked this six-mile path clockwise and barefoot, especially on the eleventh lunar day of the waxing and waning moon. This ancient practice is known as *parikrama*.

However, I noticed that a few pilgrims, instead of walking, covered the entire distance by doing continuous whole-body prostrations to the earth. I watched them with awe, as they neglected the physical hardships of heat, fatigue and the rough, stony earth.

Prostrating themselves on the ground, they extended their arms above their head to place a stone as a marker. Then standing up behind the stone, they picked it up and prostrated themselves again, repeating this over and over, thousands of times. If done with humility and devotion, an incredible inner transformation takes place, and one emerges a different person. It's also said that whatever wish one has made will come true.

A prostration, called a *pranam*, is a simple, but powerful, yoga practice that has largely been lost in translation in the West. When done with the entire body, it is known as *dandavat-pranam*, or literally, "Stick-Like Prostration".[9] It's one of the oldest yoga practices. As I was to discover later, this yoga movement is a physical representation of the most confidential teachings of the *Bhagavad Gita*.

In this quiet practice, we lay down our burdens and literally embrace the earth. Eight specific parts of the body touch the ground: thighs, feet, hands, chest, mind, head, speech and eyes. As our own belly touches the belly of the earth, we feel a primal connection; we experience the surrender of our own individual self.

In this act of letting go, we're able to hear a voice that differs from the endless chatter of the mind, one we couldn't hear before: the voice of the Soul of the Universe, present within the heart of all beings. By closing the outer ear, we awaken the inner ear. And when we speak, our words come from a heart purified by humility and devotion. This is the ground from which the most potent prayers emerge.[10]

If Stick-Like Prostration could speak, it would say, "I've spent my days lost in self-interest, following the dictates of the illusory ego. This has only enlarged the problems of my life. I now surrender my ego unto you, Soul of the Universe, and dedicate my body, mind and words in your service. I lie before you like a stick in full dedication, touching the ground with eight parts of me to make it true. Today, let me be your instrument."

It was November and extremely cold in the early mornings. A bitter fog covered the landscape. At 4:30am, I made my way to the path that circled Krishna's town. In 1991, the path was sandy and lined with beautiful trees and flowering shrubs.

I found a smooth, ochre stone on the side of the path and, holding it to my heart, I fixed my intent for the yoga practice I was about to begin. This is the confidential art of making a *sankalpa*, which we'll discuss further in these pages. The Sanskrit *sankalpa* means "definite intention", "resolve" or "vow". When performed correctly, a *sankalpa* has the power to reshape our destiny.

Having set my intent, I began my first prostration. And my second. And my third. After two hours, I looked back: I had covered a short distance only. This was going to be extremely difficult.

I made my way along the old sandy riverbed where the Yamuna River once flowed. It was lined by beautiful bathing ghats with steps that led into golden sands.

The sun began to rise on the eastern horizon. My knees felt numb. My muscles ached. Soon I was passing the reddish sandstone steps of Keshi Ghat, where the Yamuna still flows. I paid homage to the sacred river, sprinkling some of its water on my head, and continued on my way.

As the pathway around Vrindavan became more challenging, laced with sharp stones, I wrapped a cloth around my head like a turban, to protect myself from the sun. With every prostration, I felt my illusory ego, my false sense of self, weakening and dissolving. A tender humility was beginning to sprout in the heart.

In the *Bhagavad Gita*, when Arjuna asks Krishna, "What is knowledge?" he responds with a series of esteemed qualities, the first of which is humility. The root of all virtues, humility is also the foundation of yoga. Bending to the earth in sincerity, we open our hearts, minds and energy to the service of others, and above all, to the service of sacred love.

As I continued with my prostrations, I recalled at one point the events in my life that had led me to this place. Trials in our life, sometimes in our childhood, can lead us to question life and to search for deeper truths beyond the prosaic and mundane. They can propel us on a quest for deeper wisdom, a journey of the soul. For me, that defining event was losing my mother at the age of 4 years.

With sincere devotion, I continued offering prostrations, tolerating the heat, traffic, fatigue and sharp stones. It took me three days to complete the full six miles around Vrindavan. Filled with joy and spiritual strength, I closed the circle with a final prostration. I held the smooth, ochre stone—my little companion on this pilgrimage—to my heart. Tears in my eyes, I remembered my *sankalpa*, my deepest desire, one last time and returned the stone to where I had found it.

A few days later an elderly monk of the highest order, a master-practitioner in the Bhakti tradition, visited Vrindavan. Born in 1921, and dressed in simple cotton the colour of the rising sun, he was effulgent with piercing blue eyes. In his hand, he carried a *danda*, or stick, representing paramount surrender: full dedication of one's body, mind and words.

The moment I saw him, I knew I had found my teacher. In my heart, I offered Stick-Like Prostration at his feet, and my body followed automatically, all eight parts of me touching the ground in his direction.

As my forehead touched the earth, I remembered my *sankalpa*. Shri Radha, the Goddess of Sacred Love, had heard me.

My teacher looked at me carefully, his blue eyes gazing into the depths of my being. I had the strangest sense he was looking through my physical body, staring directly at the naked soul. He seemed to be scanning my past and future, the trials and tribulations of a thousand lives.

"Don't worry," he said at last. "Remember always, I am your mother."

−4−

Most people today come to yoga through yoga poses, called *asana*, like "Downward Facing Dog" or the "Warrior". Yoga poses are intended to unite body and breath, the physical and the internal, forming a bridge between our posture and our consciousness.

When performed as part of a genuine yoga practice, yoga poses can be vehicles to a deeper awareness of ourselves. They awaken dormant aspects of our being, helping us develop "divine" qualities—especially love and compassion. In that sense, yoga postures are a precursor, a warm-up, for a deeper practice that takes place in the arena of our everyday life.

Initially, there may be a disconnect between our yoga practice and our life as a whole. But what if we could *unite* our expression on the yoga mat with our thoughts, words and actions on the field of our everyday life? After all, the Sanskrit word *yoga* comes from the verbal root "to unite" or "to connect".[11] Yoga is about making *everything* we do a skilful act. What we do on our yoga mat is only a starting point for our yoga practice.

In the West, we're becoming increasingly aware that there is far more to yoga than physical and breathing exercises. For thousands of years, yoga has been a deep philosophy of life, a way of living skilfully.

Yoga is not only about self-discovery, but also about applying that self-knowledge in our everyday life. We each hold untold promise and potential; we each have a unique contribution to make in the world. To understand and manifest that potential requires great skill. That *skill in action* is called yoga.[12]

But can yoga also be about darkness? Can it be about crisis and despair?

In ancient India, soul-searching crisis was not concealed or imbued with shame, but viewed as an important time of transition, a deep rite of passage. The rishis, or sages of India, called it *vishada*, which in Sanskrit means "despair". They understood that periods of great tribulation, while difficult to bear, can serve as pivotal moments of growth.

If you're a pilot, your skill as a pilot is not tested or deepened when the airplane functions on autopilot in clear blue skies. Rather, your skill is deepened in the face of adversity—a fierce storm, the loss of an engine, the sudden failure of your instruments. In these moments, amid life's turbulence, yoga becomes an effective tool in navigating the storm.

Recognizing the immense value of adversity, the very first system of yoga in the *Bhagavad Gita* is the "yoga of despair".[13] The *Gita* begins with its hero, the warrior Arjuna, falling into a debilitating personal crisis. So deep is Arjuna's despair that he even questions remaining alive. At this point, Krishna guides the warrior through his dark night experience, teaching him the secrets of yoga.

Regarding the dark night as a potent metaphysical experience, the sages of ancient India, masters of potentiality, mapped the landscape to help us take this journey, birthing our full potential as wise and compassionate "warriors" on the field of life.

Unfortunately, with a strong and legitimate emphasis on positivity, the value of despair is often forgotten in contemporary presentations of yoga. Coming to face a period of darkness when we're already practising yoga or a spiritual path might feel bewildering. "This shouldn't be happening to me," we may think, feeling confused, ashamed or even let down by our practice. At times we may attempt to dismiss or invalidate our despair by taking shelter in pop psychology and easy spirituality, with mantras such as "Think positively", "Get over it", "Let it go", "Choose happiness".

But the ancestral roots of yoga are filled with accounts of wise seers and powerful warriors who transgressed deep despair. Alongside Arjuna, renowned seers and sages like Narada, Vyasa and Valmiki demonstrate the extraordinary transformative power available to us when we recognize that difficulty can also be a form of yoga. Teaching by example, their despair became the catalyst to their greatest work.[14] Arjuna's despair led to the *Gita*, one of the most practical and deeply insightful wisdom texts of all time.

Of course, suffering is not something we would wish on anyone—not least on ourselves. There is a notion that authentic spiritual growth requires some great tragedy or suffering. The yoga texts of ancient India don't promote suffering in this way. Yoga is foremost about kindness to oneself and to others. It's about utilizing the lessons of our suffering to achieve a transcendence and an awakening to our fully flourishing powers.

−5−

"What is a dark night of the soul?" you may be asking yourself. A dark night of the soul is not a temporary setback or a bad day at work; it's a period of intense, disorientating inner turmoil. Such an experience strikes us at the core of our existence. Almost all of us will go through at least one period like this in our life. There's little, if anything, in our upbringing or education to prepare us for it.

A dark night may have different triggers: the death of a loved one, the break-up of a relationship, being made unemployed, bankruptcy, illness, domestic violence, even war and displacement. Sometimes the internal crisis may simply creep up on us, without any external friction at all. We sometimes call that a mid-life crisis. Either way, the dark night experience is always an *inner* crisis. There may be external triggers to that crisis, but the real challenge occurs *within*.[15]

The phrase "dark night of the soul" originates from St John of the Cross, a sixteenth-century Spanish poet and mystic in the Carmelite order.[16] Since then, the term has been used broadly to describe a loss of meaning in life. In this book, I use the phrase to describe a personal life crisis such as that faced by Arjuna, and by almost all of us at some point.

Yoga and the Dark Night of the Soul looks at what such a crisis really is, how it unfolds, what its common features are, and how best to navigate the experience, allowing it to transform us. In doing so, I focus specifically on the yoga teachings of ancient India, especially from the *Bhagavad Gita*. This book aims to make the *Gita's* practical wisdom teachings easily accessible for contemporary readers and yoga practitioners.

While I'll draw upon stories and examples from the yoga texts, I'll also share contemporary examples of ordinary people like you and I, who have gone through, or are presently going through, crisis. These examples of everyday people will help illustrate the nature of a dark night, as well as helpful and unhelpful ways of dealing with life's challenges.

To protect the privacy of those who have shared their experiences with me, I've changed some of their names and details, while trying to remain as faithful as I can to these real human experiences.

Many of these stories, as you'll soon see, reveal the extraordinary potential that lies within each of us, which we can access through yoga. They show us how we can use a set of timeless teachings to make our way through life's most difficult periods.

While this book closely follows the original yoga systems taught by the yogis and seers of India, these teachings are not tied to any specific culture. They can be applied by anyone at any time, in any part of the world. The rishis held the view that there is only one wisdom in this world, which doesn't belong to any single nation or culture.[17] We can discover that wisdom, or at least fragments of it, in all civilizations and traditions.

As a text, the *Bhagavad Gita* can be difficult to access, partly because it was composed thousands of years ago. Its teachings are contained within the words and context of a very different culture and time. Most approaches to the *Gita* tend to be philosophical and academic, with numerous Sanskrit technical terms, limiting its accessibility to scholars or long-time students. While such approaches are certainly valid, they often hide the text's everyday tangible wisdom that anyone can at once use in their life to a formidable effect.

After all, the *Gita* is first and foremost a tool for practical application in the world. After hearing the *Gita* from Krishna, Arjuna doesn't retire to the forest to contemplate philosophy; he moves into battle. The teachings of the *Gita* are designed to help us live, right here and now, in the often chaotic and turbulent environment of everyday life.[18]

Yoga and the Dark Night of the Soul traces the soul's spiritual ascent from fear, lamentation and confusion to sacred love and compassion for all beings. It's an inner voyage that follows

Arjuna's own journey through his dark night experience.

To help his friend through his crisis, Krishna teaches him different, complementary yoga paths, each suited to a different kind of practitioner. But having heard these teachings, Arjuna is still not at peace. Krishna therefore shows Arjuna how to make his entire life a work of devotion. He offers Arjuna a beautiful definition of yoga as "the unwavering offering of love".[19]

Although set on a battlefield at the onset of war, the *Bhagavad Gita* is really a guidebook on sacred love.[20] The *Gita* teaches us that the dark night of the soul is our call to love; yoga is the way we get there.

Personal crisis is a unique opportunity, a sacred juncture, for addressing the soul's true need, unconditional love. The purpose of this book is therefore to lead readers to soul fulfilment, by awakening the alchemical potential of the heart through yoga.

Notes
Prologue: The Journey

1   The Latin *homo* derives from an Indo-European root for "earth", and has the sense of "earthling". It is usually translated as "man" or "human". *Sapiens* means "wise" or "knowing". *Homo sapiens sapiens* is the name of our sub-species.

2   The *Bhagavad Gita* forms part of "The Book of Bhishma", the sixth book of the *Mahabharata*, or great tale of the Bharata dynasty. The *Mahabharata* is the longest poem ever written, with about 1.8 million words. The text predates Christ, with references to it found as early as the 4th century BCE. According to archaeoastronomy, the events of the *Mahabharata* unfold some 5,000 years ago.

3   The traditional colophon that ends each chapter of the *Bhagavad Gita* identifies the text as an Upanishad on yoga. In the original Sanskrit text, the word *yoga* appears 78 times as a noun and 36 times in its verbal form as *yukta*, while the word *yogi* appears 28 times. In using the term *yoga*, the *Gita* doesn't refer solely to teachings similar to those recommended by Patanjali in his *Yoga Sutra*, but adopts a far broader usage.

4   Nisargadatta Maharaj and Robert Powell, *The Nectar of Immortality: Sri Nisargadatta Maharaj's Discourses on the Eternal* (2004), p. xv.

5   The *Bhagavad Gita* is often referred to as *Gitopanishad*, indicating its equal status with the Upanishad texts of the Vedas. The *Gita-mahatmyam* (verse 6) of Shri Shankaracharya describes the *Gita* as the essence of all the Upanishads. This makes the *Gita* the essence of the Vedas. The *Gita* is one of the three canonical texts of Indian philosophy (known collectively as the *prasthana-traya*, the three foundations), especially for the Vedanta schools.

6   For example, the *Brihad-aranyaka Upanishad* (4.4.21) distinguishes between perfect knowledge (*prajna*), which manifests in action, and the knowledge of books, which it describes as "mere weariness of the tongue".

7   *Bhagavad Gita*, 4.2.

8   *Bhagavad Gita*, 4.34: *tattva-darshinah* ("truth seer").

9   Stick-Like Prostration is similar to Shavasana, or "Corpse Pose", a yoga posture that normally comes at the end of a yoga session. Corpse Pose represents saying *yes* to life, allowing what is to be. Stick-Like Prostration is also a pose of surrender, but is imbued with the beautiful qualities of deep humility, dedication and devotion.

10   To learn more, see Shiva Rea, "Welcome Summer with Shiva Rea's Solstice Prostration Practice", Yoga Journal [website], published 17 Jun. 2016.

11   The Sanskrit term *yoga* derives from *yujir*, meaning "to unite" or "to connect" (*yujir yoge*), as well as from *yuj* in the sense of stilling (*yuj samyamane*) and of enlightenment (*yuj samadhau*). In the *Bhagavad Gita*, the word *yoga* is used in varied ways, but these all derive directly or indirectly from the sense of yoking, uniting or connecting. See Surendranath Dasgupta, *Philosophical Essays* (1982), pp. 89–91.

12   *Bhagavad Gita*, 2.50: "yoga is skill in action" (*yogah karmasu kaushalam*).

13   Each of the *Bhagavad Gita's* eighteen chapters is traditionally named according to the specific system of yoga it sets out. There are no chapter titles in the original text of the *Gita* or in the *Mahabharata*, for that matter, but over time similar or identical titles have been assigned consistently to its chapters. Chapter 1 is commonly entitled *arjuna-vishada-yoga*, "The Yoga of Arjuna's Despair". Arjuna's dark night experience, while painful and highly disorientating, simultaneously creates the opportunity for his inner transformation and spiritual deepening. By studying Arjuna's despair and how he emerges from it, we engage in a process of yoga ourselves.

14   For instance, Narada's despair led to Sanat-kumara's profound teachings in the ancient *Chandogya Upanishad*. Narada had a student named Vyasa. At the height of his literary accomplishments, Vyasa was consumed by a feeling of utter emptiness. His teacher, Narada, guided him out of his dark night. The result was the *Bhagavata Purana*, a twelve-volume work of astonishing beauty. Then, the despair of Narada's student Valmiki led to the *Ramayana*, one of India's great epics, made up of nearly 24,000 verses.

15   This is illustrated by Arjuna's dark night of the soul in the *Bhagavad Gita*, which is characterised not just by outer difficulty, but above all by inner conflict. Arjuna's outer crisis is described in verses 1–27 of Chapter 1, while his inner crisis is described in verses 28–47.

16   St John of the Cross (1542–1591) was a Spanish mystic in the Carmelite order. Born in Fontiveros, near Ávila, he composed a poem entitled *Dark Night of the Soul* (*La noche oscura del alma*) during his own dark night experience in 1578 or 1579, while imprisoned for trying to reform the Carmelite order. St John was held in isolation and darkness in a tiny stifling cell barely large enough for his body, and was subjected to brutal public lashing at least weekly. St John also wrote a commentary on this poem by the same name in 1584–85. His poetry and studies on the growth of the soul are widely regarded as masterpieces and the summit of mystical Spanish literature. For further details about St John's life, see Richard P. Hardy, *John of the Cross: Man and Mystic* (2004).

17   The *Rig Veda*, for instance, states, "Truth is one, though the learned speak of it in many ways" (1.164.46). The *Bhagavata Purana* similarly advises (11.8.10), "As the honey-bee extracts nectar from all flowers, big and small, a discriminating person should take the essence from all sacred texts."

18   Indeed, this represents a key distinction between Patanjali's *Yoga Sutra* and the *Bhagavad Gita*. The *Yoga Sutra* offers prescriptions especially suited for ascetics, who have disengaged from the world. Often naked and strangely adorned to assert their freedom from social stricture, Indian ascetics are commonly wanderers. They frequently take vows of silence and may retreat to isolated hideouts in the jungle, desert or mountains. By contrast, the *Gita* offers yoga teachings directed specifically at those who are in active engagement with the world, like Arjuna.

19   *Bhagavad Gita*, 13.10: *bhaktir avyabhicharini*, "the unwavering offering of love". Krishna advises Arjuna to pursue no other form of yoga.

20   Catherine Ghosh makes this insightful observation in "Yoga in The Gita: Love Changes Our Perception", Elephant Journal [website], published 25 Mar. 2012.

PART

I

ARJUNA'S DESPAIR
ON THE FIELD OF BATTLE

The Dark Night of the Soul

I

Born into the royal Kuru dynasty of Northern India thousands of years ago, the prince Dhritarashtra was blind from birth. In an age when a king was expected to lead on the battlefield as well, this precluded him from inheriting the throne, and the kingdom was passed to his younger brother Pandu, "The Pale One". But who in this ancient tale of intrigue would inherit after Pandu? That depended on which of the two brothers had an heir first, Dhritarashtra or Pandu.

Under pressure to see their own offspring reach the throne, the brothers now competed to produce an heir. When Pandu's wife gave birth to a child, Dhritarashtra's wife, Gandhari, pounded her stomach in frustration and gave birth to a hardened mass of grey flesh. She appealed to the mystic Vyasa, who produced 101 embryos from the mass, each engineered to become a brutal warrior.[1] The first to emerge from his artificial uterus vessel after two years of incubation was named Duryodhana, meaning "dirty fighter".

Upon Duryodhana's birth, he began to bray like an ass.

Hearing that sound, asses echoed his cries, jackals howled and vultures screamed. The wind blew furiously, while raging, fierce fires sprang up around the city. When such omens appear at the birth of a child, the royal seers revealed, the child will be the exterminator of his own dynastic line.

Some years later, King Pandu died unexpectedly and the Kingdom of Kuru reverted to Dhritarashtra. But Pandu had five sons, now young princes, known as the Pandavas. Among them, the warrior Arjuna grew up to be an archer of unequalled prowess and dexterity. Kings feared him, warriors revered him, and parents would tell their children of his valour and exploits.

Duryodhana's natural rivalry with his cousins, the sons of Pandu, turned to deep-seated hate. He attempted first to poison one of the brothers, and upon failing he conspired to burn all five alive in a fortified, highly flammable palace, specifically designed to trap them in billowing flames. Finally, through trickery in a rigged game of dice, the power-hungry and ambitious Duryodhana succeeded in depriving the Pandavas of everything they owned: their extensive land, property, titles, wealth, horses, weapons, and even the jewels and royal garments they wore.

Laughing loudly, one of Duryodhana's brothers then dragged the Pandavas' wife, the beautiful and accomplished Draupadi, by her hair into the royal court. He tried, unsuccessfully, to strip her naked. In that terrible assembly, the Pandavas vowed to find justice. In the end, the elderly Dhritarasthra and his sons exiled the Pandavas from the kingdom for thirteen years.

When the Pandava princes returned from exile, they requested their land back—or at least, a humble grant of five hamlets. But Duryodhana declared he would not bequeath them so much as a pinprick of land.

War now seemed inevitable, with all the kings of the earth taking sides. Duryodhana amassed an immense army on the great plains of Kurukshetra. The army of the Pandavas was smaller, but nonetheless formidable. Elephants, chariots, cavalry and infantry now faced each other in military formation as far as the eye could see. The two armies were about to converge.

Faced with imminent battle, Arjuna turns to Krishna, his friend and charioteer, and asks him to drive the chariot between the two armies, so that he may see the faces of those who have chosen to fight for the sons of the blind king.

Krishna is the complexion of a dark blue sapphire or a monsoon raincloud, and his beauty enchants the heart. Dressed in armour and precious gems, he's regal. He's also steady and wise. Unwavering.

An unequalled archer, Arjuna is tall, handsome, strong and powerful. He's valiant and heroic, with "the gait of a lion". Idealized by the public, he's also a little brash and boastful. Arjuna isn't so steady as Krishna.

As requested, Krishna directs the chariot between the two

armies. There, among the great generals and kings of the earth on both sides, Arjuna sees his teachers, uncles, cousins, fathers-in-law, grandfathers, brothers, nephews, sons, grandsons and friends. Setting eyes on those he holds most dear, ready to forsake their lives, Arjuna hesitates. He suddenly grasps the full horror of what he is about to do. Overcome by grief, Arjuna's world begins to collapse into crisis.

Arjuna turns to his friend, Krishna. For the first time, he begins calling into question his strongly held beliefs. Does he really care for victory? Not anymore. Not at this cost, anyway. Is he even entitled to fight and slay the sons of the elderly Dhritarashtra? He is not so sure anymore, in spite of their covetous ambition and deceit. Will killing them lead to happiness? He thinks not.

"I do not desire victory, nor a kingdom, nor happiness. What is the use of pleasures or purpose in living?" he declares. Arjuna is reeling from the shock of one who has suddenly seen the falsehood of his perception and thus the madness of this world.

The dark night of the soul is a term used to describe a collapse of perceived meaning in life. This is what Arjuna now faces: his narrative, or life story, has suddenly been ruptured by events. All his notions of who he is and what he is supposed to do have fallen around him, and he is cast adrift in darkness. Everything looks void and meaningless.

Tormented by sorrow and confounded by doubt, Arjuna now finds himself paralyzed. He no longer knows what to do. Looking to the future, he sees only signs of chaos and terrible reversals.

"O Krishna, seeing my relations standing nearby ready to fight, my limbs have become heavy and my mouth has become dry," he says. "My body trembles and the hairs on my body stand on end. My bow, the Gandiva, slips from my hand and I feel my skin burning. I find myself unable to stand steadily and my mind seems to be reeling."

The once formidable warrior Arjuna now sits down in his chariot, having cast aside his bow and arrows. Sapped of his former strength and will, Arjuna longs to retreat from life. He even wonders whether he should maybe rush into battle unarmed and be cut down by his enemies without fighting back. Alternatively, he could quietly leave the battlefield now, before war has begun, and take up life as a beggar.

Arjuna finds himself in an abyss of despair. He is unable to cope with what has arisen in his life. He finds himself entirely helpless, unable to pull himself out of his grief. His troubled eyes full of tears, he says to Krishna, "I shall not fight!" and falls silent.[2]

This sudden crisis that Arjuna experiences doesn't occur in the privacy of his home or within a solitary forest during his exile. It happens in the middle of a battlefield, at the most critical time for action. This is a very public meltdown in front of Duryodhana and all the kings of the earth, who look on at this unexpected turn of events in utter disbelief.

If ever there was a personal crisis, it doesn't get much more dramatic than this. It's with this acute crisis that the *Bhagavad Gita*, one of the most important yoga texts from ancient India, begins.

ONE

The Story and the Storyteller

—1—

Monty's skin looked dry, wrinkled and discoloured. He had lost a lot of hair. What had *happened* to him? He looked like he had been ravaged by a disease.

And then it struck me: *time* had happened. I hadn't seen Monty for twenty-five years. Monty had simply aged, as we all do. Monty was probably having the same thoughts about me as we greeted each other at this college reunion.

I soon found myself talking to strangers, some of whom used to be my friends. We began sharing memories and trading details about our lives. We each had a story to tell.

Melanie, a classmate, had selected a striking yellow Prada summer dress to wear. Always the achiever, she began enumerating her successes: her large new house in the Hamptons in New York, the growth of her legal practice, and the work of her art collector husband.

"If you really want something, just go and get it!" she exhorted. "Like when my husband teamed up with Richard Eagleton, who remodels homes. He's a friend of Barrack

Obama's. So, they were just starting out, and really had no idea how they were going to grow their business; but now they're so popular, they actually have to *turn down* work. Just imagine. *Everyone* on Long Island wants their home refurbished by them."

"That's really impressive," Lisa said kindly. "I always knew you would achieve big things." Melanie thanked her with a smile.

Monty, self-assured and articulate, was discussing politics in the Middle East. He was a staunch supporter of former Prime Minister Tony Blair. Lisa didn't like Blair's war in Iraq. She interjected a few times, but Monty cut her down like a lawyer.

"As an argument, that's not only silly, but irrelevant," Monty declared with finality. Lisa was about to push her point further, but thought better of it.

"Do you remember Jim Elms?" Emma interrupted. "You know he committed suicide a couple of years ago, right?"

"Jesus! No way!" Melanie exclaimed. "Of course I remember him. What would make someone do that?" Her words tailed off, as if she were whispering to herself. There was a sombre silence.

I noticed that Bertha didn't say much. She was the only single woman in our group who wasn't a mother. Later she confided she wasn't leading the impressive life she had planned on twenty-five years ago; and she wasn't up to repeated interrogations about it.

Actually, Bertha had at first disposed of her invitation to the reunion. The prospect of attending this event had filled her with a mixture of curiosity and dread, not unlike that of a blind date. I suspect the last person she had wanted to meet was Melanie. They had been college rivals, and Melanie had stolen her boyfriend from her in the second year.

And then there was I, eager to please. Amiable and smiling politely, I nodded and agreed with the others, even if I wasn't sure I did agree. I wanted to fit in and be liked.

As I listened and watched, I experienced a shift in consciousness. I found myself looking on with the perspective of a distant observer. It felt just like watching a movie and involuntarily becoming aware that what you're seeing, with its drama and twisting storyline, is just a movie. As the audience gasps when the hero is in peril, you are left undisturbed. This is because you no longer identify with the lead character.

While growing up in temples and monasteries in India, I had learned from my teacher that in life we each create a story in our mind. That story is like a movie. Not only are we the author of our story, but we're also the lead character in it.

The sacred texts of India identify the powerful hold our narrative has on us as one of life's greatest illusions. The Sanskrit word for illusion, *maya*, means "not that". The delusion that we are the lead character in our story causes us to live in a feverish dream.

We take our stories extremely seriously; we're prepared to fight for them, even lose friends over them. We carry that story with us wherever we go; we can't escape it. Our story is the script from which our life unfolds.

So much of our story is inherited and then enforced, coerced and impressed upon us by society. From a young age, we're told what to be like, how to behave, what to want and hope for, and what to fear. We internalize these ideas, often unthinkingly. We come to believe we are what we wear, what we drive, what we watch and what we watch it on. We work very hard to keep up appearances. We try to live up to so many expectations and pressures. Slowly, imperceptibly, we build the walls of our own confinement.

With everyone living out their personal story, we are in the end simply interacting with each other's projections. We view everyone else through the lens of our own story, and our stories can conflict and collide. We find our friends in those who support our personal narrative, and enemies in those who challenge or undermine it. If we start altering our own story, or if we move out of it, our action affects the stories of others. It creates ripples of disturbance in their world.

Lost in our story, we experience a continuous compulsion to define who we are to ourselves and to others. Through Facebook and social media, we now have the technology to refine and polish our image of ourselves. We forget that the lead character in our story is birthed by the mind. The ancient texts of India refer to this fictitious self as *ahamkara*, which in Sanskrit means literally, "I-making". Mostly, we live from this illusory, constructed self. We, the storyteller, remain undiscovered.

Because the false self is created by the mind, circumstances in the world can test that identity, challenge it and even shatter it. If my story is about being a successful achiever, that story is undermined if I suffer misfortune or if others view me as a failure—say, if I lose my job, face bankruptcy or suffer a nervous breakdown. If I see myself as highly attractive, my story is challenged if others no longer find me as beautiful as before, maybe because I've put on weight or suffered illness. When the lead character in our story, with whom we identify, is in trouble or fails, we become fearful, confused and dejected. When the lead character triumphs, we're temporarily jubilant. The more we believe our story, the more we are its prisoner.

That we create a personal story is an almost inevitable part of life; this is how we make sense of the world. But when we take our story so seriously that we forget it's just a story, we begin to lead small, anxious lives. We're then blind to the quality of the narrative we create. Whenever we find ourselves caught up in fear, anger, jealousy or frustration, we've fallen victim to the delusion of the false self.

Not only individuals possess stories, but entire communities and nations create and promote them too, as they construct false shared identities. Religions may do the same, propagating narratives that unite or divide. When these collective stories clash, it leads to conflicts and war.

So, what happens when events challenge our story so profoundly that we can no longer hold on to it? What happens if our story collapses? We are propelled into deep darkness and despair. We find ourselves cast adrift in a world without meaning. This is a dark night experience, a crisis of despair.

This is exactly what happened to Arjuna at Kurukshetra.

–2–

On that fateful day at Kurukshetra, Arjuna was poised for battle. He had prepared for this moment very carefully for more than thirteen years, acquiring the deadliest of weapons. He blew his conch shell loudly, signalling his presence on the battlefield and intent to fight, and took up his bow.

Requesting Krishna to position his chariot between the two armies, Arjuna sees his family members, elders and dear friends, all willing to face death. This is the trigger that leads to Arjuna's despair.

Arjuna is deeply loyal to his brothers, headed by Yudhishtira. They have suffered piteously, as has his dear wife, Draupadi. Shamed, banished, mocked and driven into hiding, they were forced to take up positions as servants in a foreign kingdom. They now depend upon Arjuna to win this war. To do so, he'll have to fight against his own dearly loved teacher and grandfather. Both now face him as generals in Duryodhana's army.

Until now, Arjuna has been confident about his cause, sure that he and his brothers hold the moral high ground. The public insult to Draupadi, the many years of suffering in the forest, and the attempts on their lives have led to this great battle. Through deception, Duryodhana had unjustly stripped the Pandavas of everything they owned. The Pandavas had tried repeatedly to compromise with Duryodhana and find a pathway to avoid war; but Duryodhana had always interpreted these attempts as signs of weakness, becoming only more avaricious and belligerent.

On many occasions, Arjuna had vowed to defeat Duryodhana and crown his older brother Yudhishtira as emperor. The time had finally come. Surely, Arjuna thought, he now had a right to claim the kingdom back for Yudhishtira.

But when Arjuna sees his dearly loved family members and respected elders ready for battle, he has very serious doubts. The sheer number of soldiers on both sides makes him question whether such a war can be justified. His moral compass is thrown into confusion.

Shocked by his own thoughts and actions, Arjuna turns to Krishna: "Ah yes! How strange it is that we're resolved to enact such great misfortune. Driven by greed for the happiness of royalty, we're intent on killing our own people."[3]

Arjuna had believed that with victory he and his brothers

would finally be happy. They would reclaim their kingdom and at last find peace. This was his narrative. But now Arjuna is not so sure. How could he enjoy the spoils of such a war? How could he find any happiness in a world without friends and relatives—those he had himself killed or had allowed to be killed in such a battle?

Arjuna's crisis is not the result of a newfound morality or sense of meaning in his life. It's the result of a breakdown of meaning, leading to a loss of purpose, doubt, lack of resolve and paralysis. Casting aside his bow and arrows, Arjuna sits down in his chariot, overcome by despair.

TWO

The Four Signs of
a Dark Night of the Soul

— I —

Heather woke up one morning to find a letter on her pillow: her husband was leaving her for another woman.

I've known Heather since I was 14. We went to the same high school together. Even back then, I knew she was someone who would devote herself to her family and to whomever was lucky enough to be in her life.

Heather now had three children, one of whom was still living at home. She had given up a career as a journalist to raise them.

I came to visit Heather at her home just after 11am. She was still in her pyjamas. She looked thin. Her eyes were swollen and red, like she had been crying. I made her a soothing cup of camomile tea and we went into the living room.

Heather was normally meticulously tidy, but there were dirty cardboard pizza boxes and chocolate wrappers on the floor and coffee table. I cleared up.

"Why is this happening to me?" Heather kept saying. She began questioning all the decisions she had made in her life.

"Maybe I gave up too much to have a family," she said at last. Her voice was filled with regret. I could sense her deep pain; she was tormented.

"Things will get a bit easier. Just give it some time," I offered softly.

"I think it's too late for me to start again. At my age, I'm not sure anyone will find me attractive. If only I could have my old life back." Heather broke down crying.

"Are you all right, mum?" It was 13-year-old Theo, who had heard the commotion and decided to investigate.

"Just leave me alone! I told you to stay in your room," Heather snapped, before checking herself. "I'm sorry, Theo. I'm sorry. It's been really difficult…"

Theo retreated.

"I just don't know who I am anymore," Heather said by way of explanation, holding her head in her palms. "I feel completely lost. Sometimes I wish I could just die."

The things Heather used to love doing—eating out, going on country walks, taking photos, spending time with her friends—no longer made her happy. Life seemed repetitive and pointless.

Months passed, and Heather's family, who were sympathetic and supportive at first, struggled to understand why she couldn't just pick herself up and forge ahead with life. Irritable, embittered and dispirited, she had become difficult company and would often snap at her family. Preferring isolation, she avoided them.

Heather was experiencing a dark night of the soul.

I knew there was little I could do to help Heather, except listen and try to understand. And in making the effort, I noticed surprising parallels to my own experience of crisis. Although Heather's circumstances were different to mine, the symptoms of her dark night were strikingly similar. These were also the same symptoms Arjuna describes in the *Bhagavad Gita*.

A dark night of the soul can arise in many ways, and it can pass quickly or last for many years. Nonetheless, the sages and seers of India recognized that the dark night experience itself, the dissolution of our world, has certain shared features. If we examine Arjuna's crisis closely, we find four main symptoms:

1. *Suffering associated with the three phases of time*
2. *The revealing of our dark side*
3. *A strong impulse to retreat from life*
4. *Complete helplessness*

—2—

I awoke in the middle of the night with a start. A sharp pain swept across my foot, like an electric charge. I looked about and saw nothing. Had I just been bitten by a rat or maybe even a serpent?

I was in India, and like the other monks, I slept on a thin

straw mat on the floor. I tried to go back to sleep, but was bitten again. My foot throbbed with pain. I lifted my straw mat, and out scurried a small millipede. It made for the bathroom drain, faster than anything I had ever seen. My foot was beginning to swell and lose sensation.

There's a type of millipede in India that is extremely poisonous. If it bites you, the pain is so intolerable that people have been known to put their arms or legs in boiling water out of sheer desperation.

During my own dark night experience some years later, I went through acute suffering. I remember thinking that I would rather be bitten repeatedly by hundreds of millipedes than go through what I was experiencing. The suffering of a personal crisis can feel unendurable.

In the case of such inner torment, there's usually no visible accident scar, no lost limb, no debilitating disease. Without an obvious cause for your ordeal, there's a social expectation that you merely get on with life. The lack of validation of your experience by others can cause the suffering to feel all the more acute.

Suffering related to the three phases of time is the first main feature of a dark night experience. Fear is suffering related to how our story will unfold in the future. Lamentation is suffering related to how that story has unfolded in the past. And confusion is suffering related to the present. It arises from identifying so resolutely and ardently with our story, even as it falls apart.

During Arjuna's crisis on the battlefield, he is overcome by these three types of misery. Perceiving signs of a terrible reversal, Arjuna fears the future. He laments the past, his troubled eyes full of tears. Turning to his friend Krishna, he confides just how utterly confused he is.[4] Arjuna's mental anguish is so intolerable that it manifests outwardly as an overwhelming panic attack in front of all the kings of the earth: his body begins to tremble, his mouth dries up, the hairs on his body stand on end, and his skin feels as if it is burning. Arjuna has trouble even standing.[5]

In a dark night experience, most of our suffering stems from our attachment to our personal narrative, even as it disintegrates. The central character of our story, the illusory ego, now faces annihilation in some form and is fighting fiercely for its own survival. As we resist the destruction of our world, we react to events in the present through an identity strongly defined by the past. This is, of course, a natural and very human response to what is a type of death.

When refining gold at high temperature, all the impurities in the gold separate into a layer on the surface of the molten metal. Called dross, this mass of solid impurities can then be removed, leaving pure, refined gold.

Similarly, ghee, a form of clarified butter, is prepared by

simmering butter on a medium-low heat. In the process, solid white froth separates from the butter, and is skimmed and discarded. This yields a clear liquid resembling molten gold, used for thousands of years in traditional Ayurvedic medicine.

A dark night of the soul is a period of purification and transformation. Like the process of refining gold or making ghee, parts of us that may have remained concealed from others, and even from ourselves, rise to the surface during a dark night experience. This is the second main feature: the revelation of our dark side.

During a dark night, we may become intensely irritable, angry, impatient or resentful. We may fall into guilt, self-pity and even self-loathing. This is often our response to the suffering we're experiencing. We may even feel hatred towards those who we believe contributed to our crisis.

We all have a dark side, an "ungodly" side, which only those closest to us may know. Sometimes the dissolution of our world can reveal things about us that surprise even ourselves. We suffer the death of who we thought we were, while encountering those parts of us we have kept hidden— qualities, behaviours and motivations that may be difficult for us to acknowledge. In a dark night, we come face to face with what we can no longer hide.

Some, for instance, become aware of how much anger they carry. Others must face the unbearable truth that ultimately, they don't really care about others. These inner revelations can be difficult to acknowledge or bear. In my case, following the breakdown of my first long-term relationship, I realized how selfish I was capable of being, how oblivious I had been to the suffering of others. It was one of the most important moments of clarity in my life. I wept with shame and contrition. I longed for forgiveness.

During his dark night, Arjuna must face his own dark side. As his older brother Yudhishtira explains later in the *Mahabharata*, Arjuna's main weakness was his intemperate pride in his own ability as an archer and the vain belief that no one could ever match him.[6] Indeed, Arjuna's own teacher, Drona, had promised his pupil that he would make him the greatest archer that ever walked the earth.

However, during his public meltdown on the battlefield of Kurukshetra, Arjuna, celebrated by the name "Holder of the Bow", struggles even to keep hold of his weapon. By the end of Chapter 1 of the *Bhagavad Gita*, he has deliberately cast aside his bow and arrows, his mind tormented by sorrow. He is broken, a feeble shadow of his former self.

It can't get much worse than this for a renowned warrior, famous as the "Scorcher of the Enemy", "Hero of the Kurus" and "Tiger Among Men". With Duryodhana and all the kings of the earth looking on in disbelief, the previously undefeated warrior now breaks down into tears.[7]

Surrounded on all sides by warriors and kings, and in plain sight of his nemesis, Karna, son of the sun god, Arjuna would have been all too painfully aware of his previous arrogant boasts about his prowess in battle and his proud warrior's promises.

What would Duryodhana and the great archer Karna have been thinking? What would all the kings of the earth have been saying at that moment?

Krishna reminds him: "People will certainly speak of your undying infamy, and for a person of high repute, such infamy is worse than death. The great chariot warriors will think you have withdrawn from battle out of fear, and those who previously held you in high regard will come to take you lightly. Your enemies will say many unspeakable things about you, disparaging your ability. What could be more painful than this?"[8]

Defeated in front of all his enemies, even before a single arrow has been shot, Arjuna would certainly have been looking directly into the eyes of his own demons.

–4–

In her dark night of the soul, Heather had stopped cleaning her home. She struggled to feed herself or her family. All the things she used to love doing no longer made her happy—and she didn't know why. If you remember, Heather just wanted to disappear, to exit life. She even contemplated suicide.

This is the third main feature of a dark night experience:

a strong impulse to retreat from life. This impulse is partly the result of acute suffering and partly due to a loss of personal direction, leading to paralysis. When the ego is being destroyed, the result is often intense angst and a strong desire to disengage from life. It can extinguish even the desire to remain alive.

Like Heather, Arjuna's immediate and natural impulse during his dark night is to retreat from the field of engagement. He wants to escape his troubles at Kurukshetra. In front of all the Kurus, the "Hero of the Kurus" wants to flee from the battlefield of the Kurus.

Questioning the purpose of remaining alive, Arjuna considers rushing at the opposing army unarmed to be slaughtered by the sons of Dhritarashtra, without resisting.[9] In my own dark night experience, I remember wanting to retreat too; but there was nowhere to go. "If I could just die," I thought, "that would be a welcome relief."

Arjuna casts aside his weapons and wonders whether he should take up life as a beggar. Never mind what people will say about him.[10] Retreating from the field of battle in this way is also a form of suicide for Arjuna; it is the killing of his reputation and of his identity as a heroic Kuru. More than this, it is the abandonment of his purpose or calling as a warrior, symbolizing the death of the human spirit.

–5–

On the east coast of India, in the Bay of Bengal, lies the sacred city of Jagannatha Puri. The ocean along the shores of Jagannatha Puri can be perilous, especially at certain times of the year. Powerful rip currents can drag even the best swimmers out to sea. I've never seen an ocean behave so wilfully, and with such unpredictability and ferocity.

Gaura, a tall and handsome monk, was a strong swimmer. When we went to bathe in the ocean, he would dive into the tumbling waves, unafraid. But on one such dive, the ocean waves suddenly receded and Gaura landed badly on his neck. Gaura disappeared out of sight, until a pilgrim spotted his body bobbing up and down like a corpse, tossed this way and that by the incoming waves.

Gaura couldn't move; he couldn't feel; he could barely breathe. He was rushed to the local hospital, which resembled a medieval dungeon filled with the cries of patients clinging to life. This was the only medical facility for miles.

As Gaura fought to remain alive, his inner world was hurled into chaos and confusion. Gaura experienced the same symptoms as Arjuna on the battlefield of Kurukshetra— suffering associated with the three phases of time, the revealing of one's dark side, a strong impulse to retreat from life, and complete helplessness.[11]

When our inner world collapses, we're entirely powerless,

like a shell tossed about in the waves of the ocean. It's an inner helplessness. In Gaura's case, this helplessness also manifested physically: the accident left him paralyzed from the chest down.

During my own dark night experience, I felt I would never find my way out. Darkness extended in all directions. There was no light in the distance to give me hope, no landmark or distant star to guide the way. My strength and skill could not rescue me. I found myself utterly helpless and alone.

I had studied the wisdom of ancient India for some years. But in my dark night, all my book knowledge couldn't help me. I realized how little, if anything, I actually knew. The experience was deeply humbling. This complete helplessness is the fourth main feature of a dark night experience.

The dark night breaks down and defeats even the strongest of us. Remember, Arjuna is the most powerful warrior of his time, but he faces a humiliating, public impasse. There's absolutely nothing he can do about it.

The reversal on such a public stage is so pitiable to see that even Krishna at first tries to make Arjuna snap out of it. He urges Arjuna to pull himself together: "From where does your bewilderment come at this time of crisis? Don't yield to this pathetic weakness. It doesn't befit you, Scorcher of the Enemy. Stand up!"[12]

But Arjuna can't snap out of his crisis, however much he wants to. On the battlefield at the onset of war, when prowess is most needed, the powerful Arjuna suddenly finds himself utterly powerless.

Nothing Arjuna *knows* can help him. He has studied under the wise brahmin Drona and assimilated knowledge from his older brother Yudhishtira, from his grandfather Bhishma and wise uncle Vidura, and from numerous sages and seers. But in his dark night, Arjuna finds himself stripped of all strength and clarity. The mighty warrior, "Scorcher of the Enemy", now finds himself scorched by the flames of despair. He feels utterly helpless.[13]

A dark night of the soul is a true life crisis. A temporary setback in our life allows us to remain within our existing paradigm of thought and attitude. A life crisis is different: it's a position of utter vulnerability, when we experience and acknowledge our own complete helplessness.

Most people will have at least one dark night experience in their life; some may go through several. That the struggles of despair we each go through should have the same symptoms as those described several thousand years ago in India's yoga texts is astonishing. If these texts accurately describe the dark night experience, might they also hold the secret for navigating such experiences? Might these ancient texts contain a "map" for traversing the dark landscape of the underworld?

DHRITARASHTRA SAID:
HAVING ASSEMBLED ON THE FIELD OF DHARMA AT
KURUKSHETRA, SEEKING BATTLE, WHAT DID MY SONS AND
THE SONS OF PANDU DO, O SANJAYA?

—Bhagavad Gita, 1.1

THREE

The Blind Emperor:
The Invisible Dark Night of the Soul

—I—

The stone steps of the temple monastery had just been washed, and glistened in the afternoon sun. They carried the worn and polished indentation of thousands of pilgrims.

I made my way past a large, powerful bull, who lingered in the street. It reminded me of the bull Nandi, the carrier of Shiva, god of destruction. Seemingly impregnable, it moved slowly, taking its own time, aloof to the continuous, futile motion of life. If only I could be like that. I watched for a few moments in awe.

I had travelled to the ancient town of Mathura in India to see my teacher, Shrila B. V. Narayan Goswami, an elderly master-practitioner in the Bhakti tradition. Born in 1921, he joined the monastery in 1946, and was initiated into an unbroken line of Bhakti masters going back thousands of years. These spiritual lineages transfer deep knowledge on overcoming the dark night of the soul from master to student. By "master", I don't mean someone who commands others; I mean someone who has mastered the mind and senses, someone who has mastery over fear, lamentation and confusion, the three types of suffering related to time. Deeply learned in the *Bhagavad Gita* and other sacred texts of the Bhakti tradition, he embodied their teachings in his everyday life.

That day, I decided to ask my teacher about the dark night of the soul. I wanted to know where these experiences spring from.

The ancient texts of India speak extensively about crisis and despair. Great sages and yogis describe their journey through such experiences. But the sacred texts also speak about a permanent dark night of the soul that is invisible to us. All crisis in our life emerges from and falls back into this underlying, invisible dark night of the soul, our conditioned state of being.

I asked my teacher where crisis and suffering come from. And what is the invisible dark night that the sacred texts refer to?

"The darkness that covers spiritual knowledge and causes suffering is called *avidya*, ignorance," my teacher explained. "It's our inability to see things as they are. Our primary duty is to develop spiritual perception and overcome this darkness. When it is dispelled, nothing in this world can trouble us. Suffering cannot touch us. Fear, lamentation and confusion cannot affect us.

"Our physical body is just a vehicle—one that changes shape, grows old, and dies. It's not who we truly are. Our false ego also is not who we are. These are like dark clouds that cover our perception. When these clouds disappear, we can see who we are, the soul, just as the sun becomes visible in a clear sky."

The nights are darkest when the sky is filled with clouds, I remembered. At that time, the moon and stars are no longer visible. But when the clouds of confusion and false perception are dispersed, we can see the full beauty of the night sky, as it is.

My teacher explained that the purpose of crisis is to set us on our spiritual journey. The soul longs for freedom. Difficulties in our life can propel us on our spiritual journey, our path of yoga. For this reason, despair is sometimes referred to as a form of yoga.

I was shocked. *Life itself can be an ongoing state of darkness.* If I could overcome this underlying dark night of the soul, I could eradicate crisis in my life altogether. I may face difficulties externally, but these events would no longer affect me in the same way. No more fear, lamentation and confusion. Imagine that.

The yoga teachings of the *Bhagavad Gita* are designed to forge warriors capable of surmounting any earthly challenge, yoga warriors who exist in this world, but are not of it, not affected by it. Like Arjuna, we're all on the field of life, but we're not necessarily warriors yet. A warrior is skilled. A warrior is wise. A warrior is self-controlled. Our battles are always first and foremost within us. A true warrior, one who has conquered the inner world through yoga, has nothing to fear from the outer world.[14]

My teacher directed me to study the *Bhagavad Gita*. Among all the texts from ancient India, this, he said, is the classic text on the dark night of the soul.

"Look carefully at how the *Bhagavad Gita* begins," he advised.

−2−

Look carefully at how the Bhagavad Gita *begins.*

It begins with Emperor Dhritarashtra amid the lavish comforts of his palace in Hastinapura, a hundred miles from the field of engagement. The sightless Dhritarashtra, now powerless to affect the outcome of events, anxiously asks his minister Sanjaya how his own sons and the sons of Pandu acted on the battlefield of Kurukshetra.[15] His fear is palpable.

Until now, I had focused only on Arjuna's overt crisis on the battlefield. But it seems there is an altogether different type of dark night, one we may experience throughout the full duration of our life without our even being aware of it. This dark night is entirely invisible to us. It's the dark night of Dhritarashtra.

Like Dhritarashtra, we are all kings and queens. Our life is our kingdom. That kingdom can flourish or flounder depending upon how we rule, depending upon the choices we make. We guide the direction of our "kingdom", and this makes us rulers. Like Dhritarashtra, we may not have the vision of wisdom. When the mind is blind, what use are the eyes? Like a blind king, we may not be fit to rule.

Dhritarashtra was blind from birth, both literally and figuratively. His blindness represents folly, or "ignorance": an unwillingness to see. The opposite of wisdom. Largely responsible for the great civil war at Kurukshetra, Dhritarashtra is caught up in his story and paralyzed by attachment to his ambitious son Duryodhana. While Dhritarashtra represents attachment to the story we create in our mind, his son Duryodhana embodies greed, the offspring of attachment.[16]

Dhritarashtra is the most powerful Kuru alive, and yet there is something lifeless and impotent about him. When we take our human story so seriously, we become a prisoner to it, confined within its narrative walls and governed by it. We trade away our inner freedom. We may end up passing an entire lifetime never truly having started living. As Oscar Wilde observed, following his own dark night of the soul, "To live is the rarest thing in the world. Most people exist, that is all."[17]

The name Dhritarashtra signifies both "powerful ruler" and one who has seized the lands of another.[18] Having usurped the Kuru throne and taken the lands of his nephews, the Pandavas, Dhritarashtra is a blind emperor in a false empire.

The blind emperor seeks his power by what he can control *around* him, instead of *within* him. Paradoxically, the *more* we need to control what is happening around us, the *less* in control we feel.

Listening to my teacher speak, I realized that I am like Dhritarashtra. I'm a blind emperor clinging to a false kingdom. I came into this world with nothing and I'll leave this world with nothing. But while I'm here, I cling fiercely to my ideas of ownership. I try to accumulate for my own enjoyment and to further my own interests. I'm a false king in a false kingdom.

The aim of my life is to possess, to accumulate. It is this insatiable desire that led Dhritarashtra and his sons to battle. All our problems in life stem from this delirious pursuit to make the acquisition of material goods the aim of our life and the determinant of our own worth. We think that without accumulating things, such as money, status and achievements, we are nothing. As such, we're pulled into a world of enemies and friends, a world of exploitation and conflict.[19]

I am so caught up in my story, which I believe blindly and unquestioningly, that I'm prepared to fight for it till the end. Like Dhritarashtra, I've created my own battlefield. I've turned my life, the sacred field of the present moment, into an arena of competition and struggle. Rather than a field of love and affection, a field of giving and serving, it has become an arena for taking, for grasping.

Our fictitious sense of self in our narrative, and our deep attachment to that identity, gives rise to the obsession of

"I" and "mine". We become deeply attached to outcomes and events, fixed on the idea that our story must unfold in a specific way.

The deliberate failure to see, the deliberate avoidance of truth, is represented in the *Bhagavad Gita* by the blind emperor Dhritarashtra. His are the first words of the *Bhagavad Gita*, spoken in fear, lamentation and confusion, the three types of suffering associated with time.

The type of dark night that Dhritarashtra experiences is so pervasive and affects our lives so deeply that the *Bhagavad Gita* begins with it. Any other inner crisis we may have during our life emerges from this deeper and darker night of the soul.

Dhritarashtra was born into a lineage of the wisest sages and philosopher-kings.[20] Wisdom ought to run in his blood. He has received counsel from the wisest of advisers, and as such, the blind emperor is not short of knowledge.[21] His deficiency is his incapacity to act on what he knows. This is the great tragedy of Dhritarashtra's life.[22]

The sages of ancient India called such folly *avidya*, often translated as "ignorance". In using this word, they meant something far more profound than a simple lack of knowledge. Many of us know a great deal, but in our everyday life we choose to *ignore* it. Ignorance is to wilfully shut our eyes to what we don't wish to recognize.

A few years ago, my brother was diagnosed with stage-four cancer. He underwent intensive chemotherapy at St

Bartholomew's Hospital, London, in a fight for his life. I would visit him at the hospital and when I walked in through the side entrance, I regularly encountered one or two patients with lung cancer, pale and deathly from their chemotherapy, puffing away at cigarettes in the bitter cold. It was a startling sight.

Our ability to ignore is astonishing. It is itself a form of disengagement, or retreat, from life.

−3−

Every year, monks and pilgrims from all over India travel on pilgrimage to the old town of Navadwip. Situated on the bank of the Ganges, Navadwip was once the flourishing capital of Bengal's great Sena kings and one of the leading centres of learning in all India.

The occasion presents a special opportunity each year to listen to some of the wisest monks share their deepest insights. With a small group from my temple monastery, I crossed the breadth of India and arrived in Navadwip, wondering what treasures I might take into my heart.

I don't know if you've ever seen a banyan tree. They're magnificent. They drop adventitious roots from their branches, which tumble to the earth, like the matted locks of a rishi, or sage. I have read about entire forests in times past made up of a single enormous tree.

Hundreds of monks had assembled under two large banyan trees on the bank of the Ganges. In the distance, Ganges dolphins leapt periodically out of the water. The sun and moon were visible in the same sky, which was daubed in vivid pinks and streaks of red.

One elderly monk, dressed in cotton garb the colour of the rising sun, stood up to speak. He began telling a story.[23]

"Once, there was a young prince, the future ruler of a prosperous land. Carrying a bow and quiver of deadly arrows, he entered deep into the jungle on a solitary hunting expedition, on the back of a beautiful, swift steed. Deep in the forest, he spotted a deer.

"As the prince fixed an arrow to his bow and took aim, a tiger suddenly roared loudly, piercing the silence. The prince's horse rose on its hind legs in a panic, hurling the prince to the ground, and bolted. As the prince picked himself up, he saw a Bengal tiger approaching slowly, its eyes locked on him like golden embers.

"His heart pounding, the prince fled for his life. The jungle had many trees with long, fearsome thorns, which extended like knives. As the prince crashed through the jungle, he slashed his arms and legs. Repeatedly, he fell to the ground; but he picked himself up and kept running. In the distance, he saw what looked like a clearing. Perhaps he would find a settlement or house there.

"But there was no shelter to be found. If anyone had lived here, they had long since left. As the prince ran into the open clearing, he found himself falling into a dark abyss.

"In his rush, the prince had failed to spot a disused well, now covered by long grass. He plummeted into the darkness. Somehow, as he fell, the prince caught hold of two overhanging roots of a banyan tree. These roots broke his fall.

"The prince found himself dangling half way down this abandoned well. He peered down, his eyes adjusting to the darkness. The well was deep and held no water. At its base was a nest of slithering serpents and quivering scorpions. He could hear their anxious hissing. The prince looked up: the tiger was circling the mouth of the well.

"'That's really no problem at all,' the valiant prince thought to himself. 'I'll simply hang on tight and wait. Sooner or later, the tiger will lose patience and leave. I'll then climb out of this hazardous hole and retrace my steps back to my kingdom.' He began imagining the relieved reception he would receive. What a tale this will make for the young princesses at the palace!

"The prince's brief reverie was disrupted by a scratching, grating sound. He looked up. A white rat was gnawing away at one of the two branch-like roots that supported him; and a black rat was eating away at the other hanging root. The prince tried to shake them off, but they seemed unperturbed.

"'Now I'm in real trouble,' the prince thought.

"But just then, something moist dripped on to the prince's face. It rolled down his cheek to the corner of his lips. It tasted, unexpectedly, so very sweet. The prince stuck out his tongue. Another drop fell squarely into his mouth. Honey! He opened his mouth for more.

"When the prince fell into the well and caught hold of two overhanging banyan roots, his fall had disturbed a bees' nest high in the tree. Drops of honey were now falling from the ruptured hive. The prince looked up. 'When will the next drop fall?' he thought expectantly.

"In that moment, the prince forgot all his troubles. He became oblivious to the very real and dangerous predicament he was in. As he searched intently for his next drop of honey, it was as if a spell, a type of sightlessness, had overcome him."

And with that, the monk fell silent and sat back down.

What did this story mean? I looked around me. Pilgrims were glancing at each other, puzzled and curious. I saw one elderly monk who was smiling. Clearly, he understood the deeper meaning of this story. He now stood up and began to speak.

"We are each the prince," he said. "You and I have a kingdom—the territory of our life. Like a prince or a princess, we are of royal descent. We have the potential for greatness. But we've not yet taken guardianship of our kingdom, because we've not yet mastered our perceptual world, the kingdom of our life.

"The prince goes out hunting in the jungle, where he injures and kills defenceless animals for sport. Similarly, our world spins on exploitation. With great ease, we're ready to inflict pain on others, or at least remain oblivious to the suffering of others, in the pursuit of our own trivial ends.

"The prince enters the jungle as a hunter, but he ends up being the hunted. The tiger symbolizes death. Throughout our life, we're mostly oblivious to death. But every so often we hear its loud roar. Maybe a friend or family member becomes ill or dies; maybe we have a narrow brush with death.

"The prince falls into an abandoned well. This is the small human story that imprisons us, causing us to suffer in this world. The prince manages to catch hold of two overhanging branches. These represent the good and the bad in our life that we cling to.

"What do the two rats symbolize? The white rat represents daytime, and the black rat, night. We don't know how much time we have left in this world, but two things we do know for sure. The first is that whatever time we have left is limited. It is finite. And the second is that this finite amount of time is being eaten up with every passing day and night. Suddenly, we become aware of just how precious human life is.

"What are the drops of honey? They symbolize the comforts available to us that allow us to forget the perilous situation we're in. We each have a set of habits and preferred pleasures that create a false sense of comfort for us. This can include even our relationships, our job, our retirement plan and other false securities. They allow us to become oblivious to the passage of life, so that we stop truly living. Like the prince, we remain suspended in an abandoned well, far from the kingdom we are to inherit.

"Searching for a few drops of honey in the sky, the prince has forgotten who he is and that this dry, perilous well is not actually his home. He's become blinded even to the fact that he's in mortal danger. Instead, he loses himself in the search for a few drops of fleeting pleasure. This forgetfulness, or ability to ignore reality, is a type of sightlessness. The ancients called it *avidya*, ignorance. It's the invisible dark night of the soul."

This story affected me deeply. It roused me. I may have experienced crisis in my life, but I thought I'd crossed over these dark periods. Here was a deep, dark night that I was in right now, even as I imagined I was free. This was a dark night I couldn't even see.

Sometimes when I share this story in workshops or at yoga studios, someone rightly asks, "How does the story end?"

"Nothing in the well can save the prince," I reply. "To get out of our predicament, we'll need help from outside the well. We'll need something higher than the conditioned thought processes that have placed us where we are. Krishna's yoga teachings of the *Bhagavad Gita* come to us from outside the dark well of our current troubled existence."

–4–

There is a further secret teaching in the opening verse of the *Bhagavad Gita*. When I understood it, I became very excited about my yoga practice. It's about the real, tangible benefits we can expect from yoga.

Dhritarashtra, brimming with both anxiety and anticipation, asks his minister Sanjaya what took place at Kurukshetra. He doesn't know yet that Bhishma, the invincible commander-in-chief of his son's army, has already fallen. The war is now more than halfway over, and without Bhishma, victory seems almost assured for the Pandavas. Sanjaya has rushed back to the palace in Hastinapura to convey the news. Dhritarashtra's opening question is therefore full of irony.[24]

The hidden teaching here is that when we adopt a similar mindset to Dhritarashtra's, one of blind attachment to the story we create in our mind, then defeat and loss have already occurred—even if, like Dhritarashtra, we may not be aware of it yet. Likewise, when we adopt higher principles in our life, when we live wisely, victory is already assured, even before events have begun to unfold.[25]

As we'll explore further, the conflict at Kurukshetra represents a battle within each of us: a battle we're sure to lose if, like Dhritarashtra, we remain blinded by attachment to our story. Our own victory or defeat is contained, like the DNA within a seed, in the very mindset we carry into life.

The dark night of the soul has four symptoms: suffering associated with the three phases of time, the manifesting of our dark side, disengagement or retreat from living, and helplessness. These are background conditions of life. We may not always be very aware of them, but they become especially pronounced, acute, and impossible to ignore during an overt life crisis like Arjuna's.

The seers and sages of India drew an important conclusion from this. They recognized that despair can help us on the path to deep wisdom. It can help us become aware of, and ultimately even dispel, the underlying, imperceptible dark night of the soul that affects us all. Thus, crisis itself is an important yogic path.

If we were to experience only unabated enjoyment and success, we might spend an entire life oblivious to our underlying dark night, our spiritual sightlessness. Like Dhritarashtra, we would be at the height of our power and prosperity, but we would really be in the darkest night of all.

We each have higher and lower qualities. We each carry the divine and the destructive within us. The outcomes we experience in life reflect the potential we choose to act from. Love, gratitude, harmony, truthfulness, beauty, humility, kindness, patience, hope, compassion, courage and generosity: these are divine qualities. Anger, hate, fear, shame, arrogance, self-pity, greed, contempt and resentment are destructive qualities. When we exercise our divine potential, we experience divine outcomes.[26]

Like Dhritarashtra, I realized I am prone to exercise my destructive potential. It's not surprising, therefore, that my life is a battlefield, a place of inner conflict. I am easily caught up in fear, lamentation and confusion. Like the sightless emperor, I am alone in my palace. I have created my own Kurukshetra war.

Thinking about this, I wept. Like Dhritarashtra, I was born blind. This was my true dark night, beyond any crisis or confusion I may experience in my life. I was eager to understand how to cross this underlying dark night of the soul.

If we can overcome the underlying dark night, if we can attain an enlightened state of being, we eradicate all forms of crisis in our life. We may face difficulties externally, but these events no longer affect us in the same way. We awaken our inborn prowess as a warrior on the field of life.

At the end of the *Bhagavad Gita*, Sanjaya tells Dhritarashtra the results of applying Krishna's yoga teachings: good fortune, unusual triumph, strength, and abiding wise conduct.[27]

Good fortune, unusual triumph, strength, and abiding wise conduct. Who would not welcome these?

These are the fruits of one who overcomes Dhritarashtra's condition, the dark night of *avidya*. These are the results of the yoga of despair. In counselling Arjuna, Krishna not only helps him through his specific one-off crisis; he helps him cross the underlying dark night of the soul from which all crises spring.

Thinking about this, my heart began to race. The natural results of the yoga of despair annul the four symptoms of the dark night of the soul! Fear, lamentation and confusion disappear, leading to one's *good fortune*. A strong impulse to retreat from life gives way to *unusual triumph*, complete helplessness is replaced by *strength*, and the revealing of our dark side leads to *abiding wise conduct*.

The opening verse of the *Bhagavad Gita* describes the perspective of blindness and attachment. The closing verse of the *Gita* describes the perspective of enlightenment. Thus, the opening and closing verses are in fact antithetical, serving to define not only what we are, but what we might become.[28]

This sacred text, I realized, takes us on a journey of discovery: a journey from darkness to illumination, from sightlessness to enlightenment. It's a yoga text that specifically explains how to cross the dark night of the soul.

FOUR

Krishna's Counsel on the Battlefield

**Set out on the journey of the soul.
Let every step be its own reward.
Let discernment be the warrior's sword.
Let sacred love be your only goal.**

—I—

In the sanctuary of a monastery, a yoga studio, or a tranquil spot in the countryside, it's easier to feel at peace with the world and ourselves. But what happens when we step into the chaos and stress of everyday life? What happens when we face crisis and despair? I have known monks, who have practised for their entire life, to stumble and fall in the face of life's sharp and purifying challenges.

The yoga teachings of the *Bhagavad Gita* were not delivered on the pleasant bank of a river or in a forest grove; they were spoken in the middle of a battlefield. These teachings are meant for the most difficult and demanding action. The battlefield setting represents an engagement with the swift and sometimes turbulent environment of everyday life. This is the best arena for practising yoga.

The *Bhagavad Gita*, a dialogue between Krishna and the warrior-prince Arjuna, is a book about fighting the adversaries within and winning. These are the obstacles that prevent us from manifesting our full potential.

How do we become a "yoga warrior"? To find out, I decided to travel to Kurukshetra, the place where Arjuna in the *Gita* had asked the very same question.

In Kurukshetra, under an old banyan tree, I encountered a sadhu, or holy man. The vertical clay markings of the Bhakti tradition adorned his forehead. His eyes closed in meditation, he was reciting the poetry of the *Bhagavad Gita*, visibly free of all cares and troubles related to this world. The sadhu's voice was deep and soulful like the ocean, and the melody of his song enchanted me.

As a young boy, I memorized the Sanskrit poetry of the *Gita*, but the boundaries of my own experience limited my capacity for understanding its deeper truths. Listening to the sadhu's recitation, my soul, the centre of consciousness, was hoisted on a journey, even as my physical body remained where it was. I found myself next to the sadhu in the landscape of the sacred, that transcendent realm beyond time and temporal suffering.

When the sadhu finished his recitation, the sun, a large chalice of fire, was dipping into a flaming horizon of pinks and orange-reds. This was my very first visit to India, and I knew little about Kurukshetra, other than it had been the battlefield upon which Krishna had spoken the *Bhagavad Gita* and upon which the fate of the Kuru lineage had finally been decided. I asked the sadhu to tell me more about Kurukshetra and its deeper significance.

"Kurukshetra is a place of illumination," he began, "but it's also where Arjuna fell into confusion and despair. It is therefore the place that holds the secret for crossing over from crisis to illumination through yoga.[29]

"Like Arjuna we each have to face our own individual battles within and outside of us. Our external battles occur only because of our inner battles, as our external challenges reflect the unresolved conflicts within us. External conflict confronts us with the aspects of ourselves we are least conscious of and often least wish to recognize."

"How should we go about facing these conflicts? How should we act?" I asked.

"The teachings of the *Gita* are all about action," the sadhu explained. Kurukshetra is the field of action. *Kuru* in Sanskrit comes from *kri*, meaning 'to act', and *kshetra* means 'field'. In that sense, each of us is in Kurukshetra, the field of action, at all times. The real question is how will we act on that field? Some forms of action support us and lead to beneficial outcomes, while others bring us down, leading to unhelpful or harmful results."

We may not have control over what occurs in our life, but we can control what choices we make and the actions we take.

The sadhu explained that in ancient India the sages and seers had a name for "right action", or action that manifests our full potential. They called it "dharma". Yoga, or skill in action, naturally leads to dharma, "right action". It makes the field of action a sacred place.[30]

"Don't think that Kurukshetra is limited only to a physical location in India," the sadhu added. "If you make each moment in your life sacred, then you'll begin to make your entire life sacred. Making your life sacred is called 'yoga'."

I now understood something about the *Bhagavad Gita* that had always eluded me. We need to create a sacred space to act even amid the greatest chaos and confusion.

Our present situation is always the perfect place for practising yoga—although at times we may struggle to recognize that. It's easy to practise yoga when we experience tranquillity in our lives, unhindered by challenges. Our yoga is developed when we step beyond our comfort zone and go right to the centre of the field of action. And that field of action is in some ways remarkably like a battlefield: it can be turbulent and unpredictable, with sudden and unexpected changes in fortunes. Yoga on the battlefield? Definitely.

—2—

Unlike *The Art of War*, the ancient Chinese military treatise by Sun Tzu, the *Bhagavad Gita* is a book about overcoming the adversaries *within* us.

Like Arjuna, we face fierce hordes of powerful enemies: toxic, disabling forces like rage, fear, lamentation, unease, confusion, jealousy, boredom, arrogance, self-pity, greed, contempt, resentment, judgment, hate, unkindness, and perpetual want and discontent. These are the deadly, sabre-wielding servitors of Dhritarashtra, who represents the absence of wisdom, and they hinder us from ruling wisely and enjoying a kingdom that is prosperous and free from misery. They have one objective only: to prevent us from manifesting our full potential.

In the opening verse of the *Bhagavad Gita*, Emperor Dhritarashtra, eager to understand what transpired on the battlefield between his forces and those of the Pandavas, asks his minister Sanjaya: *What did they do?*

Sanjaya does not answer this question with a description of *external* killings between the two armies facing each other. Instead, he describes Arjuna's crisis and then shares 700 verses of yoga teachings that illuminate the *internal* "killings" that help Arjuna on his journey through his dark night, allowing him to pick up his weapons and re-engage with life.[31]

The mind can be our enemy or friend. It can help us or harm us. The Pandava army represents the mind that helps us, our higher potential. The Kaurava army represents the mind that hinders us, our potential for self-destructiveness. The Kaurava army is much larger, indicating that our mind is more prone to incite harmful action than helpful action.[32]

Like Arjuna, we find ourselves positioned directly between both armies, wondering whether to engage in this momentous battle or turn away from it. Dhritarashtra is hoping Arjuna will not fight. It's a difficult battle that lies ahead. Do we have the strength and courage to fight it? Do we possess the will?

We look at the opposing side—rage, fear, lamentation, unease, confusion, jealousy, boredom. We are very close friends with some of these. We've grown up with them, and they are our kinsmen, our family. How can we kill them? Even to fight them is difficult. They are dear to us. Like Arjuna, it's hard to imagine ruling our kingdom, the territory of our life, without these qualities that have so far been so influential in creating it.

Like Arjuna, we feel weak in the knees. We drop our weapons, and sit down in our chariot. Dhritarashtra, eager to win this battle by default, is delighted.

The warrior is forged in war. The battle scars define him or her. Likewise, the warrior in life emerges from active engagement with life's refining challenges.

In our engagement with life, our field of action is the present moment. Kurukshetra is the field of now—the only place in which anything can occur.

The field of now shifts between tranquil and turbulent, and yet, the yoga warrior is not afraid to engage with whatever discord and turmoil arises. How Arjuna, the Hero of the Kurus, chooses to act on the battlefield of Kurukshetra will determine the fate of the House of Kuru. In the same way, how we choose to act in the field of now will determine our own fate and fortune.

As we drive our "chariots" on to the field of now, faced with an army that is numerically superior, what weapons will we choose? The most powerful weapons we can have are the ones Krishna gives to Arjuna, the yoga teachings for crossing the dark night of the soul.[33]

With the help of my teacher, I began studying Krishna's poetic teachings to Arjuna. I believed that if I could trace Arjuna's journey through the dark night of the soul, I would then have a map to guide me on my own inner journey. Maybe I too could be trained as a yoga warrior.

−3−

In India, there are ancient temples of breathtaking beauty, the vestiges of a forgotten age. Many of these temples have secret teachings built into their *vastu*, or sacred architecture.

As you approach the temple's entrance, you encounter first a grand exterior with towering fort-like walls and a large gateway. You step in. Now standing in a magnificent enclosure, you discover another gateway in the distance that leads to a more confidential part of the temple. You cross that threshold and find yourself in a compound more grandiose and ornate than the first; but you haven't yet reached the heart of the temple complex. Further ahead is another temple, and within that, at a point of complete equilibrium and harmony, is the sacred inner sanctum—known as the "womb chamber".[34] The temple complex is a temple within a temple within a temple, leading to this confidential cave-like heart. This inner sanctum is considered a sacred bridge between the earthly and the divine.

"Like an ancient temple, the *Bhagavad Gita* has many levels of yoga teachings, some more secret than others," the sadhu in Kurukshetra said. After sharing standard recommendations, Krishna discloses secret teachings; then teachings that are still more secret; and finally wisdom that is the most secret of all, until Arjuna encounters the heart of yoga, which are Krishna's words on sacred love.

Krishna takes Arjuna on a journey of yoga that ultimately leads to this inner sanctum. The following are his four main teachings for navigating the dark night of the soul:[35]

1. *Set out on the journey of the soul.*
2. *Let every step be its own reward.*
3. *Let discernment be the warrior's sword.*
4. *Let sacred love be your only goal.*

After asking Krishna questions and receiving clarification, Arjuna agrees to adopt these four teachings.

Upon discovering this, my heart raced with delight. I realized that dark nights offer immense potential for growth, for soul expansion. The yoga of despair is specifically designed to help us let love and kindness be the axis of our existence. The result of sacred love is soul fulfilment. According to Krishna, love is the most powerful light for countering darkness; it's the easiest way to cross the dark night of the soul.

When Arjuna's world collapses on the battlefield, he's quick to dominate the conversation, expressing his fear and despair, clinging to his story, justifying his position, trying to find all the reasons he can to abandon the field of battle. But in realizing his complete helplessness, he takes shelter of his friend Krishna—and something interesting happens. Arjuna stops speaking so much and puts greater energy into listening. He opens himself to deeper wisdom and inspiration.

Krishna discloses to Arjuna that he is not an ordinary human. He is the Soul of the Universe, present within the heart of each of us. We are not alone on the field of life. The Universal Teacher, the source of all wisdom, resides within us.

In connecting with the Universal Teacher and being open to the wisdom of yoga, Arjuna has set out on the journey of the soul.[36] Instead of avoidance, denial or escapism, he chooses to embark on a journey of *consciousness*. He has begun a rite of passage or initiation in which the illusory ego dies. In doing so, he has stepped across the first threshold into the temple of yoga. This is the first of four powerful yoga teachings in the *Bhagavad Gita* for crossing the dark night: *Set out on the journey of the soul.*

Arjuna is a warrior, a man of action. But at Kurukshetra he finds himself suddenly confused as to how he should act. Krishna therefore begins by teaching Arjuna the secret to skilful action, which he defines as yoga.[37]

Currently, all our actions arise from our story. We do the things we believe will further our own small, imaginary narrative. If something yields a result that supports our story, we're delighted; if not, we're frustrated and unhappy. Even when our narrative falls apart in a dark night of the soul, we try our best to cling to its pieces and to act from it. We may even create another story around our despair. The more we hold fast to our fractured story, the more we suffer.

Krishna teaches Arjuna the secret of action that doesn't bind us, action that doesn't lead to suffering. This is action performed for its own reward, without an attachment to the results. This is a powerful form of yoga, called Karma-yoga, and is the second of four principal yoga teachings on the journey of the soul: *Let every step be its own reward.*

When we identify intensely with our story and believe unquestioningly that we are the main character in that story, we are forced into action. Our story compels us to act in a particular way. Discernment, or the ability to see things as they truly are, summons a phenomenal freedom and spaciousness into our everyday life. It allows us to transcend the small narrative we create in our mind, which we may otherwise spend an entire lifetime defending and sustaining. Krishna teaches Arjuna how to develop such knowledge or discernment, which he likens to a sword: "With the sword of knowledge belonging to the self, rise in yoga!"[38] This is the third of four principal yoga teachings on the soul's journey through the dark night: *Let discernment be the warrior's sword.*

But Krishna wants to advance Arjuna further into the magnificent temple of yoga. In the *Bhagavad Gita*, he shares many complementary yoga paths, each suitable for a different kind of practitioner and the goals such a practitioner has. Some yoga paths require the intellect, others use the body, and still others focus on discipline of the mind. But of all the yoga paths, Krishna explains, the ultimate and most potent is Bhakti-yoga, the yoga of loving service.[39] Krishna advises Arjuna to take shelter in sacred love, transforming his entire life into a work of devotion.

So much of our personal story has been inherited and hasn't been authored with awareness or conscious intent. The disintegration of that story in times of crisis and despair creates an opportunity to rewrite our story with love and affection at its foundations. It's an opportunity to make sacred love the guiding principle in our life.

This, then, is the ultimate spiritual lesson on the journey of the soul: *Let sacred love be your only goal.*

This is the inner sanctum, the confidential heart, of the

temple of yoga. Krishna explains to Arjuna that sacred love is the most secret teaching of all, as well as the most easily performed. When our purpose is an expression of sacred love, there is nothing more nourishing or fulfilling in all the world. This is because sacred love is the nature of the soul.

Although set on a battlefield at the onset of war, the *Bhagavad Gita* is really a guidebook on love.[40]

Notes
Part I: Arjuna's Despair on the Field of Battle

1 Gandhari's 101 children born through ectogenesis included Duryodhana, ninety-nine other sons and a daughter (*Mahabharata*, Book I [*Adi-parva*], Chapters 107 and 108).

2 Arjuna's despair on the battlefield of Kurukshetra is described in verses 1.21 to 2.9 of the *Bhagavad Gita*. In the Bhakti tradition, Arjuna is regarded as a warrior who has overcome fear, lamentation and confusion. By the arrangement of Krishna, who we learn later in the *Bhagavad Gita* is the Universal Teacher seated in the heart of all beings, Arjuna goes through this dark night of the soul so that Krishna may disclose the secrets of yoga.

3 *Bhagavad Gita*, 1.45. Text numbering in the second half of Chapter 1 varies slightly according to the edition of the *Gita*. Unless indicated otherwise, all English translations of Sanskrit verses from the *Bhagavad Gita* in *Yoga and the Dark Night of the Soul* are the author's. The presentation of the *Gita's* teachings herein follows the ancient Bhakti tradition, as taught to the author by his teacher within an authentic wisdom lineage (*sampradaya*).

4 Indications of Arjuna's fear: *Bhagavad Gita*, 1.30, 1.35–36 and 2.5–6. Arjuna's lamentation: *Bhagavad Gita*, 1.27, 2.1, 2.10–11 and 1.46. Arjuna's confusion: *Bhagavad Gita*, 2.7 and 2.11. Although Arjuna appears to speak words of wisdom, he is in fact utterly bewildered, as Krishna recognizes and tells him. If Arjuna were in a state of clarity, he would not be overwhelmed by sorrow and he would know exactly what to do. Arjuna's confusion leads to a loss of meaning and purpose, doubts as to what he should do, lack of resolve, and complete paralysis.

5 Arjuna's physical symptoms are described in *Bhagavad Gita*, 1.28–30 and 2.1.

6 At the end of the *Mahabharata*, long after the great battle at Kurukshetra, the Pandavas and Draupadi retire from royal life and travel north on foot. On the steep slopes of the great mountain Meru, when Arjuna drops to the ground, lifeless, Yudhishtira reveals that Arjuna's failing was his pride in his own heroism, leading him to disregard all other bowmen and to utter boastful words that proved untrue (*Mahabharata*, 17.2.21–22).

7   Some of Arjuna's epithets in the *Bhagavad Gita*: "Scorcher of the Enemy" (2.3, 2.9, 4.2, 4.5, 7.27, 9.3, 10.40 and 18.41), "Hero of the Kurus" (11.48), "Tiger Among Men" (18.4) and "Holder of the Bow" (18.78).

8   *Bhagavad Gita*, 2.34–36.

9   Arjuna questions the purpose of living: *Bhagavad Gita*, 1.32. Arjuna considers going into battle unarmed: *Bhagavad Gita*, 1.46.

10   Arjuna casts aside his weapons: *Bhagavad Gita*, 1.47. Arjuna considers a life of begging: *Bhagavad Gita*, 2.5.

11   Based on notes from an interview with Gaura on 15 Nov. 2013, supplementing my personal observation of the tragedy and its aftermath.

12   *Bhagavad Gita*, 2.2–3, paraphrased. Arjuna has just presented some viable arguments against engaging in battle, but Krishna's first response is to dismiss the whole case as being just an emotional outpouring, and not worthy of a reasoned reply. Rather than seeking to answer Arjuna's arguments, Krishna turns immediately to the emotional trauma at the heart of them.

13   In particular, see *Bhagavad Gita*, 2.7.

14   That is why at the end of the *Bhagavad Gita*, the visionary Sanjaya declares that wherever there is Krishna, the Lord of Yoga, and wherever there is Arjuna, there will surely be unusual triumph (*Bhagavad Gita*, 18.78).

15   *Bhagavad Gita*, 1.1: "Dhritarashtra said: Having assembled on the field of dharma at Kurukshetra, seeking battle, what did my sons and the sons of Pandu do, O Sanjaya?" This opening verse, which is full of deep significance, serves to establish the perspective of spiritual blindness. Through the emperor's inquiry, it establishes at the very outset the foundational theme of the entire *Bhagavad Gita* as one of action—the type of action that leads to optimal outcomes.

16   One meaning of the name Duryodhana is "dirty fighter". Duryodhana was adept at using underhand and nefarious means to gain an advantage, a quality symptomatic of greed. In Chapter 16, Krishna will tell Arjuna that greed destroys the self and is one of the three passages to a tormented existence (*Bhagavad Gita*, 16.21).

17   Oscar Wilde, *Soul of Man under Socialism* (1891); published in Oscar Wilde, *Collected Works of Oscar Wilde* (1997), p. 1046. Interestingly, Oscar Wilde made this significant remark after going through a deep crisis of his own, which helped him understand life with greater clarity.

18   Dhritarashtra is a compound word derived from *dhritam rashtram yena saha*, "one who has plundered someone's land".

19   The *Bhagavata Purana* (11.23.59) explains that the perception of friends, neutral parties and enemies, and the life built around those perceptions, is "constructed out of darkness". In other words, this mindset betrays our own spiritual sightlessness, the invisible dark night of the soul.

20   Dhritarashtra is the son of the great sage Vyasa himself, author of the *Mahabharata*, which contains the *Bhagavad Gita*.

21   Dhritarashtra's advisers include great seers and sages like Sanjaya, his brother Vidura, Bhishma and his father Vyasa.

22   The aging emperor previously witnessed Krishna's wondrous Universal Form, revealing Krishna's identity as the Soul of the Universe, in the royal court of Hastinapura before the war. This was a form similar to the one Krishna will show Arjuna in Chapter 11 of the *Bhagavad Gita*. Dhritarashtra will also hear the same *Bhagavad Gita* as Arjuna, narrated to him by Sanjaya from within the palace compound. Yet the blind king, who does not possess the qualities of a genuine seeker of wisdom, clings to his cherished illusions. The opening verse of the *Bhagavad Gita* therefore sets out the characteristics of the unqualified listener, in contradistinction to those of the paradigmatic pupil Arjuna.

23   This allegory is often used to elucidate the teachings of Shri Prahlada in *Bhagavata Purana*, 7.5.5. The seer-child Shri Prahlada highlights how we experience ongoing anxiety when we accept our illusory stories to be real (*asat-grahat*, "grasping the unreal"). This retelling of the allegory from memory combines details from other renditions I have heard over the years. In *Bhagavata Purana*, 7.5.11, Shri Prahlada explains that the powerful hold our narrative has on us is a product of "illusion". The Sanskrit word for illusion, *maya*, means "not that".

24   The *Bhagavad Gita* is contained in the part of the *Mahabharata* known as *Bhishma-parva*, "The Book of Bhishma". When Dhritarashtra asks Sanjaya

what happened at Kurukshetra, the battle is already on its tenth day and Bhishma has been brought down. Interestingly, it was on this same battlefield that Parashurama, Bhishma's own military teacher, single-handedly annihilated the single largest army of warriors and kings; and it was here that Parashurama fought his pupil Bhishma for 27 days, unable to defeat him. Dhritarashtra and his son Duryodhana therefore pinned their hopes for victory on the seeming invincibility of Bhishma, who had the power to choose the time of his own death. And yet, significantly, as Dhritarashtra speaks this opening verse of the *Gita*, the mighty Bhishma has already fallen.

25 This is further reinforced by the story-within-a-story narrative structure of the *Mahabharata*, the epic tale within which the *Bhagavad Gita* is situated. The *Mahabharata* is recited by the sage Vaishampayana to King Janamejaya, who is the great-grandson of Arjuna. In other words, when Krishna speaks the *Bhagavad Gita*, the reader or listener already knows that the great battle of Kurukshetra, fought to determine which family lineage will inherit the throne, will result in Arjuna's descendants continuing the Kuru dynasty and inheriting the earth. When Dhritarashtra asks his opening question in the *Bhagavad Gita*, we know that Arjuna's future is already secured for at least four generations.

26 Krishna differentiates between the divine and destructive qualities in Chapter 16 of the *Bhagavad Gita*, entitled *daivasura-sampad-yoga*, literally, "the yoga of the wealth of the gods and of the ungodly".

27 *Bhagavad Gita*, 18.78 (the closing verse of the *Gita*): "Where there is Krishna, the Lord of Yoga, and where there is Arjuna, Holder of the Bow, there is good fortune, unusual triumph, strength, and abiding wise conduct. That is my conclusion." This, ultimately, is Sanjaya's answer to Dhritarashtra's initial question. Good fortune: translates *shri*, which can also signify "prosperity", "happiness", "wealth" or "beauty". Unusual triumph: translates *vijaya*. The prefix *vi-* is often used to denote something special or unique in quality or significance. Strength: translates *bhuti*. The word can also mean "might", "power", "well-being", "prosperity", "wealth" or "fortune". It often refers to the extraordinary power developed by yogis. Abiding wise conduct: translates *dhruva niti*. The word *niti* signifies, among other things, "wise conduct" or "ethics".

28 A traditional approach for understanding an ancient Indian text is to compare the opening verse of the text with its closing verse. In the first verse of the *Bhagavad Gita*, the sightless Dhritarashtra, now powerless to affect the outcome of events, asks Sanjaya what has taken place at Kurukshetra. The verses that

follow are Sanjaya's narration of what has occurred. The closing verse of the *Gita* (18.78, presented in the previous footnote), however, is Sanjaya's personal response directed at the intent behind Dhritarashtra's opening question. Thus, the opening verse of the *Gita* serves as an anchor, allowing the narrative to come full circle. In doing so, this verse provides a sharp contrast between the perspective of attachment and the perspective of enlightenment.

29 The location in Kurukshetra where Krishna spoke the *Bhagavad Gita* is known as Jyotisar, or that place which illuminates the dark night of the soul. In Sanskrit, Jyotisar means "Essence of Illumination".

30 Early on in the *Bhagavad Gita*, Krishna defines yoga specifically as "skill in action" (*Bhagavad Gita*, 2.50). The word yoga itself derives from the Sanskrit root word *yujir*, meaning to connect, to join together, to unite. Yoga allows us to unify, or unite, the field of dharma (*dharma-kshetra*) and the field of action (*kurukshetra*). All action occurs in the present moment, the field of now. Therefore, when we make the field of now a sacred place, we are practising yoga. And through yoga, we can connect with Krishna, the source of wisdom and the guardian of dharma.

31 Catherine Ghosh expresses this well in "Are You Hiding Depression Behind Your Yoga?" Elephant Journal [website], published 2 May 2011.

32 See Shri Shrimad Bhaktivedanta Narayana Maharaja, *The Essence of Bhagavad Gita* (2000), pp.14–15. Renowned commentators in the Bhakti tradition employ allegorical interpretations as an additional perspective to illuminate inner teachings of the *Mahabharata* and *Bhagavad Gita*. For example, Shri Madhvacharya (CE 1238–1317) highlights the allegorical meaning of the warriors on both sides of the battlefield in his *Mahabharata-tatparya-nirnaya* (2.144–9).

33 See *Bhagavad Gita*, 4.42.

34 In Indian temple architecture, the innermost sanctum is called the *garbha-griha*, which means, literally, "womb chamber", from the Sanskrit words *garbha* for womb and *griha* for house. This inner chamber represents a microcosm of the universe, and is where the temple deity resides. Two temple domes usually rise above this "womb chamber", one above the other, forming a vertical axis that symbolizes the axis of the world.

35   In his *Gitartha Samgraha*, Shri Yamunacharya, a senior contemporary of
Shri Ramanujacharya, divides the *Bhagavad Gita* into three equal portions of six
chapters each (1–6, 7–12 and 13–18). The first teaching, "Set out on the journey
of the soul", encapsulates the introductory verses of the *Gita*, in which Arjuna
describes his dark night of the soul and sets off on his inner journey, requesting
Krishna to be his yoga teacher. "Let every step be its own reward" encapsulates
Krishna's teachings on Karma-yoga, found in the first six chapters of the *Gita*.
"Let discernment be the warrior's sword" encapsulates Krishna's teachings on
Samkhya in the final six chapters of the *Gita*. And "Let sacred love be your only
goal" encapsulates Krishna's most confidential instructions on Bhakti-yoga in the
middle six chapters of the *Gita*, teachings he again emphasizes at the very end of
the *Gita*.

36   In seminars and workshops on the *Bhagavad Gita*, participants usually
identify as being spiritual, although not necessarily as religious. When I ask
what they mean by "spiritual", they offer different but complementary insightful
replies, and usually a common thread is a deeper understanding of oneself. In
Sanskrit, a similar word to "spirituality" is *atma-gatih*, "the path of the soul" or
"the journey of the self". By this elegant definition, spirituality is everything that
takes us forward on our journey of the soul.

37   *Bhagavad Gita*, 2.50: *yogah karmasu kaushalam* ("yoga is skill in action")

38   *Bhagavad Gita*, 4.42

39   *Bhagavad Gita*, 6.47.

40   Catherine Ghosh makes this insightful observation in "Yoga in The Gita: Love
Changes Our Perception", Elephant Journal [website], published 25 Mar. 2012.

PART

II

THE FIRST AGREEMENT:
"SET OUT ON THE JOURNEY OF THE SOUL"

Sharanagati,
The Soul's Gateway to Sacred Love

11

We want to resist the dark night; just like Arjuna, we want to flee. Our every instinct is to avoid discomfort.

But Krishna advises, "No! Go into the heart of the difficulty." In the *Gita*, we learn to take our "chariot" into the centre of the conflict. Yoga teaches us how to tolerate the discomfort, without acting or reacting from our small human stories.

In remaining on the field, Arjuna surrenders the need to control life. He surrenders the shattered identity he's been holding on to, looking instead for shelter in his dear friend Krishna's yoga teachings. Rather than being a "hero" in his small, imagined story, Arjuna now becomes a seeker, a traveller, at the beginning of his yoga journey.

The first agreement is about saying *yes* to the spiritual journey as it unfolds. But this is not a one-time agreement. It needs to be renewed continuously. At every step, we can choose to abandon the field.

Arjuna shows us that the first agreement includes three things:

1. Honour the dark night as a rite of passage.
2. Trust your inner guide.
3. Surrender the need to control.

We can't set out on the journey of the soul unless we believe the journey is worth taking. This begins with an understanding that the dark night of the soul is not a dangerous experience, but a natural, if not necessary, process. It's a rite of passage, a spiritual initiation.

We drive our "chariots" on the field of life. The chariot is our body. The five horses are our five senses. Although our illusory ego is currently the charioteer, we are not without the presence of Krishna, the Universal Teacher seated in our heart. The Universal Teacher is the intuitive voice of truth guiding us from within.

If we allow Krishna to guide our chariot, rather than the ego, then we're invincible and unassailable, whatever may happen on the often riotous and turbulent field of life. In other words, if we can guide our chariot by the higher wisdom of yoga, we're sure to achieve victory and success.

Krishna is Arjuna's mentor throughout the dark night, his guide, his shaman. Krishna is also Arjuna's best friend. He's not some unknown guru. Rather, Arjuna *knows* he can trust Krishna, and as such hides nothing from him. As Arjuna discovers later in the *Bhagavad Gita*, Krishna is also no ordinary person. He is the Soul of the Universe, the Universal Teacher within each of us. Taking shelter of a higher knowledge is known in India as *sharanagati*, "the way of surrender" or "the way of taking refuge".

Unlike Arjuna, Emperor Dhritarashtra is closed off to spiritual guidance. He hears the same *Bhagavad Gita* that Arjuna hears, but it has no effect on him. This is because he never sets off on the yoga journey. He never enters into the first agreement: "Set out on the journey of the soul." Locked up in his palace in Hastinapura, he is trapped in his egoic story, a false emperor in a false kingdom.

Higher knowledge or wisdom is of no value or purpose if we're not receptive to it. Just as Arjuna trusts Krishna, who always has his best interests at heart, the Universal Teacher has our best interests at heart. Trusting our inner guide, who manifests in our life in myriad ways and reveals yoga's secrets to us on our journey of the soul, is an important part of the first agreement. Without such trust, we never truly embark on our yoga journey. This is a voyage into the unknown. Guided by the ancient yoga teachings, we'll need to surrender the urge to control.

THERE IS NOTHING TO LOSE HERE,
NOR CAN THERE BE ANY FAILURE;
EVEN A LITTLE PROGRESS ON THIS PATH
FREES ONE FROM GREAT DANGER.

—*Bhagavad Gita*, 2.40

FIVE

Honour the Dark Night as a Rite of Passage

−I−

Meredith read the letter a fifth time. Her hands felt clammy. Initial bewilderment turned into anxiety and nausea, which she struggled to suppress.

Meredith had joined a small fashion firm in London at the age of 16. For more than thirty years she'd devoted her life to the company, helping it grow into a leading label in the UK. Having worked countless long days and weekends, Meredith had risen in the company, gaining a senior management position. Yet the company was about to be acquired by a large retail chain; and that day, Meredith learned she had been made redundant.

After three decades, the employment market had changed. Without a university degree, Meredith's work applications were being rejected off hand. As the months drifted by and rejection letters kept arriving in the mail, Meredith became increasingly desperate. She entered a dark night of the soul.

At the fashion firm, Meredith had felt pride in her success, validated by her executive role and high salary. The loss of these sureties in her life shook her sense of identity, leaving her humiliated, angry and resentful. Staying in bed until midday, Meredith began drinking, often heavily, and attempted to blunt the pain of rejection in excessive clubbing and one-night stands. Yet still she felt estranged and alone.

Nothing in Meredith's education had prepared her for this. Knowing that the loss of a job was commonplace and incomparable to the tragedies faced by many others, Meredith observed her own reaction to life's events with surprise and shame. Why did it hurt so much?

Meredith dismissed the suggestion that she see a counsellor or psychiatrist, reluctant to entertain the idea that she was mentally unwell. Instead, Meredith went to her general practitioner, who prescribed Prozac for her mood swings and Valium for her panic attacks. She retreated from her old work colleagues and wished only to mask her own grief.

In our culture, crisis is treated much like excrement. What is a natural process to all living things is, for us, hidden behind closed doors. If exposed, the release of waste matter (be it physical waste or the emotional waste that surfaces in a crisis) is met with shame, and even the slightest scent can be deemed offensive.

And yet, just as beautiful, fragrant flowers grow out of dung or fertilizer, some of our greatest gifts may emerge from our darkest and most difficult periods. In ancient India, this is represented by the lotus flower, which grows out of the muck. No muck, no lotus.

In our society, there's no understanding of, and no space for, the dark night of the soul. We disguise our sorrow: no one wants to go to work looking "mental"; no one wants to be labelled with a nervous breakdown.

There's often no one to turn to for help either. Well-meaning friends will say, "Pull yourself together!" "Let it go!" "Just move on with your life." Doctors can't really help; they lack the wisdom to treat the root cause of the suffering. They'll simply medicate. Where is our shaman; where is our teacher; where is our Krishna?

Our society tends to view dark nights in clinical terms as obstacles to be overcome as quickly as possible. Tough times and dark episodes are readily medicated with little thought, or else brushed under the rug. But periods of darkness, despair and emptiness are just as much a part of human life as periods of clarity and meaning. We do a disservice to ourselves when we treat these periods of despair as a deviation from the normal and healthy life we idealize. In doing so, we suppress and avoid a necessary element, not just in human life, but in all life, that permits regeneration after a period of decay.

We need a view of life that includes the darkness just as much as the light. Spells of unknowing and emptiness leave their mark on us; yet they can add depth to our life and make us a person of compassion, kindness and wisdom. Dark nights offer an opportunity for soul growth.

The first step of the yoga of despair is understanding and acceptance—rather than avoidance, denial or escapism. These dark episodes need to be honoured. When we suppress uncomfortable emotions, something tragic happens: all other emotions go into hiding. We shut down the entire faculty of emotion and begin to feel lifeless.

Of course, that doesn't mean a dark night experience is easy. It can be excruciatingly difficult. But it's a rite of passage of sorts and a life experience embraced in earlier societies. The ideologies of dominant Western thought have laid waste to this wisdom.

We tend to think of our life as a continuous line from birth to death. Along this line, we sometimes flourish, while at other times we fall into stagnancy. When life is viewed as a series of transformations, or traditional rites of passage, as it was in ancient India, our emergence from each of these crises births new capacities and talents.

As innately spiritual beings, we are infinitely greater than the protagonist in our small and invented earthly narrative. In the dark night of the soul, the old self dies or is cast away, and a larger, greater sense of self can emerge.

In the end, the dark night of the soul reshapes us. We may emerge a different person. We may finally give up the simplistic persona we had until now used.

If the dark night is a rite of passage, our job is to allow the transformation to take place.

–2–

The sage Valmiki established his ashram, or hermitage, on the banks of the Tamasa River that flowed near the Ganges. Word of Valmiki's learning and wisdom spread across the land. Students would travel from distant kingdoms to apprentice with him.

One day, Valmiki left his ashram with a few students. The crystal waters of the Tamasa River flowed gently, and turning to his student Bharadvaja, Valmiki compared that clear and calm current to the mind of a wise person.

While looking for a suitable place to step into the river to bathe, the sage came upon a pair of cranes lost in affection for each other.[1]

The fine-looking male, with strong wings and a proud red-coloured head, was dancing about the female, preening and showing himself off in a courting display. These two beautiful cranes were obviously very much in love. Completely at ease, they moved about with a natural elegance and grace that was spell-binding.

Suddenly, the male crane, midway through his dance, began shrieking loudly and writhing on the ground. He had been pierced by an arrow. Blood flowed out of his chest on to the river bank, as he flapped about helplessly, struggling for life. Within moments, he lay unmoving, a glazed look in his lifeless eyes.

From a concealed place a fowler now emerged, eager to claim his kill.

Rather than fly away to safety, the female began circling the dead male, wailing pitifully. In utter despair, she moved around the blood-stained carcass of her companion, hoping he would return to life and resume his courtship dance.

Cranes are known to select a single mate for life. The sudden, violent loss of her partner during his courtship dance shattered the beautiful female's world and threw her into the depths of mortifying sorrow. Out of deep empathy, Valmiki, an enlightened sage, now experienced the same acute grief and despair as the female crane.

As a young man, Valmiki had been a merciless highway robber, greatly feared by travellers. He went by the name Ratnakara. But the great sage and mystic Narada had transformed his heart, helping him to cross his own dark night of the soul and enter the yoga teachings on sacred love. As a result, he had developed profound empathy for all beings.

Observing the lovelorn female circling and crying in grief, the sage also cried out piteously, cursing the fowler for his cruelty. However, what emerged from Valmiki's mouth was not ordinary prose, but a verse that mirrored perfectly the wailing of the bereaved crane!

Valmiki knew he had invented a new form of poetry, a type of verse capable of transmitting heart-rendering pathos. Never before had rhythmic verse with such symmetry been heard.[2] The sage Valmiki went on to use this four-line stanza, born of anguish and despair, to tell a story of separation and sorrow that would become one of the greatest literary epics ever written—the *Ramayana*, or "The Story of Rama". Made up of nearly 24,000 verses, this too is an account of deep love, separation and despair.

Some of the greatest wisdom texts of India have emerged from despair, such as the *Bhagavad Gita*, the *Ramayana*, part of the *Chandogya Upanishad*, and the *Bhagavata Purana*. Despair, as a form of yoga, can lead us to profound wisdom and even bring about our greatest contribution to the world. There are ancient lineages of masters who used despair as a medium to deepen their wisdom and go on to produce their greatest work.[3]

The most beautiful poetry in the Bhakti tradition are outpourings of despair, where crying itself is considered one of the highest devotional songs. Valmiki's despair upon seeing the senseless slaughter of a beautiful dancing crane led to the first epic in poetic form. The sage became known as the father of Sanskrit classical poetry.[4]

–3–

Artists, authors and musicians may have great technical skill, but if they're not deep souls, having gone through a dark night of their own, their art or music fails to stir the soul.

In the sixteenth century, Thomas More sat in prison for thirteen months before his execution. During this time, he wrote some of his best philosophy. Nelson Mandela served twenty-seven years in prison, initially on Robben Island, before finally being released in 1990. It was during this time that he readied himself to be an extraordinary leader. Many of the most moving works of art, such as the paintings of Lucian Freud, Francis Bacon and Frida Kahlo, portray the dark side of life. They give it a certain stunning beauty.

We too are artists—artists of our own life. We create our own life story. The dark night of the soul can help us create a life story that has immense depth and that shines with a rich radiance from within.

Dark nights are difficult periods. I don't wish to romanticize them or to deny their hardships. But if they arrive, there are gifts that may come with them too. They reveal to us the full depths of the soul. I have learned so much more about those depths from periods of pain and despair, than I have from times of comfort and false security.

The purpose of a dark night is not to try artificially to impose meaning on crisis or difficulty, but we may recognize in retrospect that our impasse was our metamorphosis, a necessary catalyst to spiritual growth.

We don't choose a dark night for ourselves. It is given to us. The dark night of the soul is something that *happens to us*. Nonetheless, the experience prompts us to begin a journey of consciousness. Understanding that this spiritual process can be a profoundly good thing is the first step in setting off on the journey of the soul.

Arjuna doesn't feel guilty or ashamed for having his crisis. He doesn't run from the field, even though he wants to. Running away from the dark night of the soul stunts our spiritual growth. Bestselling author Thomas Moore puts it well: "Flight from the dark infantilizes your spirituality, because the dark nights of the soul are supposed to initiate you into spiritual adulthood."[5]

Interestingly, it's not only individuals who go through the dark night, but also couples, institutions, nations and entire societies. According to the ancient texts, we're currently undergoing a societal dark night of the soul, called Kali-yuga, an age of broken narratives and existential angst. In this age of spiritual darkness, the teachings of yoga become more important than ever.

We tend to view yoga as being principally about peace and well-being. Yoga can certainly lead to these things; but it's also about facing difficulty and coming to terms with darkness and despair. The idea that yoga is about feeling good is very much a modern Western contrivance, and one based largely on a culture of avoidance. Yoga doesn't assume that we won't have to face astounding ordeals at some point in our life. Rather, yoga *anticipates* that we will.

Fear, sadness, fatigue, despair—these are friends on the path of yoga. They teach us what isn't working in our life. There's nothing like darkness to bring yoga practice to life. Some people think we need to discard or bypass these natural emotions to be able to begin yoga. No, in yoga everything becomes a tool for our enlightenment.

Despair is one of life's greatest change agents. Without it, we're likely to shelter in easy spirituality or comfortable yoga routines our entire life.

SITUATED WITHIN THEIR VERY BEING AND
MOVED BY COMPASSION, I VANQUISH THE DARKNESS
ARISING FROM THE ABSENCE OF KNOWLEDGE WITH
THE EFFULGENT LAMP OF KNOWLEDGE.

—Bhagavad Gita, 10.11

SIX

Trust Your Inner Guide

—I—

"He is your killer," my heart said to me.

I was surprised by how clear and unambiguous the message was. It frightened me. The circumstances were odd, to be sure, but was I simply imagining the worst?

It was the dead of night and I had just arrived into Mumbai en route to Delhi. This meant travelling from the international airport across the city to the domestic airport. My flight into Mumbai was late, so there was very little time to make the connecting flight. I couldn't wait for the next shuttle bus and had to catch a taxi immediately.

One of the Air India attendants accompanied me to the airport exit and, after a brief exchange with a local driver, instructed me to follow the man. I was travelling on my own. It was 2am. I accompanied the driver to his car parked some distance away, pulling a heavy suitcase behind me.

When we reached the car, I was concerned. The car had no taxi markings. It looked just like a regular car. As I got in I noticed there was already someone in the front passenger seat.

There was little time and I had been introduced to the driver by an Air India official, so I decided to ignore the warning. Maybe this is how things rolled in Mumbai?

The taxi left the international airport and entered the solitary darkness of the night. There were few cars. I felt very alone and suddenly, very exposed.

"Are we even driving towards the airport?" I wondered. It seemed to me were heading for some remote outback.

After a quarter of an hour of silence the driver began to assert that the cost of the taxi ride would be $200. I needed to pay up now. I reminded the driver that the agreed price, as indicated by the Air India attendant, was 200 Rupees; but he began raising his voice, insisting I had misunderstood. To diffuse the situation, I said I would pay whatever the price was, once we were at the domestic airport.

At this point, I sensed a strong message from the core of my heart that I was in mortal danger. I began to recite mantras for my own protection, which I had learned in the temple monastery. These mantras are most powerful when invoked from the depth of one's being.

The driver was now on his cell phone. He seemed to be arranging a meeting. After another fifteen minutes of driving we began to enter an area that was pitch black and isolated. The car slowed to a halt behind a black taxi cab. There was no one else in sight.

"You will go into this car. We are changing taxis," the driver announced.

Emerging from the black car was a burly man with a large handlebar moustache, more commonly seen in rural areas.

"He is your killer," my heart said to me. The circumstances were odd, to be sure, but was I simply imagining the worst? In that moment, I surrendered to my inner guide. The mantras I had been chanting had strengthened my connection to the guide within, whom I now trusted with my life to see me through this situation.

A voice within, tranquil, but deep like the ocean, told me to remain calm and play along. I did that. The driver popped open the boot, instructing me to shift my suitcase over to the black car. I raised it out of the boot, forty kilos of rare sacred books together with almost everything else I owned.

In that moment, I was filled with a surge of strength and courage. Adrenalin rushing through me, I lifted the large, heavy suitcase with ease, and still holding on to my carry on, made a dash into the darkness.

There was shouting. I heard the two cars start their engines in a hurry and tear away behind me in pursuit. I reached a main road, a dual carriageway with a lot of fast-flowing traffic. Suddenly I spotted a small break in the traffic and dashed across the busy road, now running against the flow of traffic. The two cars pursued me for almost a kilometre on the other side of the road.

At a large crossroads with traffic lights, I hopped into an auto-rickshaw, a small yellow motor-vehicle with three wheels. As the lights changed to green, I knew I had found safety.

At the domestic airport, I reported what had occurred to the officials. They told me I had been extremely lucky. Pulling out a newspaper, they showed me a story that shocked me: a woman from Canada had been found dead at the side of a busy road a week ago, stripped of all her belongings, just ten miles from the airport. She too had been travelling from the international airport in Mumbai to catch a connecting flight. She had stepped into an unmarked car posing as a taxi.

There had been give-away signals, but what if I hadn't been alert to them? I was outnumbered three to one. This story could have ended in several ways. The ending I experienced was the only good one.

What was it that warned me so clearly and definitively? What had told me to feign cooperation? What had helped me make a dash for my life, signalling the moment to do so? I felt I had been protected. I had listened to my inner guide and that had saved my life.

On the connecting flight, I turned to the *Bhagavad Gita*. I opened the page where Krishna reveals his true identity to Arjuna as the inner guide and the source of all wisdom: "I am seated in the hearts of all: from me come remembrance, knowledge and forgetfulness."[6]

The embodiment of the wisdom of the ancients dwells in

our own heart. In that sense, all wisdom is situated in our heart. We have a golden thread to this wisdom, a natural connection to the Universal Teacher within us.

Later, Krishna shows Arjuna his form as the entirety of existence across all space and time. In this form, Arjuna sees the birth and annihilation of all beings. He sees even himself. Krishna says that this form of his has manifested from the yoga of his own being.

Krishna is Vishvatma, "The Soul of the Universe", and he is Yogeshvara, "The Lord of Yoga", because he gives the results of yoga.[7] Just as Krishna, the Soul of the Universe, is present within Arjuna's chariot, so too is the Soul of the Universe present within our heart, within the chariot of our body. We are not alone on the field of life.

I felt deeply thankful for the inner guide, who had directed my movements—the same teacher who guided Arjuna through his dark night.

Over the years, I've developed great trust in the voice of truth from within. My inner guide has always had my best interests at heart, helping me surmount the greatest difficulties, leading me to wise teachers, revealing the secrets of yoga, and always supporting and nurturing me on my personal journey of the soul.

In traversing the dark night of the soul, trusting our inner guide is essential. Our inner guide is the light that illuminates the path on this journey through the dark.

–2–

E. O. Wilson, Professor Emeritus at Harvard University, expressed it poignantly: "We are drowning in information, while starving for wisdom."[8]

We have more information available to us than at any time in human history. But the problems of life seem as challenging and intractable as ever. When we're in a crisis, in real personal difficulty, what we're looking for is not information, but wisdom.

Wisdom is yogic perception. Wisdom is the deeper perspective we possess as we progress on our journey of yoga. Marcel Proust put it well:

> We do not receive wisdom, we must discover it for ourselves, after a journey through the wilderness which no one else can make for us, which no one can spare us, for our wisdom is the point of view from which we come at last to regard the world.[9]

Life's most important lessons require that we, ourselves, set out on an inner journey. There is no shortcut.

In setting out on this yoga journey, we will traverse a terrain we have never encountered before. We need a compass, a guide. For Arjuna, that guide is Krishna.[10]

There are many categories and levels of guides or advisers—

from a caring teacher at school who sets us in the direction of our life's purpose, to a dear friend who speaks to us with candour, to a wise rishi of the highest level, the kind that once mentored kings and queens. According to the esoteric teachings of India, all teachers in our life are expressions of the same archetype, the Universal Teacher within each of us.[11]

The Universal Teacher assumes different forms in our life to lead us towards the fulfilment of our highest potential through yoga. If we're not aware or open, we'll fail to honour the Universal Teacher in our life.

The yoga texts explain that the Universal Teacher manifests in our life in three different ways. The first is as our inner guide, the voice of truth directing us from within.[12] At the centre of our being is a well of wisdom. All the answers to all the questions we'll ever ask lie here, because this is where Krishna dwells.

The people of ancient India developed a great respect and sensitivity for wisdom revealed in the heart. Whenever we have what we sometimes call a "light-bulb moment", a moment of awakening to a deeper way of seeing, we've heard and recognized the voice of truth. We have the innate potential to recognize truth. When we develop this faculty, we're able to hear the Universal Teacher speaking to us from within.

Hearing our own inner guide is not always easy though. Often our mind speaks so loudly that we can no longer hear the voice of truth. To hear this voice requires an inner stillness and a special kind of listening, known in India as "surrendered" listening. This is when we listen with an open heart, and with a genuine desire to honour truth in whatever way it reveals itself.

Usually, our mind, the voice of the ego, is continually speaking to us. What does it say?

"They all have more than I do. I'm not good enough. I must work harder."

"I must show that I'm doing well. I must make myself attractive and lovable."

"I mustn't lose this. Without this, I'm nobody."

"This person is helping me get what I want. She's my friend."

"That person is my competition. I must overcome him. What if he gets there before I do? I mustn't allow that to happen."

We repeat and reaffirm these messages again and again— and we act on them. This leads to suffering.

When the mind becomes dominant in our life, we struggle to hear our inner guide. The voice of the Universal Teacher within is drowned out by the domineering voice of the mind, by the officious will of the ego.

The dark night of the soul offers a special opportunity to hear the Universal Teacher in our life. This is because the dark night crisis dismembers our ego and fractures our story. In the stillness that follows, if we desire to listen, we can hear the voice of truth speaking to us through all things.

The people of ancient India referred to the inner guide as the Supreme Self, the Soul of all souls. They sought through yoga to connect with that source of wisdom.

During the dark night of the soul, what could be better than to connect with the Soul of all souls? During the dark night, when we have lost all power, what better refuge is there than with the source of all potency and wisdom?

Imagine we have an extraordinary natural gift—say, we were born to play the violin.[13] Our talent will at first be raw. We can begin developing our skills by practising the violin on our own. Our music teacher at school will be able to set us off in the right direction, but she'll be able to take us only so far.

Now imagine we were given the chance to train under Itzhak Perlman, or another master of his level. We would soon develop incredible tone, flawless technique, and a unique presence as a violinist. Our latent potential would emerge and blossom fully.

We may not all be natural musicians, but each of us was most definitely born to fulfil a particular purpose. Whether that purpose is "big" or "small", it is inexpressibly marvellous and deeply fulfilling for us. When viewed from the perspective of endless time and space, any purpose in life will appear very tiny. But when expressed perfectly, our purpose has breath-taking beauty, like an unfurling flower in the wilderness or the emergence of a navigational star on a dark, lonely road. We each have the unique potential to contribute something of special worth to the world.

The second way the Universal Teacher manifests in our life is as a caring mentor. This can take the form of a parent, teacher or advisor. Anyone who guides us through difficulty in our life, who shifts our perspective in a way that inspires us to participate more fully in life, is a yoga teacher, whether they know it or not.

In India, such a person is traditionally called a "guru", or mentor. A real mentor will always place the interests of the student before his or her own. Importantly, a guru can help a student only as far as the level he or she is at herself. Thus, gurus are of many types with different capacities. The texts of India advise that we try to learn from a guru of the highest degree.[14]

The ancient texts set out very clearly the qualifications of such a guru. These remarkable qualities have for thousands of years been considered a prerequisite to teaching the sacred lore of the rishis. They are the benchmark against which any mentor should be measured, and the standard to which all genuine mentors will aspire.

Importantly, the *Bhagavad Gita* describes a true yoga

teacher as a "truth seer".[15] In other words, this is a person who has herself crossed the dark night of the soul. She knows the inner landscape. The wisdom such a teacher transmits gives a student the ability to truly see, especially in the dark night of the soul.

The *Skanda Purana* explains that the syllable *gu* stands for "darkness" and *ru* for "illumination". A true guru is therefore someone who dispels the darkness of illusion with the light of transformative wisdom.[16]

A guru's knowledge of the sacred texts will be realized knowledge, and not merely intellectual learning.[17] In other words, it will be reflected in the way he or she lives. Thus, the ideal guru will possess mastery over the mind and senses.[18] They will not be driven by a desire for money, fame or followers. In the *Skanda Purana*, Mahadeva warns pointedly:

> Numerous are the gurus who rob their students of their wealth. But I consider it rare to find a guru who instead steals away the miseries from the student's heart.[19]

Another text similarly explains:

> One who desires to obtain wealth, fame or service from his students is not fit to become a guru. A true

guru is an ocean of compassion, is fulfilled within himself, and works tirelessly for the benefit of others.[20]

For Arjuna, that mentor is Krishna, his charioteer. Krishna is Arjuna's dearest friend, someone Arjuna knows he can trust. Arjuna therefore allows himself to be completely vulnerable. Arjuna doesn't open himself up to a stranger, an unknown guru.[21]

Likewise, Arjuna doesn't delegate responsibility for his life to someone else. After Krishna has explained the yoga teachings to Arjuna, Krishna tells him that having understood these teachings, he should act as he chooses.[22] In other words, Arjuna must *choose* the direction of his life. He must *own* his journey. Ultimately, like Arjuna, we each bear responsibility for our own life.

–4–

The third manifestation of the Universal Teacher is the environment, which is overflowing with wisdom.[23] Water, for example, teaches us fluidity and adaptability. The past teaches us humility. Stillness and silence teach us clarity. Young children teach us authenticity and playfulness. Our teachers are everywhere. They speak to us through all things. We hear their wisdom in our heart.

Suffering is an important teacher too. Many of us spend

our whole life running away from it, but suffering deepens us, teaching us compassion, empathy, and non-attachment.[24] Most people move through at least one period in their life marked by intense difficulty and pain, often acknowledging in retrospect that it was the period in which they learned the most about life—and even about death.

In facing the multifarious deaths that arrive with the dark night of the soul, we're pulled into realms of understanding that might not be readily available during prolonged periods of care-free comfort. Krishna tells Arjuna in the *Gita* that he is Death, and in doing so, reveals how we can understand the dark night of the soul to be a manifestation of our inner guide as well.[25]

It took me many years to begin appreciating that my environment might actually be supporting me at all times. To aid my understanding, my teacher told me about a powerful king named Yadu, who crossed paths with a young and effulgent brahmin, or priest of sacred learning, while travelling through his kingdom.

The king approached the brahmin and said, "Dear brahmin, although all people within this world are burning in the great forest fire of desire and greed, I see that you remain free and aren't burned by that fire. You are just like a mighty elephant who takes refuge from a blazing forest fire by standing in the cooling waters of the Ganges. Please tell me how you became enlightened, so I may learn from you."[26]

The brahmin replied, "I have learned from twenty-four different gurus. They include the earth, wind, ocean, honey thief, hawk and arrow maker. By taking their lessons to heart, I have attained complete freedom from suffering."

The brahmin then explained to King Yadu what he had learned from each of his teachers. "I observed that the earth provides for everyone's needs," he said, "even when humans plunder her resources, turn her lush forests into wasteland, and soak her surface with blood in the most savage of wars. From the earth, I learned the quality of tolerance. Similarly, the trees of the earth give their bark, roots, fruits, leaves, wood and shade, without any expectation of return. This taught me the quality of dedication to others. It taught me to make the welfare of others the sole reason for my existence."[27]

The brahmin continued: "The wind travels everywhere, sometimes passing through a waterfall, a fragrant sandalwood forest or a crematorium. The wind crosses dark and forbidding places, yet remains unafraid. It carries the aromas of different locations, but remains unentangled and undisturbed. From the wind, I learned that while we may find ourselves in challenging and troublesome situations in life, we can remain fearless and undisturbed, thereby transcending 'good' and 'bad'.[28]

"From the ocean, I learned that whatever life brings our way, we should remain undiminished in who we are. During the rainy season, the rivers rushing to the sea are overflowing; and during the summer, they dry up. But the ocean always remains unmoved and inexhaustible. Similarly, a wise person is never shaken, even in the midst of the greatest difficulties. She remains at peace whether she meets with success or failure. This is because she doesn't seek her identity in these things. Therefore, they don't define her."[29]

The brahmin continued: "One day, I happened to see a person in the forest breaking open a bee hive to collect all the honey that the countless bees had spent their entire lives producing. From this I learned about the dangers and futility of needless accumulation of capital, which simply creates greed, danger and fear. Humans can be like bees who struggle to produce a large quantity of honey, which is then stolen by a more powerful capitalist for his own enjoyment or benefit. If our wealth is not lost during our life, death will in the end surely take everything from us. I concluded that I shouldn't make the amassing of capital an end in its own right. Rather, the primary purpose of wealth is to help others.[30]

"One day, I observed a group of large hawks in flight. Unable to find any prey, the hawks suddenly joined forces to attack a weaker hawk that was carrying some meat. The weaker hawk soared, dodged and dove to save itself. At last, the weaker hawk, its life in peril, gave up the meat it was holding on to, and at that moment it was freed from misery. Seeing this, I understood that humans form deep attachments to objects and outcomes, which they believe will make them happy. But these attachments are a source of suffering. As soon as we relinquish our possessiveness and attachment, we become liberated.[31]

"Another time, I observed an arrow maker at work. Suddenly drums, trumpets and other musical instruments could be heard, as a large procession approached. Despite all the commotion, the arrow maker was so absorbed in his work that he didn't even notice the king, who passed right next to him. This filled me with wonder. Most of us, I thought, are continually distracted by the commotion of daily life. If we could practise yoga with the undivided focus and absorption of the arrow maker, how our life would be transformed.[32]

"In this way, I learned from twenty-four different teachers. I took their teachings to heart and began applying them in my own life. This is how I attained enlightenment."

Hearing this, King Yadu accepted this effulgent and fearless brahmin as his guru. The king developed the same qualities as the brahmin and began ruling his vast kingdom as a philosopher-king.

I learned from this story that there is beauty and perfection in all things. If we're awake to the voice of truth, if we hear that voice speaking to us through all things, we realize that the environment is always friendly. It is not hostile. A person committed to the path of yoga perceives opportunity all about her, even in times of difficulty. As William Shakespeare eloquently put it: "Sweet are the uses of adversity, Which like the toad, ugly and venomous, Wears yet a precious jewel in his head."[33]

In every challenge or difficulty, a precious jewel awaits us. Most of us see only the outer form of the circumstance and never look for that hidden jewel. We're unable to see it because it lies in a direction we don't often look: *within*.

THE SELF, DELUDED BY THE FALSE EGO,
THINKS, "I AM THE DOER."

—*Bhagavad Gita*, 3.27

SEVEN

Surrender the Need to Control

—I—

As I underwent my own dark night, I wondered whether I would make it through. Everyone was out enjoying the sunshine, but I felt utterly alone and desolate. The laughter of children and the chirping of birds felt jarring. My world was filled with darkness.

Immersed in that state of internal desolation, I wandered into a solitary cemetery on a hill. I wanted to be alone. I wished it were I who was dead. The gravestones, upright and silent, stared at me like impassive monuments of shattered lives. I felt at home here, among the graveyard phantoms, the fragments of dreams, the broken stories and forgotten memories.

But something caught my eye: a bright orange butterfly on a twig. It had just emerged from its glossy skin-like case. Filled with life, the creature disrupted my misery. It felt like a message.

Nature has its own powerful wisdom. The rishis and yogis realized this and looked to nature for inspiration and learning, to help them live in harmony and balance. They considered the natural world to be a teacher, and created yoga poses inspired by animals and plants to imbibe their lessons.[34]

Nature doesn't fight its own processes. An acorn transforms into a mighty oak; an embryo morphs into a baby; and a caterpillar becomes a butterfly, following its own internal blueprint. We, by contrast, are continuously fighting our own natural processes, including the natural rite of passage that is the dark night of the soul.

To become a butterfly, a caterpillar undergoes a wondrous transformation, casting off its old self. Inside the cocoon, the creature digests itself, causing its body to die. During this partial death, some of the caterpillar's old tissues are salvaged, and these remnant cells are used to fashion a new form. The caterpillar's nibbling jaws become a long tube, and twelve beady eyes meld to become two. Now there are antennae and wings. The exquisite colours of the butterfly begin to manifest.

Its final metamorphosis accomplished, the butterfly emerges from its translucent case. The brown hairy caterpillar has transformed into a new being—one of nature's most stunning paintings. Rather than spend its life crawling on the ground, this creature can now rise into the sky, and even cross continents. Rather than feed on poisonous milkweed, it will spend the rest of its days drinking nectar.

I learned later that the caterpillar sheds its skin numerous times, whenever it outgrows it. The creature's transformation into a butterfly is its final and most wondrous metamorphosis.

While animals and plants go through a biological metamorphosis, we experience ours on a spiritual level. In our metamorphosis, all that is false dies away; only the permanent and true can remain.

The universe is self-organizing and self-correcting. It supports life moving forward all the time. The dark night of the soul is a self-correcting mechanism. Like the caterpillar that sheds its skin, we cast away the small human story and identity we've been clinging to. It can no longer serve us. We enter a period of incubation, a partial "death", which allows renewal and growth. Upon our return to the world, we're no longer limited by the same small narrative we inhabited before.

In the dark night of the soul, we're "deworlded". This is frightening to us, naturally. We want to resist the dark night, to avoid it at all costs. But can we learn from the butterfly? The caterpillar has no way of knowing what it will become. The butterfly's magnificent colours, its ability to visit new continents, its capacity to taste nectar—these are all beyond the imagination of the ungainly caterpillar. Yet during its transition, the caterpillar allows the transformation to take place.

We too have no way of knowing how we will emerge from a dark night experience. The ability to say *yes* to the dark night of the soul, the ability to allow the transformation to take place, requires a level of trust or faith that the universe will ultimately support us.

I marvelled at the bright orange butterfly on the twig. It was stretching and unfurling its newly formed wings. It seemed perfectly adjusted to the world.

"If nature can handle the death and rebirth of this butterfly," I thought, "then surely, I too can have faith, and surrender to whatever process I'm undergoing."

Watching the little creature brought peace into my heart. I would learn from this little friend.

–2–

In the dark night of the soul, we may learn more about ourselves and about the nature of life than in all the combined years of our life. But how do we deal with the initial pain and suffering that comes with the collapse of our perceptual world? It's easy to say, "Just have faith." What about our pain? How do we deal with that?

Krishna's first instruction to Arjuna on pain is to neither react to it nor to run away from it. Pleasure and pain are both a natural and inevitable part of being human. Krishna reminds Arjuna that whatever pain or discomfort he's experiencing is sure to pass. Like heat and cold, these sensations are impermanent and are born of our engagement with this world. The wise learn to endure these sensations, without being distracted by them.[35]

This is an important teaching. Krishna is making an implicit distinction here between *pain* and *suffering*. Pain is an inevitable part of life. We may not have much control of pain, such as the pain of a wound, but suffering? Suffering is our mental response to our experience of pain.

When I remained in India through the scorching summer months, I learned that the hardest part was not the temperature above one hundred degrees Fahrenheit, but the insufferable voice of the mind. The heat is a form of pain; the constant resistance of the mind to that pain is suffering. The two are not the same. I learned that while I couldn't control the summer heat, I could control the relentless nagging and dissatisfaction of my mind.

Pain is inevitable; suffering is optional. This is why Krishna advises Arjuna to learn to endure his pain without being distracted, without creating a story around it. Krishna advises Arjuna not to struggle against struggle, but to allow struggle to be, because struggle is an inevitable part of life. We can't escape it.

As Krishna explains, we can learn to work with pain *skilfully*. One of the most powerful ways to approach pain is simply to remove our resistance to it and enter a more graceful place of acceptance.

This approach to pain actually releases it, detoxifying us and transforming the energy of our pain. Quick to react to our pain, we often view it as our enemy. We try to banish or suppress it. But what if we looked at our pain as though it were, say, a little child who needs our nurturing? What if we let go of our resistance to it?

The main cause of our suffering is warring with reality: not wanting things to be the way they are. As yoga author Stephen Cope explains:

> Through practice I've come to see that the deepest source of my misery is not wanting things to be the way they are. Not wanting myself to be the way I am. Not wanting the world to be the way it is. Not wanting others to be the way they are. Whenever I'm suffering, I find this "war with reality" to be at the heart of the problem.[36]

The ability to annul suffering is an important part of yoga. In the *Bhagavad Gita*, Krishna defines yoga in several ways, and one of them is "breaking the connection with suffering".[37] In other words, yoga, the art of living skilfully, is designed to free us from misery associated with the past, present and future.[38]

Rather than running from pain, the solution is to make a 180-degree turn in graceful acceptance and enter the heart of the experience. This is the only place where there is peace. The practice of saying *yes* to life, of allowing what is to be, is represented in yoga by Shavasana, the "Corpse Pose". This is a yoga pose that normally comes at the end of a yoga session. In this pose, the yoga practitioner lies on her back with her arms at her sides in a state of complete acceptance.

While Corpse Pose may look easy, its full benefits come with finding complete release. This yoga pose is extremely beneficial to the psyche. Corpse Pose's full surrender to the process of death is what we need in the dark night of the soul.

If Corpse Pose could speak, these might be its teachings: "Let go of projection and resistance. Let go of your stories and identities in this world. Be your own best friend. Above all, never forget that you're a child of the universe, as much as the stars and the trees; you deserve to be here. You're protected and supported. Die into life."

The ancients developed great trust in the self-organizing and self-correcting principle of life. They called such trust *sharanagati*, "the way of surrender". This is when we make the Soul of the Universe our protector and maintainer.

The word "surrender" comes from Old French *surrendre*, which means "to give (something) up".[39] What is it we are called upon to give up in the dark night of the soul? Our story. Our false identity.

We came into this world without anything. We then created a complex story of who we are and what we own and what we must do. Surrender is a return to our naked origin, the recovery of an original state *before* our story.

Most of our life we take refuge in our small human story. But in the dark night of the soul, this story is shattered. The dark night of the soul puts us in a place where we have no choice but to surrender. This surrender is not about being beaten down or giving up, nor is it about indulging in suffering. Quite the contrary. Surrender opens the doorway of yoga. It allows us to set out on our journey of the soul.[40]

Surrendered people recognize they can't control everything. Therefore, they neither attempt nor desire to force situations or other people. Instead, they focus their attention on their own behaviour, and find new, creative ways to overcome obstacles.

Comfortable with uncertainty, they are less fixated on outcomes and are able to go with the flow of life. When an unplanned situation happens, they easily shrug it off. As a result, they tend to be happier, more light-hearted and more resilient, unlike inflexible people, who are far more susceptible to anger, distress and resentment.

Surrendered individuals know how to pause, take a deep breath, and observe. Powerful without dominating, they understand that true power comes from deep listening and being respectful. Those who are surrendered don't measure themselves by how much they are liked, nor do they feel the need to compete for attention. When they sit quietly in a room, others are drawn to them naturally.

Those who practise surrender tend to be good listeners. They don't judge, building true and lasting friendships. With the ability to see others beyond temporary stories and circumstances, they engage with others at the level of the soul, the sacred self.

The English word respect comes from *respicere*, which means "to see or behold". Since surrendered souls truly see others, they truly respect others. Liberated from their stories, their sense of success isn't determined by occupation or net worth, nor do they have a driving need for money and power. As a result, they don't use others for their own advantage. They love people and use things, rather than use people and love things.

Willing to accept when they're wrong, surrendered people don't insist on being right. They're open to new ideas, and they forgive easily. The practice of surrender allows one to be more playful with life. Vibrant, alive, and a real pleasure to be around, surrendered people have a natural spontaneity and vitality that rubs off on others.

The surrender we learn during the dark night of the soul becomes a powerful way of being throughout the rest of our life. No longer desperate to manipulate life, we can allow events to unfold; we can make room for the unexpected. We stop struggling and fighting against life.

Surrender is about relinquishing the need to control, knowing we'll be guided and protected. We may be pushed down; we may be cast into darkness, unable to see any pathway ahead. But nothing can keep us from taking shelter of Krishna, the Soul of the Universe, seated in our own heart. This connection with a power greater than ourselves is called "yoga".

At the end of the *Bhagavad Gita*, Krishna tells Arjuna: "Relinquishing all forms of dharma, take refuge with me only. I will release you from all misfortune: don't despair!"[41] In other words, *sharanagati*, the way of surrender, leads to the blossoming of our highest potential. This is because it gives the yoga pilgrim entrance into the temple of yoga. There is no state of being more powerful and helpful than this in the dark night of the soul.

In the Bhakti tradition, *sharanagati* is made up of six attitudes, which the yogi or yogini cultures in her practice:[42]

1. Accept whatever supports your yoga practice.
2. Let go of whatever harms your yoga practice.
3. Depend upon the Soul of the Universe as your true protector in all circumstances.
4. Embrace the Soul of the Universe as your maintainer.
5. Surrender all false identities, including that of being the doer or controller.
6. Cultivate humility in life.

Our journey of yoga is a continuous process of accepting what takes us forward on our path and letting go of whatever holds us back. The yogi or yogini relinquishes the imaginary identity she has created in her story, which leads to suffering, and takes shelter of the Soul of the Universe, knowing she will be protected and maintained. With natural humility, she's able to travel far on her journey.

Sharanagati, the way of surrender, encapsulates the first yoga teaching of the *Bhagavad Gita* for crossing the dark night: *Set out on the journey of the soul.*

Notes
Part II: "Set Out on the Journey of the Soul"

1   Certain details in this story of Valmiki strongly suggest that the bird was a Sarus Crane. The Sarus Crane is now extinct in India.

2   Since these lines were born of grief, or *shoka*, this poetic form, the first of its kind in Indian literature, became known as a *shloka*. There are several different redactions of Valmiki's *Ramayana*. One of the oldest, the *Rigvedic Ramayana*, renders this moment in which the sage cries out in grief and involuntarily utters the first ever *shloka* in text 9.73.5.

3   For instance, Narada's despair led to Sanat-kumara's profound teachings in Chapter 7 of the ancient *Chandogya Upanishad*. Narada had a student named Vyasa. At the height of his literary accomplishment, Vyasa was consumed by a feeling of emptiness. Narada guided him out of his dark night, and the result was the *Bhagavata Purana*, a twelve-volume work of astonishing beauty. Then, the despair of the Sarus Crane, reflected in the heart of Narada's student Valmiki, led to the *Ramayana*, one of India's great epics.

4   Valmiki is known in Indian literature as *adi-kavi*, the first poet, as he is the first to have composed a set of rhythmic verses in Sanskrit and placed them in sequence within an epic.

5   Thomas Moore, *Dark Nights of the Soul: A Guide to Finding Your Way Through Life's Ordeals* (2011), p. 15

6   *Bhagavad Gita*, 15.15. The ancient texts of India explain that both the self and the Universal Teacher, the source of all wisdom, reside within the heart of all living beings, which is compared to a cave (e.g. *Katha Upanishad*, 1.2.12, 1.3.1 and 2.1.7; and *Brahma-sutra*, 1.2.11). The sage and mystic Narada explains that Shri Krishna, the Universal Teacher and Lord of Yoga, is sitting unseen within the cave of the heart of all living beings (*Bhagavata Purana*, 10.37.10–11).

7   *Bhagavad Gita*, 11.4, 11.9, 18.75 and 18.78. Arjuna also addresses Krishna as "O Yogi" (*Bhagavad Gita*, 10.17).

8   Edward O. Wilson, *Consilience: The Unity of Knowledge* (1999), p. 294.

9   Marcel Proust, *In Search of Lost Time*, Vol. 2, *Within a Budding Grove* (1992), p. 513.

10 *Bhagavad Gita*, 2.7. Arjuna accepts Krishna as his guide before Krishna begins explaining the yoga teachings of the *Gita* to him.

11 *Bhagavata Purana*, 11.29.6, as well as Shrila Krishnadas Kaviraja Goswami, *Shri Chaitanya Charitamrita, Adi-lila*, 1.47 and 1.58, and *Madhya-lila*, 22.47. In the Bhakti tradition, the Universal Teacher is worshipped as Vishnu, the all-pervading sustainer of all things. One of the 1008 names of Vishnu is Guru, or "Teacher".

12 In ancient India, the inner guide is known as Paramatma. For key references to Paramatma, see *Mundaka Upanishad*, 3.1.2; *Shvetashvatara Upanishad*, 4.7; *Bhagavad Gita*, 6.7 and 15.15; and *Bhagavata Purana*, 1.2.11.

13 The remainder of this chapter is drawn from Simon Haas, *The Book of Dharma: Making Enlightened Choices* (2013), Chapter 11, entitled "The Universal Teacher". The material has been edited and adapted for this presentation on the yoga teachings of the *Bhagavad Gita*.

14 *Skanda Purana*, "The Song of the Teacher" (*Guru-gita*), 279–81. A topmost guru is known as *parama-guru* or *sad-guru*.

15 *Bhagavad Gita*, 4.34.

16 *Skanda Purana*, "The Song of the Teacher" (*Guru-gita*), 44.

17 See *Bhagavata Purana*, 11.3.21; *Mundaka Upanishad*, 1.2.12; and Shrila Sanatana Goswami, *Shri Hari-bhakti-vilasa*, 1.46.

18 Shrila Rupa Goswami, *Shri Upadeshamrita*, 1.

19 *Skanda Purana*, "The Song of the Teacher" (*Guru-gita*), 269.

20 *Vishnu-smriti*; quoted by Shrila Sanatana Goswami in his *Shri Hari-bhakti-vilasa*, 1.45.

21 Catherine Ghosh makes this insightful observation in "Yoga in The Gita: Dynamic Participation in Your Daily Life", Elephant Journal [website], published 11 Mar. 2012.

22 *Bhagavad Gita*, 18.63

23 My teacher, Shrila B. V. Narayan Goswami once explained, "[T]here is nothing in all of existence from which some instruction cannot be taken. For an intelligent person, all the objects of the world will give some kind of instruction." Shri Shrimad Bhaktivedanta Narayana Maharaja, *Shri Prabandhavali* (2003), p. 58.

24 *Bhagavata Purana*, 11.8.38 and 11.9.1.

25 *Bhagavad Gita*, 10.34.

26 *Bhagavata Purana*, 11.7.29.

27 *Bhagavata Purana*, 11.7.37–38.

28 *Bhagavata Purana*, 11.7.40–41.

29 *Bhagavata Purana*, 11.8.5–6. See also *Bhagavad Gita*, 2.70.

30 *Bhagavata Purana*, 11.8.15.

31 *Bhagavata Purana*, 11.9.1–2.

32 *Bhagavata Purana*, 11.9.13.

33 William Shakespeare, *As You Like It*, Act 2, Scene 1.

34 According to the *Gheranda Samhita* (2.1–2), there are 8.4 million *asanas*, as many as there are forms of life. Of these, 84 are preeminent, of which 32 are especially useful.

35 *Bhagavad Gita*, 2.14–15

36 Stephen Cope, "Everything Is Already OK" in Stephen Cope, ed., *Will Yoga and Meditation Really Change My Life?* (2003), p. 291.

37 *Bhagavad Gita*, 6.23: *duhkha-samyoga-viyogam* ("breaking the connection with suffering")

38 For instance, see *Bhagavata Purana*, 1.7.7. See also *Bhagavad Gita*, 2.64–65: Krishna tells Arjuna that the self, when not governed by attraction and repulsion, attains calmness; and in such calmness, "the cessation of all one's suffering occurs".

39   *The Oxford English Dictionary* (1989).

40   For some of the benefits that spring from surrender, see Judith Orloff, "7 Habits of Surrendered People", Dr Judith Orloff's Blog [blog], published 26 Feb. 2014.

41   *Bhagavad Gita*, 18.66. The Sanskrit word *papa* is usually understood to refer to the karmic results of harmful acts, but it can also be understood in the wider sense of difficulty, suffering or misfortune. This verse effectively marks the end of Krishna's teachings, with the verses that follow being about sharing the yoga teachings with others and the benefits of hearing and studying these teachings.

42   See the verse *anukulyasya sankalpah pratikulyasya varjanam* from the *Vaishnava-tantra*, quoted in *Hari-bhakti-vilasa* (11.676), *Bhakti-sandarbha* (Anuccheda 236) and *Shri Chaitanya Charitamrita* (*Madhya-lila*, 22.100). The fifth attitude, *atma-nikshepa*, is often translated as self-surrender. The English rendition here is based on the "Piyusha-varshini" commentary of Shrila Bhaktivinoda Thakura to Shrila Rupa Goswami's *Shri Upadeshamrita*, verse 1.

.

PART

III

THE SECOND AGREEMENT:
"LET EVERY STEP BE ITS OWN REWARD"

Karma-Yoga,
Practising Skill in Action

III

Krishna's first teaching to Arjuna is that he isn't the imaginary lead character in his story.[1] The self survives the changing stories of life. We are spiritual beings, not the tiny persona we've created in our story. Remembering who we are frees us from identification with our stories.

Arjuna doesn't quite understand how Krishna's teachings about the self relate to his predicament, his inability to act on the battlefield. Krishna therefore teaches Arjuna the three secrets of Karma-yoga, the yoga of skilful action.[2]

We can't escape action, not even in the dark night of the soul, Krishna explains.[3] Even when we choose not to act, we're engaged in a form of action. The real question, then, becomes, "What is the *best way* to act? How do we act with skill?"

Yoga is "skill in action", Krishna explains.[4] This is one of the first definitions of yoga that appears in the *Bhagavad Gita*. In other words, yoga is the art of making adept choices in life. It's easy to act; but it's difficult to act *skilfully*.

When our actions are propelled by fear, lamentation or confusion, we act in a way that is unskilful. Yet, there's a way of acting that doesn't lead to suffering. Unskilful action entangles us more deeply in our story; but skilful or yogic action frees us. It creates immense spaciousness and no longer binds us to suffering.

Krishna breaks it down into three easy steps:

1. Be true to your own nature.
2. Let go of the fruits.
3. Make your work an offering.

We're each born with a particular nature, which allows us to make a unique contribution in the world. While we can spend so much of our life fighting ourselves, Krishna counsels Arjuna to be true to his nature. "Beings *must* follow their nature; what can repression accomplish?" he says.[5] Rather than pretend we're someone else or try to be what others expect us to be, the first rule of Karma-yoga is to be true to our own nature. As Krishna observes, "One's own path, even if imperfect, is better than another's path followed perfectly. By carrying out action in accord with one's own nature, one doesn't go wrong."[6]

The second step is to let go of the fruits of action. As Krishna tells Arjuna, "You have a claim only to the action itself, never to its fruits."[7]

The best way to act, Krishna explains, is to give our best and let go of the fruits, or desired outcome. This seems like a radical teaching, because usually whatever we do is *only* for the fruits. Krishna explains how being overly anxious about the results creates suffering. It's better to act with full presence and love, finding satisfaction in the action itself. Let the action, as an expression of love, be its own reward.

Letting go of the fruits doesn't mean we don't care about the results. It means we act with full commitment, but we understand that the results of our actions lie outside our control. We never know how things will turn out. We have some control over how we choose to act, but not over the results of those actions. Letting go of the fruits means giving up our attachment that something *has to happen* in a particular way. We remain open to whatever the results are.[8]

By consciously surrendering our attachment to the fruits of our work we free ourselves from the ego's need to claim success for what we do and from the ego's fear of failure. This brings out the best in us. We're much less likely to suffer crippling disappointment if things don't go as we had hoped or planned.

By contrast, if we're fixated on trying to force an outcome, it usually brings out the worst in us: our ego flourishes and we're caught in a cycle of want and frustration, tied to our story. We lament about the past, when things haven't gone as we desired, and we're fearful of the future. We're not able to live with presence in the field of now. This is bewildered action, or action that binds us to suffering.

Krishna then discloses the third component of Karma-yoga: make your work an offering. Krishna explains: "One who offers his actions to the Divine, having let go of attachment, isn't affected by misfortune, as water doesn't cling to a lotus leaf."[9]

What a beautiful teaching! By making whatever we do an offering of love, an act of service, we purify our being. We're released from misfortune.

In taking this third step of Karma-yoga, we cultivate an attitude of devotion and a mood of service in whatever we do, bringing out the best of ourselves. This is a life-changing approach. The work we do no longer binds us; it becomes the means by which we develop what is most valuable and fulfilling to the soul: sacred love.

Like all the greatest teachings, this sounds simple, and it is. Throughout our life, we've reinforced our story through our actions. This has had a *binding* effect. Yet, our actions, if skilful, can also have a *releasing* effect. This is Karma-yoga, the yoga of skilful action.

Ostensibly, Duryodhana and Arjuna are on the same battlefield engaged in the same activity; but Duryodhana is acting in a way that binds him further to his story, while Arjuna is urged to engage in Karma-yoga, which will release him from his story and help him cross the dark night of the soul.

ONE'S OWN PATH, EVEN IF IMPERFECT, IS BETTER
THAN ANOTHER'S PATH FOLLOWED PERFECTLY.
BY CARRYING OUT ACTION IN ACCORD WITH ONE'S OWN
NATURE, ONE DOESN'T GO WRONG.

—*Bhagavad Gita*, 18.47

EIGHT

Be True to Your Own Nature

—I—

"My resume is basically a list of things I hate to do."
"I like my job only marginally more than I like being homeless."
"It's not that I hate my job, but I'd rather have my eyes gouged out by a rabid beaver than work in this hell hole for a day longer!"
"I like my job to the extent that sometimes I go minutes without checking how many minutes are left in the workday."

These are some of the ways employees feel about their work. I regularly meet people who find their jobs deeply unsatisfying, even soul-destroying.

Many years ago, before setting up my own business, I was keen to gain work experience in the legal profession. I interned at one of the top firms in the world, at its London office.

Even before I walked through the glass sliding doors and passed security, I was awed by the sheer scale and polished exterior of the firm. Associates and partners, dressed in immaculate tailored suits, ascended the lifts and escalators to their designated departments. I hurried along to "Commercial", eager to impress.

As I was about to discover, not everything was as it seemed. Some people were clearly made for this workplace: they loved the law and were in their habitat. But for many others, the firm was an impersonal, soul-crushing machine that seemed to siphon off their vitality, demanding everything from them.

To take the edge off their fatigue and alienation, employees would meet at one of the nearby bars till late in the evening and get drunk. If that wasn't enough, they would head to upmarket strip clubs.

What kept them tied to work they didn't like? The reward was a lot of money and prestige. With a large salary came new expectations and standards of living: a larger apartment in a more central and expensive London postcode, a more impressive car, costly holidays to the Burj Al Arab in Dubai or to the Bahamas. These things become the new norm, and one day you realize you're locked in.

I made friends with Chris. He was scheduling his business meetings around his job interviews.

"I can't tell you how much my spirit has died since I started working here," he told me. "It feels like a slaughterhouse of the soul."

A slaughterhouse of the soul! The phrase surprised me. I would be reminded of it a few years later.

"Well, what would you like to do?" I asked Chris.

"I love plants. I was going to be a botanist, but my father convinced me it was a bad idea. Botanists struggle to pay their bills."

Like so many, Chris was in a profession that didn't suit his nature. Harried and fatigued, he would get through Mondays knowing that everyone around him was equally miserable. Chris complained regularly that he wasn't being paid enough; that others of his standing at similar firms were paid more; that colleagues advanced ahead of him because they had connections or navigated the firm's politics better.

I don't know what happened to Chris. We didn't stay in touch. But the phrase he used remained with me: "slaughterhouse of the soul". No matter how well-paid the job, I knew I didn't want to end up in a slaughterhouse of the soul.

–2–

Rather than just care for her dying patients, long-time palliative nurse Bronnie Ware thought she could maybe learn from them too. After all, these were people at the end of their life. Awareness of our own mortality has a way of altering our perspective on life, of helping us see what we so easily miss in the frenetic, feverish rush of everyday existence.

Bronnie began questioning her patients: "What went really well in your life? Do you have any regrets? Is there anything you would do differently?"

To Bronnie's surprise, there was one regret that kept coming up again and again: *"I wish I'd had the courage to live a life true to myself, not the life others expected of me."*[10]

In the *Bhagavad Gita*, Krishna tells Arjuna that it's better to strive and even struggle on your own path, than to succeed on the path of another.[11] Krishna goes further: "It's better to follow your own path *even if you perish doing so*, than to follow the path someone else expects of you and succeed in doing so perfectly."[12]Arjuna is a warrior by nature. In his dark night of the soul, he wants to give up being a warrior; it's a difficult path. He would rather choose a different calling, maybe that of a wandering monk. But Krishna teaches him about the importance of being true to one's nature: "By carrying out action in accord with one's own nature, one doesn't go wrong. One should never abandon the type of action one is born to perform, Arjuna, even if it has faults. All undertakings come with some fault, just as fire comes with smoke."[13]

By carrying out action in accord with one's own nature, one doesn't go wrong. That's a powerful statement.

To express our nature, our calling, making it our personal offering of the heart, is our birthright; it's what we were placed on earth to do. But how do we know what our nature is? We may have spent so many years, even decades, trying to live up to the expectations of others and trying to fit in that we simply don't know what our nature is anymore. What then?

We can start by looking to our gifts. If we're naturally good at something, it may offer us a clue about our nature. Every life form has a particular gift, or "power". A bee is able to manufacture honey; a hummingbird can stop mid-flight and hover in the air; a fish draws oxygen out of water; glow-worms can illuminate the darkness, like stars fallen to the earth. We too each have a unique gift and contribution to make.

But recognizing our gifts is only a starting point, of course. It's through active engagement with the world that our calling is revealed to us; it's by being of service in life that we're summoned to express our nature in a specific way. Our nature then manifests most clearly to us, as a calling.

One simple way to know if we're being true to our nature is to ask, "Do I feel more *alive*? Is what I'm doing creating vitality, or is it sapping my strength and making me feel dead?"

Imagine carrying a fifty-kilo bag of rocks back to your home, ten miles up a mountain path. The sun is beating down. After one mile, you begin questioning whether this was a good idea. How did you ever get involved in this drudgery? After two long miles, you can hardly continue. You question whether you'll be able to make it. With every step, the bag feels heavier. All your energy is draining away, and the journey is utter misery and torture. After three miles, you finally give up.

Now imagine that instead of rocks, your bag is filled with fifty kilos of gold bars or precious jewels. There's enough treasure here to last you an entire lifetime. The bag is the same weight as before. The journey up the mountain is the same distance too. But now instead of feeling sapped of strength, you'll be filled with energy and vitality. Instead of struggling with every step, you'll probably be dancing up the mountain with that bag.

This is what it feels like when we live in accord with our nature and follow our purpose, or calling. We all have some experience of this. When we truly love what we do, we can spend all day and all night doing it, even forgetting to eat or sleep. But oddly, we don't feel sapped of strength; we find we have more strength and energy than before. We experience what we might describe as "effortless effort".

−3−

Imagine spending twenty-five years—a quarter of a century—climbing the corporate ladder and finding yourself unfulfilled. When Peter was finally made a senior partner at his London law firm, the culmination of all his hard toil and sacrifice, he began, for the first time, to acknowledge his unhappiness.

Previously, Peter had viewed his simmering lack of something as the need for a promotion or pay rise. But when he finally became a senior partner, there was nowhere else for him to go; there was nothing on the horizon to hide the emptiness he felt. Peter realized he had spent two and a half decades toiling in the City in work that didn't satisfy him deeply. He was a good lawyer, for sure; but this was *not* his passion.

Peter came from a poor family. His parents had struggled to send him to university. Growing up, he sat beside children who had a lot more than he did, and this made him feel inadequate. When it came time to choose a trajectory for his life, he didn't pause to think about his purpose or his nature. He wanted a career that would give him prestige and a high income. Law promised both.

After twenty-five years, the choices Peter made as a youth had caught up with him. The realization that he had been following a path that was not his own threw Peter into a personal crisis, a dark night of the soul.

What do you do in that situation? You realign with truth, with the way you and the universe are constructed.

And this is what Peter did. "What is it I *really* want to do?" he asked himself. "If I could start all over, knowing what I know now, what would I choose?"

This brings us back to Bronnie Ware and the number one regret of her dying patients: *"I wish I'd had the courage to live a life true to myself, not the life others expected of me."* When faced with our own mortality, what stands out most clearly is the quality of the choices we've made in our life.

Peter gave up practising law at the height of his career and became a teacher. The pay was far less, but he doesn't regret his decision. Peter loves what he does. It gives him energy and inspiration every day.

Whenever I think of Peter, I remember Krishna's words to Arjuna: "One's own path, even if imperfect, is better than another's path followed perfectly. By carrying out action according to one's own nature, one doesn't go wrong."

This true story holds a special significance for me. It helped me see that law was also the wrong choice of work for me. I too come from a poor background. In secondary school, when most children went to the corner shop to buy chocolate or fizzy drinks during lunch break, I always stayed behind. Unable to afford anything, I felt left out and different. This feeling affected my career choices. I too wanted to pursue a line of work that commanded respect, that was prestigious and paid well. I wanted to be acknowledged as successful.

But I came to recognize that a career in law is not my life purpose. It's not what I was placed on this earth to do. While it has its attractions, it didn't pass the "truth test" for me. And when we aren't true to ourselves, we inflict a form of violence upon ourselves.

Like our solicitor, I too became a teacher. I now teach dharma and yoga philosophy, with the aim of making it relevant, accessible and engaging for contemporary readers and audiences. I've found my purpose. And it all started by living in accord with my own nature. I learned how to do that from the solicitor who left London to become a teacher. His personal story affected me deeply: in some way, his story was my story.

−4−

"Just be yourself, and you'll be fine. Everything will take care of itself."

I was a teenager at my sixth form college, Wyggeston & Queen Elizabeth I College in Leicester, and my English teacher decided to give me some life advice. These words of hers sank into my soul like a dart, even if I didn't fully understand them at the time.

She was the first person in my life to tell me: *just be yourself.* You don't need to try to be anyone else. In doing so, she was repeating exactly what Krishna had advised Arjuna on that clear, early morning on the battlefield of Kurukshetra.

From childhood, the media and advertising industries, our friends and even our family have been telling us what it means to be "successful". Many of us find ourselves unconsciously buying into a dream that is not our own, that doesn't accord with who we are.

If we continually try to conform to the expectations of others, we never give ourselves the chance to manifest who we're meant to be. Everything in the universe is true to its nature—*except for humans*. An acorn pushes out an oak; it doesn't try to push out lilies. As an oak, it expresses its own perfection perfectly. But we easily embrace an idea of success that isn't our own, and then allow that idea to direct our life.

One of the strange secrets of life is that no matter how hard we try, we remain incomplete and unfulfilled until we're perfectly ourselves. When we express ourselves unreservedly, we become beautiful—not just in our own eyes, but in the eyes of everyone around us. To be beautiful means to be yourself. When we ignore the seed of potential within us and try to become someone we're not, we feel unfulfilled and frustrated.

Awareness of the short duration of our life can give us the clarity and courage to put this principle into practice. Steve Jobs, former CEO of Apple and Pixar, put it poignantly:

> Remembering that I'll be dead soon is the most important tool I've ever encountered to help me make the big choices in life. Because almost everything—all external expectations, all pride, all fear of embarrassment or failure—these things just fall away in the face of death, leaving only what is truly important. Remembering that you are going to die is the best way I know to avoid the trap of thinking you have something to lose. You are already naked. There is no reason not to follow your heart.[14]

Death has a way of putting things into perspective, and the dark night of the soul is a type of death. Our story has been shattered; past meaning has been lost. We're cast adrift.

Often a person may fall into a dark night of the soul precisely because they've spent years or decades hiding from themselves. They may have pursued other people's ideas of what they should be doing and have abandoned themselves.

The dark night breaks down our story. It invites us to look at the areas in our life where we've abandoned ourselves in favour of an imaginary story. The first step, therefore, is to begin living in a way that is truer to our nature. We're invited to be more truthful. Living in accord with one's own nature is an act of self-kindness.

How we're built is part of the universal order of things. Krishna therefore advises Arjuna to align himself with that universal order and use it to his advantage to undertake powerful and effective action. It's impossible to be effective or skilful on the field of life if we're locked in a fight against our own nature. Krishna's conclusion is really quite simple: "Beings *must* follow their nature; what can repression accomplish?"[15]

The universe has built each of us in a unique way. If we're engaged in a fight with the universe, guess who'll win? The universe. Always.

–5–

One summer as a teenager, I found work at Walkers Crisps' large factory in Leicester. My job was to pick crisp bags from conveyor belts and pack them into cardboard boxes. Morning till evening.

An employee named Edward stood out to me, as he was always cheerful and energetic. He packed twice as quickly as everyone else. I watched him with curiosity and admiration; I wanted to be like him. If I owned the company, I thought, I would want employees just like him.

However much I tried, I couldn't muster Edward's enthusiasm. I kept watching the clock. Every minute on the factory floor felt like half an hour. After four days, I quit. I remember thinking that even if the wages had been doubled or tripled, I simply couldn't possibly bear another day on that packing floor.

We each find that some types of work are natural and satisfying for us, while others leave us feeling drained and deflated. Most of us will work for the greater part of our life, so if we're unfulfilled at work, we're setting ourselves up to be unhappy for the greater part of our life.

Is there a way to find happiness in our work? Is there an approach to work that generates vitality, rather than saps our strength?

Krishna tells Arjuna there is. He teaches him Karma-yoga, skill in action. The first step, Krishna explains, is to work in harmony with the gift of our nature, with the way we're built. Krishna refers to work aligned with our nature as our "personal dharma" (in Sanskrit, *sva-dharma*).[16] Ideally, this is work we're good at. More importantly, it's work that feels right, natural, and aligned with who we are.

Our personal dharma is our own exceptional way of expressing ourselves and of being of service in the world. It's our very own way of living in alignment with truth.

When we engage in work that suits our nature, even great effort has a feeling of effortlessness. It feels like we're supported in our endeavours by the universe itself. This is because the universe has designed us in a unique and inimitable way. Expressing that, and living in accordance with it, is what we're meant to do.

When we love what we do, we naturally attract abundance into our life. But we can never love what we do if we're living against ourselves. Being true to our nature is therefore the first step to attracting abundance into our life.

Krishna goes still further: "A person attains *full perfection* by devoting himself to his own particular work."[17] In other words, our work can become our daily yoga practice.

We're each born to perform a specific type of action.[18] Our personal dharma is an inherent feature of the way we're constructed. When we follow our personal dharma, Krishna says, making what we do an offering, then our work can become an act of worship.[19] Imagine that.

If we act against our nature, no matter what we choose to do and no matter how successful we may become in doing it, we'll always feel a lingering emptiness and dissatisfaction. Living against ourselves is very difficult. It requires immense effort. It's exhausting. We're forever looking for external rewards, and always awaiting the future. Our actions in and of themselves don't satisfy us.

But if we live in agreement with our nature, in a way that is truthful to ourselves, whatever we do—whether it meets with great outward success or even only limited validation—is still highly satisfying. *What we do becomes its own reward.*

YOU HAVE A CLAIM ONLY TO THE ACTION ITSELF,
NEVER TO ITS FRUITS.

—Bhagavad Gita, 2.47

NINE

Let Go of the Fruits

—I—

Traditionally in India, the fourteenth day of the lunar calendar is considered an opportune time to enter battle, to dismantle something, or to get to the heart of an issue, due its strong, disruptive energy; but it's not considered a good time to set off on a journey.

Nonetheless, I had picked this day to fly out to Costa Rica. It was more important to me that I save £65 on my flight ticket. I wasn't going to pay too much attention to what seemed like superstition.

Things started to go wrong immediately. The coach to Heathrow Airport was delayed by an hour and a half, and then got caught in heavy traffic outside the airport, coming to a complete standstill. We were taking twenty minutes to cover a few hundred yards. As each minute passed, I checked my watch in desperation, making new calculations in my mind. This was going to be really, really tight.

By this stage, I was cursing under my breath. The coach had left the M25 and was inching its way around a roundabout.

"I could run faster than this, even carrying my luggage," I thought. My shirt felt damp from a cold sweat. My heart was racing. My mouth felt dry.

Maybe there were others in my desperate situation. I looked around and noticed a little girl in a red jacket laughing and pointing. She had spotted rabbits on the grassy knoll in the centre of the roundabout. There were dozens of them, adults and babies, emerging from their burrows, oblivious to the stream of anxious drivers that encircled them. Their peaceful play contrasted sharply against my own desperation.

I was clinging to my expectation that the journey would take two hours. But this little girl, enraptured by the adventure of her journey, was carefree. There was a lesson for me here. The Universal Teacher was speaking to me through her.

The little girl made me think about my approach to life. I was fixated on an outcome; but that outcome was outside of my control. No amount of desperate willing, panicked wishing or anxious cursing was going to make our coach move any faster. So, all I was doing was deliberately making the journey as miserable as possible.

One of the big secrets of Karma-yoga is that we have a right to put all our heart into what we do, but that we have no entitlement to the fruits of what we do. This is because the outcome of our efforts is always outside our control: ultimately, we never know how things will turn out. Krishna therefore teaches Arjuna to let go of the fruits.[20]

Letting go of the fruits means shedding our attachment to a particular outcome, and opening ourselves up to whatever life returns to us. This teaching has been one of the most revelatory and transformative in my life.

I decided there and then to apply Krishna's teachings. What was there for me to lose? I was trapped on this coach, and there was nothing further I could do.

When anxious or stressed, I tend to take shallow breaths from my chest; so, consciously relaxing my abdomen, I began breathing using my stomach instead. I focused my full attention on my own breathing, allowing it to deepen and slow down. With every outward breath, I let go of my expectations, my clinging, my controlling.

As the coach finally arrived at Heathrow Airport and passengers were getting off, there was an elderly gentleman struggling with his luggage. People were brushing past him, impatient to get to their check-in queues. I stopped to help him, smiled and wished him well on his journey.

Had I been lost in panic and anxiety, I probably wouldn't have noticed him. I would have jostled past, muttering under my breath. But my way of seeing the world had shifted, and the way I was approaching life now seemed far truer to who I wish to be.

—2—

Emperor Dhritarashtra sighed heavily. He now spent his days alone on his throne, lost in thought. The omens were bad. If only news would come to him from the battlefield. Had his one hundred sons routed the enemy? Or had they finally met their demise?

At long last, the emperor's minister, Sanjaya, arrives from Kurukshetra with news. Dhritarashtra is eager to know everything that has occurred: "What did my sons and the sons of Pandu do?" His anxiety is palpable. This is how the *Bhagavad Gita* begins.

Dhritarashtra symbolizes our own deep-rooted attachment to the fruits of action, our clinginess to outcomes. How significant that the *Gita* itself begins with a blind emperor and his paradigm of attachment, his mental captivity.

Attachment gives rise to a zealous attitude of "I" and "mine". But as soon as we introduce this egoic idea, it leads to competition and conflict. This sums up the tragic circumstances that led to the battle at Kurukshetra.

The sons of Pandu and Dhritarashtra grew up together under the care of Dhritarashtra. They are all equally Kauravas, or descendants of King Kuru. Nonetheless, Dhritarashtra is intent on separating the sons of Pandu from the family heritage: "my sons and the sons of Pandu", he differentiates. Where perceived interests conflict, the egoic "I" and "mine" lead to rivalry, jealousy, greed, deceit, exploitation, fear, hatred and ultimately war.

The conflict at Kurukshetra is not just an external battle. It mirrors the internal conflict and turmoil within Dhritarashtra himself. It represents a battle within each of us—a battle we're sure to lose if, like Dhritarashtra, we remain blinded by attachment.

The battlefield Arjuna finds himself on is an arena of attached positions. Both sides are fighting for a kingdom they believe is their rightful claim, and failing to talk through their differences, they face each other on the brink of war. This startling standoff casts Arjuna into his dark night of the soul, as he realizes for the first time just how absurd this all is, and how powerless he is.

Our power withdrawn from us in a dark night of the soul, we realize we can't push life about. Learning to truly let go, we allow ourselves to flow with life without struggle or fear, and without continually trying to impose our will.

Krishna wants to teach Arjuna a skilful way to act, even in his dark night of the soul. "Don't try to control what's outside your control," Krishna teaches him. "Put your heart into what you do, make it an expression of love and devotion, and then let the results take care of themselves. This is yoga."[21]

In the *Bhagavad Gita*, Arjuna's bow is his instrument of action. If we fire an arrow, we'll need to take aim. We'll need to focus on hitting the target. But once we release our arrow, what more can we do? The arrow, like the outcome of all our best efforts, is now outside of our control. Therefore, Krishna advises, "Let go of the fruits. Don't obsess about the arrow that has left your bow."[22]

We have a birthright to live in alignment with our nature. When we focus on our birthright, we experience vitality and fulfilment. But when we become obsessed about the results of our actions, we experience clinginess, stress, anxiety, competition, fear, discontent, resentment and anger.

Rather than live life like Dhritarashtra, blinded by attachment, we can set off on our yoga journey, like Arjuna, making what we do an offering of love, without being overly concerned about what we get back.

−3−

When I arrived at the American Airlines counter, I knew I was close to missing my plane; it was going to be tight. I was alert and ready, but I wasn't consumed by anxiety and desperation anymore.

I smiled at the assistant and explained what had happened.

"Your flight is a little delayed," she said, "and it's also really full. We're offering remaining passengers the choice to catch a later flight, which leaves in two hours. It goes via Miami instead of New York. We would reroute you and pay you £100 for your trouble."

As I was considering what to do, the assistant leaned over and advised, "I would take it, if I were you. Most flights are delayed in New York for several hours due to bad weather, with many passengers stranded. It's chaos." I agreed, and she began typing away on her system.

"You look like a nice gentleman. I'll even bump you up to business class," she added with a wink.

Grateful, I made my way to Miami and had a pleasant onward journey, in business class. We never know what will happen. Sometimes the things we desire most turn out to be deceptive, even damaging; and sometimes what seems terrible to us at the time, ends up being the best thing that could have happened to us. We can only apply our best effort.

If we're trying to force an outcome, it also tends to bring out the worst in us: we get caught up in a cycle of want and frustration. We find ourselves resisting the present, lamenting the past, and hankering for the future. We're not present in the here and now. This is a disempowering way to act, which leads only to bewilderment.

Krishna therefore teaches, "Don't be moved by success or failure. Don't be attached; the outcome is not dictated by you."[23] For example, we can't guarantee how many participants will attend our Sunday workshop or yoga class. We can't control whether a book we write will be well received. Our start-up could fail, despite all the energy and money we have put into it.

Whenever we feel attached to an outcome, it indicates we're trying to control what lies outside of our remit. Krishna teaches the warrior Arjuna a new way to act, one that doesn't bind him to suffering. In breaking the connection to suffering, such action constitutes yoga.[24]

Letting go of the fruits is not the same as not caring or not being committed. Rather, it means living with strong purpose and commitment, but remaining open to whatever the results of what we do might be.

We can plant a mango tree. We can watch it grow. We can care for it and water it. But whether that tree will in the end deliver large, succulent mangoes is not something we can guarantee. The best way to act, then, is to plant your mangoes and look after your orchard with presence and love, making the action itself its own reward. Let the action, as an expression of love, be an end in itself.

If we're doing work for the sake of the work itself, rather than for a desired result, we're less likely to be plagued by constant anxiety. We're less likely to suffer crippling disappointment if things don't go as planned. The best way to act, Krishna explains, is to devote ourselves to the cause, but not to the fruits.

−4−

The monkeys in the town of Vrindavan, North India, are exceedingly shrewd. They've learned how to jump on to a person's shoulders and seize their glasses. Perched high up on a wall, they'll return the spectacles only in exchange for bananas or, better still, mango juice. When you get your glasses back, they're usually mangled and chewed up, but at least you have the costly lenses. Today, the monkeys have learned that stealing a mobile phone works just as well.

Every few years, the town makes an effort to reduce its rising population of monkeys. They capture as many as they can and release them into the forest miles away. Monkeys are traditionally captured using deceptively simple traps. You take a bottle that is just large enough for a monkey to push its hand into, and fix it to a post or wall, placing a banana inside as bait.

Sure enough, a monkey will spot the succulent banana and push its hand into the bottle. The mouth of the bottle is large enough for the monkey's little hand, but not large enough for the monkey's hand along with the banana. Now so attached to having that specific banana, the monkey won't release its grip, allowing the monkey trapper to throw a cloth bag over the primate's head.

Despite its exceptional intelligence, in the pursuit of a desired object the monkey is easily fooled. If the monkey would just let go of the banana, it would be free.

I've come to realize that we humans are like this too. We're exceptionally intelligent, until we become attached to a particular object or outcome. Our "bananas" are our projections of what our life *should* look like:

"I should have a bigger and nicer house by now, so I won't enjoy the beautiful home I'm in already."

"My partner doesn't fulfil my checklist of criteria that a life partner should fulfil, so I won't give this relationship the attention and care it deserves. Rather than focus on everything that's right about the relationship, I'll focus on everything that's wrong with it."

"Why am I not earning as much as my friends? I'll make sure not to be grateful for what I have by being resentful and angry about what I should but don't have."

"I should have achieved a lot more at my age, so I'll live in a state of restless dissatisfaction with my life."

The list of "bananas" goes on and on. But in the end, it's all just self-inflicted suffering; it's all just bananas.

The monkey, if it would simply let go, could find many more bananas elsewhere. But he can't relinquish *this particular banana*. Also, he can't relinquish his idea of what he needs to do to get this banana. The monkey is in a form of captivity even before the trapper bags him.

Krishna emphasizes the importance of letting go of our attachments.[25] At first Arjuna misunderstands: he thinks Krishna is advising him to give up the world. But Krishna explains that the secret of action is to renounce our infatuation with the world, without renouncing the world itself. Non-attachment is not that we should own nothing, but that nothing should own us.

When I first came across these teachings of Karma-yoga, they stopped me dead in my tracks. I knew what it was like to act *with* attachment to the results. I had plenty of experience of the suffering this generates. I also understood what doing things without attention or care was. But to put all my heart into something and at the same time let go of the fruits sounded radical and surprising. Is it even possible?

−5−

Vrindavan is surprisingly cold in the winter, as the temples and homes don't have heating. My Sanskrit teacher wore a thick woollen hat. His room was full of Sanskrit books. I paid my respects and sat on the straw mat laid out on the floor.

Despite his erudition, my teacher always maintained a humble demeanour. I remember once seeing him affronted by an angry man. I don't know what was bothering this man, but he was shouting and gesticulating wildly. My teacher remained calm and unmoved, replying respectfully and with a quiet affection. It was so disarming that the angry man could no longer hold on to his anger.

"Prabhu, in the *Bhagavad Gita* Krishna advises Arjuna to

follow his calling as a warrior, but not to be attached to the fruits of action. How is it possible to do something you care about without feeling attached to the results?" I asked.

"Usually, we covet the fruits of our work *before* we start any kind of work," my Sanskrit teacher replied. "We don't consider any kind of work without the promise of payment or a reward. But Krishna teaches Arjuna to follow his personal dharma and make it an act of service, an act of devotion, so that what he does becomes its own reward.

"Whether we ultimately meet with success or failure, a change of perspective can make our endeavours an act of worship. This is a beautiful and deeply satisfying way of acting, and one that doesn't bind us to this world; rather, it sets us free.

"Of course, it's important to remember that the teachings themselves won't free us. Only to the extent that we *apply* them, that we live them, will they free us."

"Can this form of yoga be applied to anything we do?" I asked.

"Yes, what matters most is not what you happen to be doing, but *how* you do it. It's about right attitude and motive— *from inception*. Then there's meaning even within difficult or frustrating tasks."

It seemed so simple, but I still had a doubt: "I'm worried that if I take a non-attached approach, maybe I'll be less effective at what I do. Maybe I won't do it quite so well."

"No, you'll be able to act more skilfully and more effectively than you can imagine. By remaining unattached and approaching all of your work with a mood of service, your best qualities will naturally emerge." My teacher explained that letting go of the fruits frees us to act impeccably; and when we act impeccably, success will find us.

Karma-yoga allows us to detach from the ego's need to claim success, as well as its fear of failure. When we let go of the results, we make a space for the action to become its own reward. In doing so, we'll remain fulfilled whatever the results.

Krishna explains that there is a way to live beyond the binaries of this world: beyond gain and loss, praise and blame, triumph and defeat. The wise person who lives like this, beyond the binaries, "awakens to the light in the night of all beings."[26] In other words, such a person crosses beyond the underlying dark night of the soul that affects us all.

"Can you tell me more about such a person?" I asked.

"Krishna compares such a person to the vast ocean.[27] During the rainy season, the rivers that rush to the sea are overflowing, and during the summer they dry up; but the ocean always remains unmoved. Similarly, whether good things flow into our life or not, whether difficulties emerge or not, a person situated in yoga remains undisturbed, like the ocean. Whether such a person has everything or nothing, they remain self-satisfied. They are never shaken, even amid the greatest difficulties. They remain at peace whether they meet with success or failure."

I longed to become such a yoga warrior on the field of life. Undisturbed by anxiety and incessant longing, such a yogi lives perfectly in the present moment. From my own experience, I knew that presence is impossible if we're overly attached to specific outcomes and results. Letting go of my obsession with the results would free up a space in which I could focus on the work itself with complete attention. It would create a sacred space in which to act.

ONE WHO OFFERS HIS ACTIONS TO THE DIVINE, HAVING LET GO OF ATTACHMENT, IS NOT AFFECTED BY MISFORTUNE, AS WATER DOESN'T CLING TO A LOTUS LEAF.

—*Bhagavad Gita*, 5.10

TEN

Make Your Work an Offering

—I—

There were things I hadn't told many people, not even my friends. One was that my mother was a heroin addict. She died when I was young, from a drug-related illness.

In writing my first book, *The Book of Dharma: Making Enlightened Choices*, I decided to share a few personal details about my life. I felt exposed and vulnerable. How would readers react to such revelations?

I had other concerns too. Would the book be well received? Would there be sufficient sales? I had been working on the manuscript for more than three years. What if someone I had showed the manuscript to published a similar book before I did? These worries and concerns all related to the fruits of the endeavour, and as such, were a cause of suffering.

On a grey, rainy day in December 2011, a close friend named Ananta came to visit, and looked over the manuscript. He read a short passage from the manuscript aloud:

"I mustn't lose this. Without this, I'm nobody."

"This person is helping me get what I want. He is my friend."
"That person is my competitor. I must overcome him. What if he gets there before I do? I mustn't allow that to happen."

These are the words of the ego, the imaginary self, caught in fear, lamentation and confusion. We began to laugh. Somehow, I was trapped in this paradigm even while writing about it. There was a disparity between my words and my behaviour. How shrewd the ego can be. I knew I would need to write from a more potent and sacred place within myself.

That night, I walked out into the darkness. I needed time on my own. I wandered through Wyggeston & Queen Elizabeth I College, where I had studied many years ago, and down the hill into the cold, starry night. I felt an overwhelming helplessness. Allowing that emotion to remain, tears came to my eyes. Had I wasted three and a half years? The thought was terrible.

What was I to do? I reached into the deepest centre of my being. Krishna, the Universal Teacher, lives in the heart of all living beings and guides their passage. I took shelter there.

What I needed to do began to unfold. I would start again. But first, I would sever my attachment to any fruits from the project. How can I truly share wisdom if I'm seeking to profit from it? I would simply be another personal development punter selling his wares.

I made a firm decision I would use any profits earned from

this writing to publish the wisdom texts of my own teacher and to contribute to other good causes, such as supporting schools for India's poorest children, especially girls.

The moment I made this resolution in my heart, I felt an unusual inner strength and lightness of being. I felt so alive! I had invoked the last principle of Karma-yoga, the yoga of sacred action.

All mental cloudiness vanished. I was now fully present to what I was doing. Returning to my desk, the words began to flow effortlessly, like a river from the soul. Whole chapters emerged in a single session of writing. I stopped being the author. I became a servant, the instrument of something much larger.

I was now more deeply committed to this book than ever, but I wasn't attached to the outcome. I no longer sought a validation of my identity or my sense of worth through the project. It became an offering of the heart, a humble attempt to serve my teacher and my readers.

I was no longer anxious about my finances either. I had initially been working on the book with the promise of some future reward, but in my case, this had become a driving motive. Having let go of the results, I felt free and unafraid about my financial future. I knew, instinctively, I would be looked after.

Like Arjuna, I had to relinquish many things. I had to abandon the idea that the book would bring financial reward. I had to let go of the desire to be recognized, even to be accepted and liked. I had to relinquish my need for the book to be well received. It was a deeply purifying and transformative process.

I accomplished more in the following six months than in the previous three and a half years, and all without worry or being attached to the results. This new approach to work was truly transformative.

−2−

The morning sun shone on to the towering sandstone temple, gleaming against the crystal in the stone. Bright green parrots flew about in pairs. The branches of a nearby tree shook, as little monkeys jumped playfully. From this vantage point in the town of Vrindavan, you can see everything for miles.

This temple dedicated to Krishna was home to many tulsi plants in clay pots, which were carefully watered each morning. This was a sacred sanctuary. Such places have a way of decluttering the soul and helping us remember what's truly important in our life.

I sat down near a tulsi plant to meditate. Within minutes, I was deeply absorbed. In a sacred sanctuary of the soul, meditation can be effortless.

In my contemplation, I could hear a beautiful song. The melody and words were enchanting, overwhelming me with joy. I opened my eyes and saw an old man sweeping the temple courtyard with a broom made of long, thin branches.

As he swept the dust and leaves, he sang to his beloved lord, Krishna, and tears of happiness rose to his eyes. Without a care in the world, without concern for who might be watching or listening, he poured his soul into song. His face radiated happiness and life, and I could see he was engaged in sacred action.

This menial task of sweeping, commonplace and humble, was filled with remarkable beauty and charm. There is a Sanskrit word for sacred action, action impelled by devotion: *seva*. Captivated, I stopped to watch for a few minutes.

I had never before witnessed how an act so menial and simple could carry so much beauty. Watching this man, I realized that it doesn't matter whether what we're doing is little or large, humble or grand. If it's an act of devotion, it fully satisfies the soul. Transcending the ordinary, it becomes a pure expression of the soul.

When the old man put aside his broom and sat down, I struck up a conversation, hoping to learn more about sacred action. What was it that transformed a simple, ordinary activity into something so potent? Was it possible to make all our actions such an expression of beauty? If so, how?

"I've seen you sweeping this temple courtyard each morning," I said in Hindi. "You seem so happy doing it. What makes this work so special for you?"

"*Seva* is the only valuable thing in my life," the old man said. "It doesn't matter what you do, if you do it with devotion, it purifies the heart. It frees you from all suffering and awakens Bhakti, sacred love, in your heart."

He looked at me intently. His eyes glistened like liquid emeralds. "Life is meant for *seva*. So many are busy accumulating money; but in the end money can't help you. This is because you're a spiritual being. Only sacred love can fulfil you."

In the *Bhagavad Gita*, Krishna tells Arjuna to make everything he does an offering of love. Krishna recommends sacred action. This is when we make our daily work a practice and a form of worship.

To make everything we do part of our yoga practice, Krishna has added the third and final teaching of Karma-yoga, the yoga of skilful action: "Turn it over to me. Whatever you do, make it an offering of devotion to the divine present within you and within all beings. In this way, what you do becomes an act of worship, a form of yoga."[28]

−3−

"Life is like a droplet balancing on a lotus leaf," my teacher explained. "At any moment, it can fall. We can't say how much time we have left. Therefore, do everything with care and attention, as if it's your last moment, your last chance."

A yoga warrior keeps the thought of death at her left shoulder. This might seem a bit extreme, but awareness of our own mortality can kindle a desire to act impeccably. It can bring our full presence to the action at hand.

The best place to meditate, my teacher explained, is known as *jivan-sandhi*, the juncture between life and death. This is where our prayers will be heard. This is where all the great masters in our line have attained perfection in their practice.

The juncture between life and death. How does one reach that place?

I was a young practitioner who struggled with *japa*, mantra meditation. There were monks who could meditate for hours on end, lost in rapture as they entered the inner landscape of the heart, the mystical realm of devotion. But this practice was new and difficult for me. My mind was easily distracted.

My teacher saw this. One morning he called me over: "Right now, your *japa* is not very effective. You should spend time in the early morning sitting in stillness for your meditation; but during the rest of the day burn in the 'fire' of *seva*. Dedicate your life to *seva,* and the doorway to Bhakti will open for you. Then your practice will become easy; you'll be completely absorbed."

From then on, I began seeing myself as a servant. I began asking, "Suppose this were the last thing I did in my life, the last opportunity to be of service. How would I perform this task?" I wanted to walk the sacred pathway between life and death.

–4–

The young Assami boy, who had been sitting quietly in the temple, suddenly began coughing up blood. At first just a few specks, but blood was soon pouring from his mouth, bubbly and bright red. Tuberculosis. Everyone stepped back in dread.

It was 1946 when this sixteen-year-old monk named Ananga Mohan fell severely ill. He was a kind-natured boy who sang very sweetly. To this day, tuberculosis (or "consumption", as it was formerly known) remains the most deadly infectious disease in the world, killing about 1.5 million people a year. Highly contagious, the bacteria is transmitted through the air.

Everyone was afraid to approach Ananga Mohan, but my teacher personally cared for him with great attentiveness and love, cleaning and feeding him, and carefully seeing to all his needs for many months, until Ananga Mohan passed away.

One of the most difficult things someone can do is tend to a dying patient, especially if they have a highly contagious disease. My teacher had, quite literally, offered his own life for this *seva*. He described this time to me as a turning point in his practice. This dedicated *seva* melted the heart of his teacher, Shrila Bhakti Prajnana Keshava Goswami, who taught him the most confidential secrets of the Bhakti tradition.

Born in 1921 in Bihar, India, my teacher Shrila B. V. Narayan Goswami joined his teacher's temple monastery in the 1940s. Since childhood he had studied India's sacred texts, and he embodied these teachings by dedicating his life to *seva*.

Whatever my teacher did, he did with utmost attention and presence. I've watched him fully immersed in his morning and evening meditation, engaging with visitors and pilgrims, and explaining the teachings of the ancient yoga texts. Both momentous and seemingly insignificant tasks commanded his full attention. He did everything as a personal offering of devotion, and that imbued whatever he did with beauty and deep significance.

I apprenticed with my teacher for sixteen years, living and travelling with him continuously for several years during that time. I saw no difference between the way he did things when he was being observed and when no one was watching. There was no discord between what he said and how he lived.

In the temple monastery, monks are taught to act with full attention and devotion. We can't make what we do an offering of devotion if we're not present to what we're doing. But if what we do is an act of love, we'll necessarily be deeply present.

For example, if we're cooking a meal for a loved one, we'll plan the menu with great care. Selecting only the choicest ingredients, we'll cook with all our heart. And when we serve out the meal, we'll be fully attentive to the needs of the person we love.

In the temple monastery, I often felt like a complete beginner. The monks do everything with such a distinguished level of consciousness and quality of intent. Most of them didn't have a formal education at university. They didn't have experience in law firms or commercial enterprises. And yet, they seemed more skilled in whatever they did than trained professionals.

The same monk could sweep the stone steps of the monastery, take charge of cooking a magnificent meal for ten thousand pilgrims, rebuild a wall at the back of the temple, arrange the reprinting of several book titles, and expertly care for an ill or dying patient. There was nothing they couldn't do. Nothing was too difficult, too menial, or too bothersome. I learned from them that there is nothing that I too can't do, if I set my heart to it.

To exercise the yoga of skilful action is to do whatever we do impeccably, with full attention, for its own sake. We're accustomed to bringing our best self to our yoga mat. But in our daily life, whether we're working at the office or preparing a meal at the end of the day, we may be distracted, inattentive, lazy or vexed.

The monks taught me that only love and affection has the power to fulfil the soul or to attract the Soul of the Universe, the Soul of all souls. And this requires attention and presence. In its ultimate expression, the yoga of action is to live through deeds of love. If we could express love in everything we say or do, how our life would be utterly transformed.

−5−

When I told Peter about making whatever we do an act of devotion, his eyes lit up. "This is what I try to do," he confided. "When I teach, I devote myself to it, as a service to my students and an offering to…" Peter paused.

If you remember, Peter was a very successful solicitor at a top-tier London law firm. At the height of his career, Peter realized that practising law was not his passion; he had been chasing an empty dream. He became a teacher.

I wondered whether Peter was trying to indicate the Soul of the Universe, that ineffable source of all existence and non-existence described in the sacred yoga texts and perceived by the rishis in their deepest meditation. In the *Bhagavad Gita*, that supreme resting place is Krishna, the Lord of Yoga, present in the heart of all beings as the Universal Teacher.

"I believe we're more than just skin and bones," Peter continued. "There's a spark of the divine that illuminates us all. When I teach, I try to serve the divine within all beings."

"How do you make what you do an offering?" I asked.

"Well, firstly, I give my full presence and attention to what I do. I don't turn up feeling as though my teaching or anything else I do is a chore. I see it as a privilege, and I love what I do. I like to think I'm not just teaching my students a subject, but also helping them create a meaningful, flourishing life.

"It's rewarding when I get a brilliant student, but it's also rewarding when I have a troubled student who finds a way to turn things around. It doesn't always work out that way, of course. I can do my best, but ultimately, I know I can't control the outcome. What's important is the attitude I bring to what I do."

"That mood of service, I imagine, helps when the work gets difficult."

"Yes, sometimes I have students who simply don't care. They talk back. They don't want to be there. Other teachers don't want them either, but I try to understand what they're going through. I used to be a difficult person too, when I was working in London. It was mostly because I was suffering. No one could see that; but I was in pain. I know what it's like to show up every day when you don't want to be there."

There was a picture of Peter on the mantelpiece, in an elegant dark frame. I asked him if this was his father.

"No, that's *me*," he laughed. "I used to be overweight. I didn't look after myself. I guess when you've abandoned yourself, you also neglect yourself physically and emotionally.

"Now things have changed, and I feel more alive than ever before. I've started looking after myself. I know that if I don't, I can't be of service and do what I truly love."

It reminded me of the monks in India. They take care to sleep well—not too much and not too little. They eat with presence and care. This is an integral part of their yoga practice.

Our physical body is the vehicle by which we can try to make our life an offering of love. It's our "chariot" on the field of life.

For someone living in a consumer society, learning how to do work as deep service can be life changing. Rather than thinking "What am I not getting?" we can ask "What can I give?" If there is something wrong with a situation, rather than dwell on its faults, we can ask ourselves, "How can I help make it better?"

There are many ways to begin developing a mood of service. We can serve the values of kindness, compassion and human dignity. We can serve the earth, or the evolution of consciousness. In the esoteric Bhakti tradition, we develop selfless love by directing our service to Krishna, the Supreme Origin, in whom all things rest. As a result, that unconditional love and affection automatically encompasses the earth, all beings including ourselves, and the evolution of consciousness.[29] It's a love that looks beyond all the temporary stories we may be living out. In the Bhakti tradition, such sacred love is regarded as the highest stage of spiritual enlightenment.

"It helps for me to begin the morning with a prayer," Peter confided, "to offer my day to the Divine, and to set the intention that my actions be beneficial to all beings. Moving through the day with this mood makes living itself a form of worship."

It reminded me of Krishna's words to Arjuna: "As people without knowledge act *with* attachment, O descendant of Bharata, so the wise should act *without* attachment, seeking the well-being of the world."[30] By such a practice, we can become rishis, or wise seers, who "take delight in the welfare of all beings".[31]

In listening to Peter, I could hear the Universal Teacher speaking through him. The dark night of the soul can be a powerful teacher.

–6–

The sage reached into his cloth bag and pulled out a handful of gemstones. He spread these on a white cloth for me to see: moonstones, sapphires, amethysts, tiger's eyes, quartz crystals, lapis lazulis and opals.

I was in Varanasi, India. The old sage was a renowned astrologer. He looked at me intently.

"The universe bestows upon us many precious gifts: intelligence, wisdom, health, knowledge, beauty, strength, skill…" the sage said. "What do we do with those gifts? There are two ways of relating with life. The first is symbolized by a closed fist."

The old man reached down and grabbed as many gems as he could fit into a tightly closed fist. He extended this fist in my direction.

"This closed fist is a *mudra*, a hand gesture that symbolizes a specific state of consciousness, a specific way of relating with the world," he explained.[32] "It's a *mudra* that represents fear, greed and attachment.

"If the *mudra* could speak, it would say: 'I'm taking as much as I can, and whatever I take, I'll keep for myself. I must hold on to it very tightly, or else someone will take it from me or I may lose it.' It's a *mudra* of competition and ego, focused on 'I' and 'mine'. In the first verse of the *Bhagavad Gita*, the blind emperor Dhritarashtra expresses this mindset.[33]

"Most of us approach life in this way. That's why the *Gita* begins with Dhritarashtra's fear-based, attached mindset. As soon as I open my fist, whatever I'm holding will fall from my grasp. This is our fear: 'I'll lose what I have.'

"The universe has so much to offer us; it's endlessly abundant in precious gifts. If we clench our hands into fists and the universe wants to give us more, we're not in a position to accept it. Our hands are tightly closed.

"Thankfully, there's a different way of relating with the universe—one that is the exact opposite of a fist." The sage now turned his closed fist by 180 degrees and opened his fingers. He extended his open palm towards me, revealing moonstones, sapphires and sky-blue opals.

"This is the *mudra*, or gesture, of giving. It's also the *mudra* of receiving. In this approach to life, there's no fear of loss. There's no attempt to seize and hold on to things. Importantly, if the universe wants to give us more precious gifts, we're now in a position to receive them. Our hands are open.

"This powerful way of relating produces results that are 180 degrees different to those of a closed-fisted mindset. Have you not experienced this? When we live with an open heart, we discover that the more we give, the more we receive. Always.

"Take a look at the figures of saints and teachers across India: they never have closed fists. Their palms are always open. This is because the palm represents the heart.

"Remember, there are just two ways of relating with the world: with an open heart and with a closed heart. The last verse of the *Bhagavad Gita* describes the open-hearted way of being, which the seer Sanjaya says leads to 'fortune, unusual triumph, strength, and abiding wise conduct'. The *Gita* is about making this 180-degree shift in consciousness from a closed heart to an open heart."

This was a striking revelation for me. I thought of the times I had dedicated myself fully with a mood of loving service and giving, without concern for getting anything in return. These were the best times of my life. They were by far the most exhilarating and rewarding. They never brought misfortune.

I also thought of the many times I had adopted a small-minded, closed-fisted approach to life. Those were times of struggle, ego, anxiety and frustration. Every time.

Mudras are like prayers translated into physical form. If we live with a closed-fisted mindset, we make that our prayer in life. But by living with an open heart, we adopt a very different quality of prayer.

"Our heart is a treasure chest filled with beautiful gifts the universe has bestowed upon us," the astrologer continued. "Our greatest treasure is our unique nature, gifted to us so we can be of service in the world. When we're consumed by fear and the desire for more, we don't appreciate what we already have. That's because we're focused on everything we *don't* have.

"We can't live in accord with the way we're constructed without first becoming aware of our own gifts. The desire to look carefully at these gemstones we hold in our heart, to honour the gifts the universe has bestowed upon us, is the first step of Karma-yoga: be true to your nature.

"The second step of Karma-yoga is to let go of the fruits. When we adopt an attached, closed-fisted mindset, we're afraid we'll lose what we have if we open our hand. We're afraid it will fall from our grasp. Inverting our fist by 180 degrees represents the shift from fear to trust. This is the second step of Karma-yoga. By trusting that the universe will look after us, we're able to let go of the fruits of our actions.

"And the final step of Karma-yoga is to open our fingers, making what we do an offering. This completes the inversion from *grasping* to *giving*, from *competition* to *loving service*. We've now brought three divine qualities into everything we do: truth, trust and love. Only with this last step of opening our fingers do we truly see, reveal and share the treasures of our heart. It's the only way we truly express ourselves fully.

"And then what happens? The universe immediately fills our open palms with further treasures. The universe never allows such open palms to remain empty."

Notes

Part III: "Let Every Step Be Its Own Reward"

1 Krishna's first teachings to Arjuna in Chapter 2 are about the soul. Krishna tells Arjuna he is much bigger than his small human story. Krishna reveals that the soul is quite wonderful: she survives the dark night, and even the death of the body.

2 Karma-yoga is the main teaching that dominates the first third of the *Bhagavad Gita*, particularly Chapters 2–5. Chapter 6, along with other passages in the *Mahabharata*, contains the earliest complete exposition of the yoga system later taught by Patanjali. Krishna explains that renunciation, or letting go of the fruits of action, is an inherent feature of such yoga practice. In other words, Patanjali's yoga system can be properly undertaken only by someone who has mentally withdrawn their mind and senses in the manner achieved by practising Karma-yoga.

3 See *Bhagavad Gita*, 3.4–8. This passage is aimed at those who say giving up worldly desires is possible only by withdrawing from the world. Krishna advises that better than physically renouncing the world is to cultivate a mood of inner renunciation while remaining active in the world.

4 *Bhagavad Gita*, 2.50: *yogah karmasu kaushalam* ("yoga is skill in action").

5 *Bhagavad Gita*, 3.33.

6 *Bhagavad Gita*, 18.47. "Own path" translates *sva-dharma*, used here to refer to one's path aligned with one's own nature. In the *Bhagavad Gita*, dharma is not just what a person ought to do; it's a reflection of a person's inner nature (*svabhava*). "Go wrong" translates *apnoti kilbisham*, which means, literally, "incurs sin or fault". The first half of this verse is repeated from *Bhagavad Gita*, 3.35.

7 *Bhagavad Gita*, 2.47. The opening verses of the *Isha Upanishad* refer to the same teaching of desireless action, which doesn't bind the performer.

8 Early on in the *Bhagavad Gita*, Krishna advises Arjuna to act without attachment to success or failure, and thereby perform yoga (2.48). A sage of steady mind, Krishna says, is free from attachment (2.56). Krishna warns Arjuna that attachment leads to intense longing, and frustrated longing turns into anger (2.62). Indeed, the subject of attachment is treated in one way

or another throughout the *Gita.* It is fitting, therefore, that the text begins with Dhritarashtra's paradigm of attachment, evinced by the word *mamakah,* "belonging to me".

9   *Bhagavad Gita,* 5.10.

10   Bronnie Ware, *The Top Five Regrets of the Dying: A Life Transformed by the Dearly Departing* (2011), pp. 34–43.

11   *Bhagavad Gita,* 18.47, paraphrased.

12   *Bhagavad Gita,* 3.35, paraphrased.

13   *Bhagavad Gita,* 18.47–8. This passage refers to Arjuna by his name Kaunteya.

14   Steve Jobs, Stanford University commencement speech, 12 Jun. 2005.

15   *Bhagavad Gita,* 3.33.

16   For example, see *Bhagavad Gita,* 18.47. Every person is born with an inherent nature (referred to in the *Gita* as *sva-bhava*), and one's personal dharma is a reflection of that nature. The broad differences in inherent natures were reflected in ancient India in the division of society into four categories: teachers and thinkers (*brahmanas*), warriors and managers (*kshatriyas*), traders and entrepreneurs (*vaishyas*), and artisans, labourers and servants (*shudras*). Of course, the sacred texts also speak about the highest dharma (known as *para-dharma*), which relates not to the temporary body and mind, but to the eternal soul. That dharma, as we shall see, is sacred love for the Divine, the Soul of all souls (e.g. *Bhagavata Purana,* 1.2.6).

17   *Bhagavad Gita,* 18.45, italics added. "Full perfection" translates *samsiddhim.*

18   *Bhagavad Gita,* 18.48. *Saha-jam* means, literally, "born along with". This indicates we are each born to perform a particular type of action.

19   *Bhagavad Gita,* 18.46. Our work becomes worship when we follow the three steps of Karma-yoga and make what we do an offering to the Divine, the origin of all beings and of all natures.

20   For example, *Bhagavad Gita*, 2.47–48.

21   Paraphrased. Krishna defines yoga as remaining the same in success and failure (*Bhagavad Gita*, 2.48: *samatvam yoga uchyate*).

22   Paraphrased.

23   Paraphrased. On success and failure: *Bhagavad Gita*, 2.38 and 2.48.

24   In *Bhagavad Gita*, 6.23, Krishna defines yoga as *duhkha-samyoga-viyogam*, "severing our connection with suffering". The wisdom of ancient India is designed to free one from suffering associated with the three phases of time (e.g. *Bhagavata Purana*, 1.7.7).

25   The subject of attachment, and of letting go, is treated in one way or another throughout the *Bhagavad Gita*. For example, see *Bhagavad Gita*, 2.48, 2.56, 2.62, 2.64, 3.7, 3.19, 3.25, 3.34, 4.10, 4.20, 4.23, 5.10, 5.11, 7.11, 13.10, 13.11, 13.15, 14.22, 17.5, 18.6, 18.9, 18.23, 18.34 and 18.51.

26   *Bhagavad Gita*, 2.69.

27   *Bhagavad Gita*, 2.70.

28   Paraphrased. As Krishna later confides, yoga is "the unwavering offering of love" (*Bhagavad Gita*, 13.10).

29   For example, see *Bhagavad Gita*, 10.8 and *Bhagavata Purana*, 4.31.14.

30   *Bhagavad Gita*, 3.25. See also *Bhagavad Gita*, 3.20 and 5.25.

31   *Bhagavad Gita*, 5.25.

32   A *mudra* may be a simple position of the hands and fingers or may involve the whole body. *Mudras* of the hands and fingers are known as *hasta-mudras*.

33   Indeed, the very first word of the *Gita* is "Dhritarashtra", a compound word that denotes one who has seized the lands of another.

PART

IV

THE THIRD AGREEMENT:
"LET DISCERNMENT BE THE WARRIOR'S SWORD"

Samkhya,
The Sword of Discernment

IV

The vast Kaurava army stretches as far as the eye can see. Wielding deadly weapons, its battle-hardened warriors are ready to relinquish their lives for Duryodhana, their king. Arjuna finds himself completely outnumbered.

Like Arjuna, we too are surrounded by deadly foes: fear, self-doubt, denial, hypocrisy, dishonesty, resentment, anger, contempt, arrogance, disrespect, frustration, cruelty, selfishness, greed, envy, hate, narcissism and perpetual dissatisfaction.[1] Servants of the illusory ego, these ungodly qualities of the lower potential are arrayed against us in the heart. They emerge from the darkness and confusion of false perception with the singular aim of preventing us from realizing our full potential—our kingdom by birthright.

Arjuna stands on a chariot given to him by Agni, the god of fire, which can't be destroyed, but what kind of chariot do we possess? Our physical body, which is subject to illness, exhaustion and death. Arjuna's chariot is pulled by steeds seemingly as swift as the wind. Our steeds are our five wild senses, which drag us in unhelpful and conflicting directions on the field of life.

Located on Arjuna's flag is the mighty Hanuman, a fierce monkey god whose loud shouts cause the hearts of the enemy to tremble. Hanuman represents dedication and devoted service, which invariably lead to victory of the higher potential over the lower. What flag do we fly on the field of life?

Arjuna has celestial weapons, including his celebrated Gandiva bow. He's an unequalled archer, having trained under the mighty warrior-maker, Drona. What training have we received?

Despite his advantages, when Arjuna finds himself between the two opposing armies at Kurukshetra, his mind becomes bewildered. "I won't fight," he decides. If even Arjuna's mind is disturbed, what is our predicament when faced with life's challenges?

To help his friend Arjuna, Krishna gives him an indestructible weapon: the flaming sword of knowledge.[2] Not just any knowledge, but a razor-sharp discernment called Samkhya.[3] This sword, when wielded by a skilled yoga warrior, severs our connection to suffering. It cuts through our false perceptions. In gifting that divine yogic weapon to Arjuna, Krishna is simultaneously bequeathing it to each of us.

Krishna devotes a full third of the *Bhagavad Gita* to Samkhya wisdom, and his main teachings can broadly be summarized as follows:

1. Remember who you are.
2. Understand the terrain.
3. Distinguish between the divine and the ungodly.

The *Bhagavad Gita* is about making choices—hard choices. Arjuna is faced with a difficult choice: "Should I fight? Should I not fight?"

Lost and confused between the two great armies, he doesn't know what to do. Krishna tells him: "*You don't know what to do because you don't know who you are.*"[4] Krishna's very first Samkhya teaching to Arjuna is to remember who he is.[5] Arjuna thinks he's the person who is sad, confused and in turmoil.

We're not this physical body we inhabit, Krishna explains, which is like a garment. Neither are we our mind-made self, with all its problems and heavy burdens, which lives between the unsatisfying past and the fearful future.

Samkhya allows us to grasp that we're not the imaginary lead character in our small story. We're spiritual beings. The dark night is a blessing, because it can reveal this to us, if we let it. Once we know who we are, undefeatable and beyond our petty, recurring storyline, we can act on the field of life with freedom, clarity and power. Whatever we do is then truly an expression of yoga.

The dark night of the soul is a type of death. It breaks us

apart; but in doing so, it allows us to find the unbroken self at our core.

The knowledge of who we are is not something to be learned, just remembered, like the person waking from a dream, who automatically remembers who he is. Krishna refers in his teachings to *disturbed memory*: "From disturbed memory comes loss of discernment, and from loss of discernment a person becomes lost."[6]

After hearing Krishna's yoga teachings, Arjuna announces, "My confusion is destroyed, and by your grace I have regained memory."[7] To regain memory is to return to a state of consciousness before we lost ourselves in our false stories and identities.

On the field of life, with all its confusions and uncertainties, powerful forces of forgetfulness sweep over us. They obscure what Krishna describes as the "eye of knowledge", rendering us sightless, like the blind emperor Dhritarashtra.[8] With Krishna's sword of discernment, we can keep illusion and forgetfulness at bay as we travel the path of the yogi.

We speak a lot about yoga, but less often about its opposite, *vi-yoga*, that which separates us from our true potential.[9] On any journey, it's important to differentiate between terrains and to be alert to dangers, such as perilous swamps, cliffs or thieves on the road. There are many optical delusions on the inner path. Like mirages, they confuse the unwary traveller, causing her to leave the path and lose her way.

Krishna's second main Samkhya teaching is, therefore, "*Understand the terrain.*" Arjuna must not only remember who he is, but he must also understand the field of action. Krishna tells him about three qualities—Sattva, Rajas and Tamas—that form the landscape of the present moment, the field of engagement.[10] These three combine in endless permutations to create the play of form in life.

This brings us to Krishna's third main Samkhya teaching: "*Distinguish between the divine and the ungodly.*" In traversing the inner landscape, the yoga traveller will need to distinguish between what helps and what harms her. We possess both higher qualities and lower qualities. Both exist within us as a potential. Krishna advises Arjuna to differentiate carefully between these two potentials.[11]

The quality of our perceptual world is shaped by the potential we choose to nurture. The best way to overcome the lower, ungodly potential is to take shelter of the divine potential. By nurturing the divine, we build a world made of love, kindness, gratitude, truthfulness, courage, sincerity, hope, generosity, humility, strength and dedication.

Arjuna is faced with great challenges on the field of engagement. Fortunately, Krishna, the Lord of Yoga and the source of the divine, is driving his chariot and guiding him on his yoga journey. That same Krishna, the Universal Teacher, is present in our own chariot too. By taking refuge in Krishna, and by giving him the reins to our own chariot, we discover that we're protected.

Krishna explains: "In this world, there is nothing as purifying as knowledge. In time, a person perfected in yoga personally discovers this knowledge within the self."[12] Krishna makes it clear that yoga is not just a philosophy, but *philosophy in action*. The knowledge or discernment that Krishna shares is something that needs to be *lived*, not merely contemplated.[13]

Putting our knowledge into practice begins in the dark night of the soul, when everything we cling to has fallen apart. As Arjuna discovers, the yoga of despair is about transmuting despair into discernment. Like the fire that forges the sword, adversity can forge the spirit and produce wisdom.

Armed with the sword of Samkhya, the same weapon of knowledge that Krishna gave to his friend Arjuna, we too can vanquish the obstacles on our path and the false perceptions that tie us to our small human story. Like Arjuna, we can then travel far on the path of yoga, without fear.

THOSE WHO POSSESS THE EYE
OF KNOWLEDGE CAN PERCEIVE THE SELF.

—Bhagavad Gita, 15.10

ELEVEN

Remember Who You Are

— I —

By the time I stepped on to the solitary railway bridge, leaving the old town of Mathura and its many lights behind me, I found myself in utter darkness. It was a long walk to the monastery at Durvasa Tila, on the other side of the Yamuna River. The sun had long set, and I had left my journey far too late.

Bands of armed robbers roamed these remote parts, and I wondered if it wasn't wiser to return the way I had come. I raised my palm to my face: I could hardly make out the contours of my hand. As I slowly felt my way along the long railway bridge that spanned the river, my eyes gradually adjusted to the darkness. I could make out sinister shapes where the river flowed.

The bridge gave way to a winding dirt track. Out here I was completely vulnerable. I could be shot with a pipe-gun, or bludgeoned, or hacked to pieces by a machete. I doubted anyone would hear my screams. A dog howled in the distance. My heart leapt.

For a while, I was quite sure someone was following me in the darkness. I broke into a light jog, and ducked behind a bush. Remaining still, I listened intently, waiting for a silhouette or a noise. Time seemed to slow down.

Several minutes elapsed; but the only thing that punctured the stillness was the pounding of my heart. A little embarrassed, I got up, peered around and continued on my journey. "Why in the world did I make this late trip?" I thought. "*What* was I thinking? I'll *never* do that again."

If I saw anyone, I decided, I would sprint for dear life. I was pretty sure I could outpace any human if they were wielding a machete. I couldn't see more than a few steps in front of me, but then, neither could an assailant. That thought gave me some comfort. It was a long walk, and I made a deliberate effort to be less on edge.

As I started to relax a little, I became aware of the vast and serene stillness of the night. I let it fill my lungs. A faint smell of jasmine seemed to cling to the night. I surrendered to the stillness, and had the strange sense something close and familiar, maybe some hidden part of me, might reveal itself.

The feeling intensified, and with it came an unpleasant, sickly feeling—dread of the unknown. My reaction was instinctive: I began drowning the unfamiliar stillness with mental chatter. It had been a long, busy day, and my mind now began revisiting what had transpired, assessing and judging the minutiae.

This manoeuvre was not lost on me. I could see the workings of my mind more clearly than usual, as an observer. Earlier, I had felt terror, then embarrassment. This incongruous overlay of emotions had given way to an unusual sense of detachment from the chatter of the mind.

The simple act of watching the mind dispassionately had brought it to a place of calm. As I breathed in the stillness of the night, I was swept away by an overwhelming awareness of my own presence, my *aliveness*.

It's sometimes said that the mind is like a pond. For most of us, that pond is dark and impenetrable, its muddy bottom stirred continually by our agitated and restless thoughts. In our hectic, results-driven daily life, we don't allow the waters of this pond to still. We don't let them reveal their transparent depths. Since the field of perception is mostly clouded and disturbed, all that is visible to us is the movement on its surface: the continual play of form in the world. We can call this "surface perception".

There's another kind of perception: "deep perception". When we allow the lake of the mind to still, we can see right through the crystal water to its magnificent hidden depths.

In a state of alert awareness, when the restless, overbearing mind is still, everything seems magnified in clarity and intensity. I felt an unusual lightness of being, a total immersion with the universe. As I looked about at the heavens filled with innumerable stars, I became aware of one familiar light shining brighter than all the rest. The light of consciousness is what illuminates all things.[14]

The centre of my consciousness, I noticed, was no longer located within my physical body, but had risen somewhere just above the crown of my head. The clarity of perception from this place was breathtaking. I felt completely free from suffering.

Everything, including my body, was an inseparable field. To my wonderment, I saw that this field was the ever-flowing river of time. Everything was connected to everything else; and everything was in constant change. But as I looked about me at this inseparable field in flux, I realized that I, the soul, am changeless. The immense river of time flowed around me, and I knew I carried eternity inside.

I longed to remain in this heightened state of awareness. What a joyful place! Could this be where the yogis throughout the ages went in their meditation?

Could I remain here? Remembering the world I would be leaving behind, I suddenly felt afraid—I wasn't ready. Immediately I was pulled back into my physical body, forcefully reabsorbed into the constraining and limiting storyline of my small human life. It felt like violence inflicted upon the soul. That immensely spacious and joyful place was lost to me.

To describe the experience now, having re-entered my mortal story, is to do it injustice. It was one of those rare moments in which we look through the waters of perception into the heart of the universe. I understood now why the yogis and sages had described that luminous part of us that exists beyond the ego—the soul, if you will—in the way that they did in the sacred texts.

I believe most people have these experiences at one time or other. By reading about them, we can grasp them conceptually, but we never truly understand them until we experience them ourselves. When that happens, it transforms us forever. We realize we're much bigger, and more wonderful, than the beleaguered human being in the small, anxious and ordinary story of our life.

When lost in our story, our life is marked by constant struggle and striving. We become creatures of anxiety. We measure our own worth by the fickle judgments of others, or by how much we own or what we can do. We lose the courage to be true to who we are; because, like Arjuna, *we have forgotten who we are.* As a result, we experience an emptiness inside that we can't seem to fill. We're always dissatisfied, despite having so much.

Sometimes it takes darkness to appreciate the light, I thought, as I continued towards the temple on the hill. The stars shine brightly twenty-four hours a day; they never cease shining. But it's only in the obscurity of the night that we see their brilliance and beauty. We speak about illuminating the dark; but sometimes it's the darkness that allows us to appreciate the light.

In that thought, I had connected with the very heart of the soul's dark night and the yoga of despair. The obscurity in a dark night experience, when what is fleeting has been broken apart, can give us a glimpse of the self-luminous soul.

—2—

Who was this unfamiliar face in the mirror? I ran my fingertips lightly across my mouth and cheeks.

I hadn't looked into a big mirror for five years. In the temple monasteries in India, there are no full-size mirrors, just tiny hand-held ones used for applying sacred markings in clay to one's forehead. Monks don't spend time gazing into mirrors.

Living a simple, austere life in the temple monastery, meditating every day, withstanding the scorching heat of the summer and the freezing cold of winter, walking barefoot for miles on pilgrimage, and practising the ancient yoga teachings—these things had enlarged the spirit and awakened the soul. They gave me a sense of my transcendent spiritual identity, beyond the small stories of this world.

I had left India to renew my five-year visa. Now back in England at the home of a friend, I switched on the bathroom light to find myself in front of a mirror so large it covered an entire wall.

Looking at the face in the mirror, I couldn't help but think, "Who is this? This mask of flesh and skin isn't me. I'm simply residing in this body for a short time. Ageless and timeless, I'm not made of destructible elements, like flesh, skin and blood."

Many people identify with their physical body, but our body is simply a covering of the self, like a garment. It's the vehicle by which we, the transcendent self, express ourselves in this world. When the self leaves the body at death, the body is inactive, like a car without a driver.

When there were no motor cars in India, people frequently used chariots. The sages and seers, therefore, give the analogy of a chariot to help us understand the self.[15] We're passengers in the chariot of our body. Driven by the mind and senses, our chariot moves across the field of life, meeting with pleasure and pain, gain and loss, enjoyment and suffering.

Just as a warrior needs to feel at ease on her chariot, so a yoga practitioner needs to be able to rest and feel at home in her body. We reside in this body for the time being and can give ourselves permission to feel comfortable in it. If we don't accept our body and mind, we struggle to find the tranquillity we need to practise yoga.

At the same time, it would be ludicrous for a warrior to believe that the chariot is who she is. Most cells in the body are replaced over a period of seven years. That means our body of seven years ago has been ecologically dispersed throughout the environment. This physical body is not who we really are.

We're not fat, thin, young or old. These attributes relate only to the body.

When we look at photos of our childhood, it's easy to recognize how we're distinct from the changing physical body. We're the life force that animates that body. When people identify too closely with the body, they think strongly in terms of bodily distinctions such as black and white, male and female, Indian and American. But all these designations refer to the body only.

While it's fairly easy to understand we're not the body, it can be more difficult to discern that we exist beyond the creations of our mind. Those who meditate find it easier to perceive this, because meditation is a practice for stilling the restless mind.

The yoga warrior on the field of life asks, "What part of me never changes? What part of me is indestructible?" I used to think of myself in one way; now I think of myself differently. My thoughts about myself are subject to change. Therefore, if I believe I'm the lead character of my story, I'm bound to be disappointed.

To help Arjuna understand that he exists beyond the play of form of this world, Krishna differentiates between what he calls the "field" and the "knower of the field"[16] The "field", Krishna explains, is the body and everything connected with the body. This includes our senses, our thoughts, our feelings, our desires, our will, and all the transformations that these may go through in life.

The "field" Krishna is speaking about is the field of perception. Krishna explains that we, the true self, are the "knower of the field". This means we're distinct from the field.

Krishna is telling Arjuna that we're not this physical body, and we're not the temporary sensations we may experience through that body either. We're not the "good" or "bad" thoughts we may have. Nor are we any of the things of this world we may perceive, desire or identify with. We're spiritual beings beyond the transient play of form of this world. Don't look for yourself in the field of perception: whatever you see there is not who you are. You are the *knower* of the field.

–3–

While wandering through narrow lanes, a woman spotted a beautiful object in the window of an antique shop: an ornate birdcage. With twenty-four rib-like pillars, the entire cage had been delicately carved from a single block of jade. There were perches of ivory, and the cage floor, which sparkled like a mirror, reflected an intricate, patterned design on the cage's domed turquoise ceiling.

"Where is this cage from? How much is it?" the woman enquired eagerly.

"This birdcage belonged once to the great Mughal emperors who ruled India," the shopkeeper confided. "It's a rare collector's item."

The woman paid a large sum for the cage. She took her collectible home and placed it in the hall, where it could be admired easily.

"The cage could do with a little polish, to bring out its splendid colours," she noted. So, she spent all evening carefully cleaning the ornate antique and marvelling at its beauty. She felt it must be worth even more than she had paid for it.

So enamoured was the woman by her antique that she failed to see the little hummingbird inside. Its breast a dazzling, iridescent green, the tiny bird hovered in the centre of the cage, like an emerald suspended in the air.

"Feed me, please feed me!" the hummingbird sang softly, but the woman paid no heed. She saw only the cage.

That night the woman dreamed of royal cages, the prized possessions of Mughal princesses and mighty Maharajas. But of all the gilded cages in her dreams, none matched the one she now possessed.

When the lady awoke, she went straight to her antique. She admired her possession for a long while. So taken was she by the cage that she again failed to hear the bird's plaintive cry: "Feed me, please feed me." The lady saw only the cage.

"I must arrange a party," the woman thought, "so that I can show off my new antique to my friends."

She went through her address book and invited all the influential people she knew. As she sent out the invitations, she could hardly contain her excitement. It would be a spectacular event.

The woman cleaned the cage until it sparkled like a pin. She decided to buy several yards of fine silk brocade for the cage. All night she stayed up sewing. In the early hours of the morning, she stood back to admire her work.

"What a splendid collectible," she said to herself with a smile.

"Feed me, please feed me," the hummingbird cried out feebly. But the lady had eyes only for the cage; she never saw the starving bird begging for food within.

Putting on her apron, the lady went about preparing for Saturday, baking currant buns and iced fairy cakes. This would surely be an event to remember.

Guests soon began to arrive in twos and threes. They gathered around the draped object, now positioned in the centre of the room. Glowing with excitement, the lady unveiled her new collectible for all to admire.

The ornate cage, gleaming in the sunlight from the window, caught everyone's attention. The guests marvelled at the object.

But a little girl began to cry.

"What's wrong, my dear?" her mother asked, trying to console her. The little girl pointed to the cage floor: lying on its side, the hummingbird, without food for days, closed its eyes. Its little wings were still.

"Feed me, please feed me," it whispered with its last breath. The tiny bird's heartbeat came to a stop.

The guests looked at each other in shock and discomfort. One guest dropped her sandwiches; another spilled his tea. The owner of the cage fell silent, embarrassed at her absentmindedness. She had so admired the jade collectible—how could she not have noticed the dying bird inside?[17]

I first heard this story in India, as a young boy. The pampered cage, with its twenty-four rib-like pillars, is the body and everything connected to the body. The bird is the soul. We think this body is everything, so we focus on the body, but starve the soul within.

Most of the things we seek in our life relate to the body and our identity in our small human story: money, influence, achievements and the admiration and approval of others. But all the vanities of life can't satisfy the soul. As a result, we feel a great lack that can be difficult to identify. We don't know the cause, but the feeling is nonetheless strong. It doesn't go away. We long to fill the emptiness in our heart.

That feeling of emptiness is the hunger of the soul. The purpose of yoga is to nourish the soul and set it free, so that it can express its own true nature.

–4–

An elderly Samkhya teacher grew weary of his student's complaining. One morning he sent his student to fetch some salt. When the apprentice returned, the Samkhya master instructed the melancholic young man to put a handful of salt into a glass of water and drink it.

"How does it taste?" the master asked.

"Terrible!" spat the student.

The master chuckled. He then told the young man to take another handful of salt and put it into the nearby lake. The two walked in silence to the edge of the large, serene lake behind the master's hermitage. The apprentice poured his fistful of salt into the water.

"Now drink from the lake," the master said.

As the water dripped down the student's chin, the master asked, "How does it taste?"

"Fresh," remarked the apprentice.

"Do you taste the salt?" asked the Samkhya master.

"No," said the young man.

At this, the master sat beside this troubled young man, who so reminded him of himself, and took his hands: "The pain of life is pure salt; no more, no less. The amount of pain in our life remains the same, exactly the same. But the amount of pain we taste depends on the container we put the pain into. So, when you're in pain, the only thing you can do is enlarge your perception of who you are. Stop being a glass. Become a lake."

The master continued: "When we live within the confines of our small human story, we're a tiny glass. Our pain takes on a very large significance, to the point of becoming unbearable. But when we remember we're spiritual beings, not the lead character of our small story, we experience immediate freedom and spaciousness. We grow from a tiny glass into a large, serene lake. The misfortunes of life no longer affect us in the same way."

We don't generally invite pain into our life; but it comes anyway. And when pain comes uninvited, we can't simply will it away. Krishna tells Arjuna that pain and pleasure come and go, like heat and cold. But if these sensations don't trouble us, then we've truly attained wisdom.[18] Becoming equal in pain and pleasure means becoming a lake. It means *remembering who we are*.

We have the mortal self and we have the mortal story. But we're more than our mortal self; and therefore, we're also more than our mortal story. When we remember who we are, we're no longer bound by mortal limitations.

Krishna, speaking of such a person who can remain equal in pain and pleasure, declares, "Such a wise person is prepared for immortality."[19] This is because such a person transcends the limitations of her own mortal story.

Thus, a Samkhya master is not someone who no longer experiences any difficulties in her life; a Samkhya master is a person who is no longer troubled by those difficulties.

−5−

One summer, my wife and I spent a week at a professor's home in Yorkshire, to look after her border terrier while she was away. It was a large, beautiful house facing the Yorkshire Moors. Each morning, we would take the professor's dog, Charlie, out on a walk. He was a ball of fur with a peculiar but sweet personality.

On these walks through the stunning moors, I would often be lost in thought on the poetic verses of the *Bhagavad Gita*. Suddenly, I would look around and Charlie was nowhere to be seen. I would call out the dog's name, anxiously scanning the moors in every direction. Imagine losing someone's dog on the Yorkshire Moors.

Wondering what to do, I would inadvertently glance at the ground beneath my feet, and to my complete surprise, discover Charlie. He had this ability to silently follow you, not in front or behind you, but directly between your feet.

It struck me that we spend an entire lifetime searching for happiness. We work very hard to find it; but as soon as we fulfil one of the desires we believe will make us happy, another emerges, in an endless chain. We're always looking in every possible direction except the most obvious one.

Our happiness doesn't exist somewhere out in the future. It lies right here, within our own being. And that's the very last place we think to look.

Now, whenever I become distracted and find myself looking for happiness in future outcomes and events, in things, in accomplishments, I check myself and remember Charlie. "You're looking for Charlie again," I tell myself. "Stop looking for Charlie."

Our habit of looking outside of ourselves for happiness can even enter our yoga practice. We're on a yoga journey; but it isn't a voyage to a distant location. The self is not something far away we need to travel to, nor something we need to become. We're the self already. Our journey is therefore really a journey of knowledge, a journey of remembering. The *Kena Upanishad* refers to "awakened knowledge".[20] Yoga helps us out of our forgetfulness of who we truly are.

Just as the natural quality of fire is heat and the natural quality of water is wetness, the natural quality of the self is happiness.[21] Not a shallow, temporary happiness, but a deep and abiding fulfilment that doesn't depend upon the play of form in this world.

Krishna explains that a person who truly knows the sacred self finds complete fulfilment and contentment in the self.[22] A yogi or yogini can directly experience this happiness through her daily practice of yoga. In other words, she doesn't need to look outside of herself for fulfilment.

Happiness is our natural state when illusion is removed or stripped away. Therefore, the way to happiness is not to try to create it, but to seek everything that *obstructs* it.

I SHALL DESCRIBE FURTHER THE HIGHEST KNOWLEDGE,
SUPREME AMONG ALL TYPES OF KNOWLEDGE,
KNOWING WHICH ALL THE SEERS HAVE FROM HERE
ATTAINED THE HIGHEST PERFECTION.

—*Bhagavad Gita*, 14.1

TWELVE
Understand the Terrain

—I—

We turned the corner, and there she was: the Eiffel Tower. I had been to this iconic Paris landmark several times, and I confess, I find lifeless monuments a little disappointing. When I'm finally in front of them, there's something oddly flat and pedestrian about them. On this summer morning, however, it was different—I had never seen the Eiffel Tower as magnificent as this, not even in pictures.

The monument hadn't changed; the city hadn't changed; I was much the same person. So, what was different? *My vantage point.*

Most tourists head straight to the base of the Eiffel Tower. This time, we had Ariana, a close friend teaching at La Sorbonne, as our tour guide. She took us to Trocadéro, perched on a hilltop on the other side of the River Seine from the Tower. Across a gorgeous park and tiled plaza, complete with gilded statues, you're exposed to a stunning, unobstructed view of the Eiffel Tower. Local Parisians were enjoying their lunch on the steps. I felt I was in on a secret.

What we see depends not only on what we're looking at, but also *where we're looking from*. In the *Bhagavad Gita* Krishna goes to some lengths to explain this to Arjuna.

❦

On a journey, it's important to understand the terrain. Some terrains offer beautiful, unobstructed views and make for an easy passage. Some are troublesome and require immense effort. Others are dark and treacherous, liable to confound and entrap the traveller.

Krishna differentiates between three types of "terrain": Sattva, Rajas and Tamas. Think of Sattva as the hilltops of life. They offer us clear, undisturbed panoramic views. When the mind is influenced by Sattva, a person feels satisfied at heart. She's no longer troubled by a million longings. Sattva manifests as mindfulness, tranquillity and wisdom. The Sanskrit word *sattva* means "beingness" and refers to a deep awareness of what is.

But it's difficult to remain on the mountaintop. We are forced back down to the more troublesome slopes of striving and attachment, and into the murky valleys of lethargy and forgetfulness.

Rajas is a vantage point on life that fills a person with a million desires, leading her to be anxious, ceaselessly striving, and forever dissatisfied. A person influenced by Rajas is always trying to reshape the world. The Rajas terrain involves a difficult climb up a steep slope, with all the exertion, longing, triumph and frustration of such a pursuit.

Then you have Tamas, the dark valleys of life, with treacherous, disorientating marshes and haunted forests of bewilderment. When lost in Tamas, "darkness", we fall into lamentation, moroseness, self-pity, resentment, frustration, anger, hatred and a myriad of other forms of negativity. This is the terrain we're likely to find ourselves in during a dark night of the soul. It can manifest as a strong desire to give up on life.

Travellers can find themselves stuck in Tamas for an excessively long time. They drift into an existential sleep, even while appearing awake. They forget why they're on the road, or even that there is a journey at all.

Millennia ago, the sages of India differentiated between Sattva, Rajas and Tamas to help us live more consciously; to help us better understand our own state of consciousness, the qualities of our environment, and how those qualities influence us. Krishna summarizes these three competing qualities by what they produce in our heart:

> Wisdom arises from Sattva; greed arises from Rajas;
> and negligence and bewilderment arise from Tamas,
> as well as folly.[23]

Krishna has already explained the nature of the self, the

"knower of the field". Now he wants us to understand the "field" itself. The yoga warrior must understand who she is, but she must also be able to navigate the field of life.

–2–

He looked at me with beady eyes. His face was pale, covered in a thick layer of ashes.

"I'm not allowed to leave the crematorium," he said. "I've lived in and around its walls for nearly two years."

We were in the ancient city of Jagannath Puri, on the eastern coast of India. I had often walked past the city's walled cremation ground, or burning ghat, on Swargadwar Road, uneasy about its proximity to the city's bustling streets. When the wind blows from the sea, an unsettling smell of burnt flesh permeates the market. The funeral pyres burn without rest.

"What do you eat? Where do you sleep?" I asked the ascetic.

"We only accept what's left behind in the crematorium. For the first year I slept in the open. Then someone left an old stretcher, and I used that to build a simple shelter."

"But *why* do you do this?" I asked.

"We believe that Tamas, darkness, is the highest quality. Sattva brings discernment: 'This is good, that is bad; this is clean, that is dirty.' We believe everything is the same, and so we want to destroy discernment. To do this, we cultivate Tamas."

"How?" I asked.

"We do things that promote Tamas. Maybe it's better you don't know."

I remembered Krishna telling Arjuna that those who culture Tamas worship ghosts and departed beings. I was beginning to feel a little afraid.

"If you're not allowed to leave the crematorium, why are you out here now?" I asked.

"I recently started having doubts about my path," the young man replied. "I've been reading teachings on yoga that explain the benefits of Sattva. Through Sattva, these teachings say, we gain higher knowledge."

The sacred yoga texts explain that Sattva, Rajas and Tamas each have a function. Tamas, for example, generates lethargy and sleep. A good night's sleep gives us renewed energy to actively engage with life. When situated within these beneficial contexts, Tamas and Rajas are not undesirable energies.

At the same time, the yogi must also choose which quality to actively *culture* in her life. The yoga texts recommend Sattva, advise us to avoid Tamas, and alert us to the shortcomings and mixed results of Rajas. But here was an ascetic who lived in a crematorium and practised the reverse: not yoga, but *vi-yoga*, that which takes us away from yoga.

The sun was beginning to set, and it was time for us to part ways. As I said goodbye outside the main entrance to the burning ghat, the ascetic pointed out his teacher some twenty yards away.

I froze in fear. Covered from top to bottom in human ashes, a large-framed man was surveying me with reddish eyes. His thickly matted hair touched the ground. He seemed intoxicated. Motionless, he stared blankly ahead, holding what looked to me like a human skull, his fingers hooked through the eye sockets.

"He has been living in crematoriums and charnel grounds for more than twelve years," the student explained. "That skull in his hand is what he eats from."

"What does he eat?" I ventured, swallowing hard.

"His own excrement mixed with milk."

–3–

"I hardly made any progress on my assignment today," my friend Wendy confided. "Every time I want to work on it, something comes up and I get side-tracked."

Wendy was in her late twenties, with three children. She had her first child in her late teens. Now that the children were older, she was taking a degree course in journalism.

Her mother Janine, keen to correct Wendy at every turn, signalled her disapproval: "If you keep letting yourself get distracted, you'll never get that assignment done. You'll end up flunking the course, and then what?"

"Why do you *always* have to criticize?" Wendy sprang back.

"Of course you'll do well, darling," Wendy's partner Horatio assured her. "I have no doubt about it. You *always* do well." Horatio wasn't as sure as he made believe, but the tension created by Wendy's anxiety made him uncomfortable, so his instinct was to stifle it with reassurance. This was easier than listening. Horatio's definitive assurance made Wendy feel under even more pressure. She felt silly for voicing her fears.

"Why don't you try blocking off some time for your assignment," Horatio now counselled. "Shut your office door, switch off your mobile, and don't log on to Facebook or check your emails."

Wendy didn't say anything. She didn't need advice; she needed to be heard.

"I know what you mean," Wendy's brother Joe declared, enthusiastically. He had been waiting for his turn to speak. "I've been getting distracted a lot lately myself. It always seems to happen when I have a big deadline looming. Just last week, I needed to complete another financial statement analysis report for my department and…"

Wendy was getting frustrated. Joe had just railroaded the conversation, making it all about him, again.

Joe's girlfriend, Susan, noticed. She was a good listener, and admired Wendy's courage in pursuing her dream to become a journalist. When Joe finished, she brought the conversation back: "Wendy, you said you weren't able to make much progress today. You kept getting side-tracked?"

"Yes, it's almost as if I'm looking for something to distract me. I think I'm afraid whatever I write might not be good enough."

Wendy paused. This was a sudden insight for her, an unexpected moment of clarity. She didn't know where her words came from. Suddenly she understood something important about herself that would no doubt serve her well in life.

In that brief interval and the conversation that flowed from it, Susan and Wendy formed a connection of trust and understanding. Intimacy even. They became friends.

Communication can be of three broad types, depending upon whether Sattva, Rajas or Tamas is dominant.

Generally, most of our conversations are strongly influenced by Rajas and Tamas. When covered by Tamas, we tend to criticize and shut others down; our words are judgmental, demeaning, undermining, hurtful or destructive.

When driven by Rajas, we try to shift the conversation to ourselves. When others are speaking, we don't really listen: we're waiting for our turn to speak. In Rajas, we're driven by our own immediate needs—the need to be liked and admired, the need to be right, the need to influence, the need to be at the centre.

In Sattva, we approach a conversation without any personal

agenda, and in doing so we're able to listen, without judgment. Communication in Sattva leads to vitality and a deeper connection between the speaker and listener. It encourages the participants to reveal their heart, and leads to trust and intimacy.

In the conversation at Wendy's home, Wendy's mother tends to fall into a pattern of criticism, activated by Tamas. This in turn provokes an angry and defensive response in Tamas from Wendy, creating further emotional distance between mother and daughter. Tamas, a destructive force, leads to argument and discord.

Wendy's brother is strongly influenced by Rajas. This manifests as a desire to steer conversations towards himself, his own needs and interests. In Rajas, as in Tamas, we're not able to listen to others. We can feign attentiveness, but we're unable to suspend our preoccupation with ourselves and enter the experience of the other person. While someone is speaking, we're busy thinking about our next statement rather than listening to what's being said.

A conversation in Rajas can seem animated, colourful and interesting, but the participants don't feel energized or vitalized by it. There's no heart-to-heart connection, no sacred bridge between worlds, no union of souls.

Horatio, too, is moved by Rajas, which leads to a failure of understanding. When Wendy expresses her anxiety or inner turmoil, he's unwilling to suspend his own needs for a moment and share her uncertainty. He *must* resolve it, and so offers unrequested advice.

Susan, however, is able to listen and open up the conversation. She encourages Wendy to go deeper into her experience. Her capacity to listen with sustained immersion in another's experience gets people to reveal their heart.

When our primary objective is to undermine someone or what they are saying, without constructive intent, our communication is in Tamas. Examples are quibbling, blaming, personal attacks and self-abuse. Such communication is fuelled by Tamasic states such as fear, jealousy, prejudice or insecurity.

When our primary concern is to establish our own position, our communication is in Rajas. We do this when we make the conversation all about ourselves or when we try to convince someone, control their actions, or establish our superiority.

By contrast, when two or more people speak to each other without judgment or agenda, really listening to what the other person says, that exchange of life energy is communication in Sattva. Such communication allows new ways of seeing to emerge. It leads to healing, understanding, insight and wisdom. Through this kind of genuine, open exchange, we energize and inspire each other. We enhance each other's lives.[24]

According to the rishis, communication in Sattva is best, while communication in Tamas is best avoided. Communication in Rajas is sometimes unavoidable, but should be tempered as much as possible with Sattva, so that it has some life-enhancing properties and doesn't degenerate into Tamas.

Importantly, these three forms of communication also apply to our private communication with ourselves, our "self-talk", which also manifests in Sattva, Rajas or Tamas.[25]

–4–

Jeremy was a young entrepreneur. He had attended several courses on how to get rich quickly, paying a lot of money for these courses. They helped him focus his energy. In these sessions, hundreds of other young entrepreneurs, fuelled by infectious desire, listened rapturously, hypnotized by the prospect of making it rich.

Jeremy began buying small single-family houses. At that time, the banks in the UK offered generous buy-to-let, interest-only mortgages. They required only the smallest of deposits. This was before the property crash, in a buoyant market.

Jeremy started off with £300,000. Remarkably, eighteen months later he was sitting on a property portfolio worth more than £7 million, with equity of more than £3 million.

For Jeremy, this wasn't enough. It was only the beginning. He felt impatient. His dream was to amass more than £100 million before his fortieth birthday. No one was going to stop him. So, he set up a real estate business.

The fledgling business was a very busy place to work. It had the same hunger and industry, the same speed and exuberance, the same unstoppable energy as its founder. It also carried the same greed and impatience, which sometimes led to the cutting of corners.

The business grew from a home operation into a larger firm with many employees. The growth was so rapid that there wasn't enough time to care for all the details. Deals were made, but documents not filed properly; negotiations were conducted, but parties not properly vetted; land was purchased, but full due diligence not always completed; opportunities were seized, but risks not always appreciated or planned for.

The energy was predominantly Rajas, with a measure of Tamas. As Krishna explains, action taken with disregard of consequences, of loss or harm, and of personal capacity is in the nature of Tamas.[26]

The sages refer to Sattva, Rajas and Tamas as the *gunas*, which in Sanskrit also means "ropes" or "what binds". This indicates the tremendous power of these qualities upon one's consciousness.

How we begin something is so important. The quality of our consciousness is carried right through to the end, in an inexorable chain that is difficult to undo.

We can begin or end anything—a relationship, an enterprise, even our day—in any of the three *gunas*. In Sattva, beginnings and endings are thought-through, deliberate, orderly and peaceful. In Rajas, they tend to be rushed to achieve some urgent purpose at all costs. As a result, they're usually poorly planned, disorderly, chaotic and disruptive. Beginnings and endings in Tamas are induced by lethargy, neglect, anger, jealousy or some other destructive tendency.

An action impelled by one *guna* will tend to yield a result in that same *guna*, if not in a lower *guna*. The results we experience tend to reflect the quality of our actions; and the quality of our actions mirror the quality of our state of mind.[27]

The results we experience can also be divided into three kinds. Actions in Sattva yield results that are positive, stable, durable, congruous, appropriate, balanced and agreeable. Actions in Rajas tend to yield mixed results, while actions in Tamas tend to deliver disempowering, destructive and disabling results. According to the ancient texts, one who acts in Sattva experiences fulfilment, one who acts in Rajas achieves mixed misery and happiness, and one who acts under the influence of Tamas is morose and dejected.[28]

The outcome of Jeremy's business was mixed. Things began to go wrong. Investors wanted their money back and partners proved unreliable, even potentially fraudulent in some cases. The company filed for bankruptcy.

−5−

I had come to the Indian Embassy in London to renew my visa, aiming to return to Mathura, India, in time for Janmashtami, the celebration of Krishna's birth. An elderly official spotted me, dressed in the simple robes of my tradition. He must have become curious, for he called me into his small office. I noticed a copy of the *Bhagavad Gita* on his desk.

After asking a few questions, the consulate official began telling a story: "A young traveller was once crossing a remote forest. He hoped to reach a great city nearby in time for Diwali, the festival of lights. At the grand temple in the heart of the city, he planned to offer a lamp, some forest flowers and three moonstones to Krishna, the beautiful lord of his heart.

"Deep in the forest, three robbers fell upon the unwary traveller. The first pulled out a large knife, intent on killing the traveller immediately, without a second thought.

"The second robber, who was more calculating, stopped him: 'Of all crimes, murder is the most serious. If we're caught, our punishment will be death. It's better we simply take everything this man has and leave him tied to a tree.'

"And so, the three robbers went through the young man's travelling bag and took whatever they deemed valuable and went on their way.

"Later that evening, the third robber returned to the crime site, alone. He found the young traveller still tied to a tree.

"'I'm truly sorry for all you've endured,' the robber said, tears in his eyes. 'I hope you haven't suffered too much. Here, let me untie you.'

"The robber, who knew the forest well, led the young traveller to a path out of the woods. In the distance was the beautiful city, lit up by thousands of lights. There were lamps in every window and on every terrace.

"The robber opened the traveller's hand and returned his three precious moonstones.

"'I'll leave you here,' the robber said, with a sadness in his eyes.

"'But no, you must come with me,' the traveller exclaimed. 'I haven't had a chance to thank you for what you've done. Come into the city. I'll tell everyone of your kindness, and you'll be rewarded.'

"The robber remained silent. He said at last, 'I'm a robber. If I go into the city, I'll be recognized and caught. This beautiful city is yours, but I must remain exiled in the woods.'"

After telling this story, the consulate official paused, looking at me intently. "The dense forest is this world," he explained. "We, the soul, are the traveller. If we're on a yoga path, we're trying to reach the great city of lights.

"The three robbers in the woods are Tamas, Rajas and Sattva. These three bind the soul in the dense forest of this world.

"Thoughtless and destructive, the first robber, Tamas, binds the soul to darkness and lethargy. Capable of great cruelty, he has little regard for the suffering of others. Rajas, by contrast, has a plan—and that plan centres around his personal gain. Rajas binds the soul through hankering and attachment.

"Sattva, the quietest of the three, feels pained to see others suffer. His function is to release the soul from Tamas and Rajas. In other words, Sattva loosens the bonds of this world. Illuminating and peaceful, Sattva can lead the soul to the boundary of enlightenment, the beautiful city of lights.

"But Sattva can't go further. Even Sattva has no place in the sacred realm of the soul. Therefore, ultimately, the yogi must transcend all three *gunas*, including Sattva."

The elderly official paused and turning to me squarely, asked, "Why can't Sattva enter the city of lights?"

"Because Sattva too is a *guna*, or thief," I replied. "Krishna explains in the *Bhagavad Gita* that Sattva binds us through attachment to happiness and to knowledge."[29]

"Yes, Sattva, the purest of the three *gunas*, is a big help on the journey of the soul; but Sattva can't enter the highest level of consciousness, beyond the play of form of this world. Sattva can only show the way," the official said.

The official was dressed in an immaculate pinstriped navy suit. I remembered that day that we can't judge someone by their outward appearance. A wise soul may be dressed in monk's robes or in a suit, dress, jeans or yoga leggings. It's easy to forget Arjuna was suited up as a warrior. So was Krishna.

There are wise souls all around us who can inspire us on our journey of yoga. Krishna, the Universal Teacher, sends them our way at the right time to help us.

The consulate official continued, "So how can we rise beyond the *gunas?*"

"Krishna tells Arjuna that he can transcend Sattva, Rajas and Tamas through Bhakti, sacred love," I replied.[30]

"Do you know what the three precious moonstones represent?" the official asked. This was the most unusual interview I had ever had.

"Well, the traveller wants to offer them to Krishna, the beautiful lord of his heart. These gemstones are taken away by Rajas and Tamas, but are returned by Sattva. I think they represent our body, mind and words. When we truly offer these with love, we transcend the three *gunas.*"

The official showed no sign of agreeing or disagreeing. Instead, he asked another question: "And someone who has transcended the *gunas*, what are they like?"

I remembered that Arjuna had asked Krishna this same question. "Such a person is equal in happiness and distress, fortune and misfortune," I replied. "They're self-contained. They don't derive their identity from this world, so remain unmoved whether praised or blamed, honoured or condemned.

They don't distinguish between friends and enemies, but see all beings equally on the level of the soul. They understand that everything in this world is simply the play of the three *gunas*."[31]

The official broke into a big smile. He opened my passport and stamped it with a five-year multiple-entry student visa.

"You're on your way to Mathura to make an offering to Krishna on Janmashtami," he said. "I'm not able to travel to that great city with you, but I'll help you get there. I certainly won't hold you back."

.

THE DIVINE QUALITIES LEAD TO COMPLETE FREEDOM,
BUT THE UNGODLY QUALITIES TOWARDS BONDAGE,
IT IS CONSIDERED.

—*Bhagavad Gita*, 16.5

THIRTEEN

Distinguish Between the Divine and the Ungodly

−I−

Rooted in the hearts of many Hindus is the belief that if you die in the sacred town of Varanasi, on the bank of the Ganges, you will attain release from the cycle of rebirth in this world. Every year, thousands make their way to this town to spend their final days.

Varanasi has three guesthouses for the dying. One of these is Kashi Labh Mukti Bhawan, established in 1908. Its manager, Bhairav Nath Shukla, has witnessed over 12,000 deaths in his forty-four years at Mukti Bhawan.[32]

Shukla observed that at the end of their life, the guesthouse residents often regretted decisions they had made driven by their lower qualities, impelled by what Krishna describes as "the wealth of the ungodly". Krishna lists six qualities that injure us: hypocrisy, vanity, egotism, anger, harshness and absence of wisdom.[33] The last of these, absence of wisdom, is the gold in which every ungodly jewel is set.[34]

Ungodly qualities are so familiar and near to us that we usually fail to see them in ourselves.

Shukla remembers the day that Shri Ram Sagar Mishra, a Sanskrit scholar, arrived at Mukti Bhavan. The oldest of six brothers, Mishra used to be closest to the youngest, but an ugly argument between the two had led to a wall being built to partition the family home.

Mishra was sure he would pass away on the sixteenth day from his arrival. On the fourteenth day he said, "Ask my estranged brother of forty years to come see me. This bitterness makes my heart heavy. I'm anxious to resolve every conflict."

Shukla arranged for a letter to be sent. On the sixteenth day, the youngest brother arrived. Mishra held his hand and begged him for forgiveness. He asked him to take down the wall dividing the house. The brothers wept and mid-sentence, Mishra stopped speaking. His face became calm. He was gone in a moment.

Shukla has seen this story replay in many forms over the past forty-four years. "People carry so much baggage throughout their lives, unnecessarily, only wanting to drop it at the very end of their journey," he says.

The heavy baggage we carry is the wealth of the ungodly. It's everything that has sprung from our own hypocrisy, vanity, egotism, anger, harshness and absence of wisdom.

Shukla explains that near the end of life many residents of Mukti Bhawan learn to appreciate the simple things, such as the chirping of birds, the fragrance of jasmine in the garden, or the soulful devotional songs Mukti Bhavan plays three times a day.

This isn't true for everyone, though. Those who are too critical or too proud struggle to find joy in small things, their minds too preoccupied. They remain caught up, shouldering this heavy burden of the ungodly, even at the very end of life.

We're truly rich and fortunate when we possess a large treasury of the heart, not a large treasury of the ego. The wealth of the gods and goddesses is a precious cache of unearthly qualities: fearlessness, purity of heart, discipline, non-violence, truthfulness, avoiding anger, non-attachment, tranquillity, compassion, kindness, humility, vitality, patience, and much more.[35]

Shukla recommends cultivating helpful habits to house helpful values. And this, he says, happens over time, with practice: "It's like building a muscle; you have to keep at it every day."

Until we consistently work towards being giving, truthful or kind every single time we're challenged, we can't expect to have attained that jewel-like quality.

Many people donate or perform charitable acts towards the end of their life, Shukla observed. This is because death is hard on them. In their suffering, they begin to empathize with others' suffering. What if we could develop these qualities not at the end of our life, when we're frail and bedridden, but when we're at the height of our energy and vitality?

Culturing these helpful qualities—amassing this type of capital, "the wealth of the gods"—is a form of yoga, Krishna explains to Arjuna. We tend to focus on accumulating money and material assets throughout our life. In doing so, we may easily and unwittingly spend a lifetime amassing the wealth of the ungodly, and find ourselves carrying a heavy burden all through life, right to death's door.

We're born into this world naked, without anything; and we'll leave this world empty-handed. There's nothing at all we can take with us. All we have is the potential of a divinely inspired life. By practising kindness and the other qualities of the gods, we'll be able to exit this world peacefully and gracefully.

—2—

After fourteen years of marriage, Claude's wife Amber left him for a yoga instructor. Claude plunged into a dark night of the soul.

During their marriage, Claude had wanted children, but Amber had been distinctly unenthusiastic. Within a few months of meeting her new yoga instructor, they had moved to San Francisco and Amber found herself expecting a baby.

Most people would have been filled with bitterness and fury, but Claude's response surprised me: he never spoke ill of Amber. If Claude's friends began disparaging her, he refused to join in. Instead, he deliberately chose to remain respectful of her, even though his world had been thrown into turmoil.

The dark night of the soul is the perfect time to develop kindness and compassion, both towards oneself and towards others, despite the pain.

Claude carried a lot of pain. But he refused to linger in self-pity, taking ownership of his life. He contemplated and acknowledged the mistakes he had made in the relationship, and how he might have contributed to the break-up. This took courage and strength.

There were still unresolved legal issues between Claude and Amber, including a third-party court case relating to their previous business together. Amber had taken the better half of their joint property portfolio, but Claude didn't look for payback. Instead, he helped Amber settle the case, without her knowing.

Divorces and break-ups can become bitter, drawn out disputes, with both parties intent on destroying each other. They easily elicit the worst in us, our "ungodly" side.

Claude was deeply interested in Bhakti-yoga, the yoga of sacred love. He studied the *Bhagavad Gita* often and sought to culture divine qualities, such as non-violence, avoiding anger, never maligning others, compassion, kindness, humility, and the absence of malice.[36]

Claude's teacher had taught him the wisdom of trees. Yes, *trees*. A tree doesn't take it personally if we don't bow down in gratitude for the oxygen it provides. It gives whatever it has to others—its shade, its flowers, its fruits—without concern about receiving anything in return. It braves the scorching afternoon heat and torrential rains without complaining, offering shelter to those in need. And if someone arrives with an axe to cut it down, it remains free from malice and the desire for revenge.[37]

By meditating on the nature of a tree, we can develop the qualities of tolerance and generosity. Claude wanted to emulate a tree, not an axe.

−3−

We passed a pack of twelve dogs facing each other in a large circle. It looked like a meeting. I had never seen dogs do that before.

Two of the dogs, both male, began barking loudly at each other, while the others watched and listened. Eventually, one of the two surrendered and left. The barking ceased.

Witnessing this, I recalled a passage in the *Mahabharata* where Arjuna's grandfather, the wise Bhishma, likens someone who speaks ill of another behind their back to a cur.[38] I knew from personal experience that if you face a hostile street dog in India, it will retreat; but as soon as you turn your back to it, the feral canine will begin barking fiercely.

Still, I couldn't quite understand Bhishma's words. I was walking on the seashore with my teacher, so I asked him.

"A dog has higher qualities than someone who criticizes others," my teacher replied. "When a dog sees another dog it doesn't like, it begins to bark loudly. But once that other dog has left, the first dog will stop barking. Humans are just the opposite: when someone we don't like enters the room, we're silent and polite; but as soon as that person leaves, we begin 'barking' loudly. And we continue criticizing that person for many days, at every opportunity."

I laughed. Unlike a dog, we rarely criticize others to their face; usually, we do so only when they're not around. When a dog shows its dislike of another dog, there's at least honesty and integrity in its barking.

Also, a dog lets go of its malice easily. We carry ours with us for many days, sometimes even years.

"What should we do if someone does something that really bothers us?" I ventured.

"If you're troubled by someone, it's a blessing. It means Krishna wants to teach you a special lesson. When we point a finger at someone, we should look at our own hand: our index finger is pointing at that person, but notice, three of our other fingers are pointing back at us.

"So, if you're disturbed by the qualities of others, look deeply at your own heart. Is that quality in you? Why are you so disturbed by it?"[39]

We tend to project unacknowledged aspects of ourselves on to others. When we're "triggered" and find ourselves criticizing others, it often reveals parts of ourselves we disown or reject.

My teacher continued, "When we judge or criticize someone, we build a bridge from their heart to our own heart, and all the faults of that person, real or imagined, cross over that bridge, taking root in our own heart. So, we should try to see the good qualities of others."

I imagined creating a bridge that allowed only the divine qualities to enter my heart. Since that day, I have been making a conscious effort to look for and appreciate the virtues of others. This has become an important part of my yoga practice.

–4–

One day a wise yoga teacher went to the Ganges to bathe. On the riverbank were a group of family members arguing loudly. The teacher observed them for a few moments and then turned to his students: "Why do people who are angry shout at each other?"

The students thought about it for a while. "We lose our cool, so we raise our voices," one student offered.

"But why would we need to shout at a person sitting right next to us? We might as well say whatever it is we have to say softly."

A few other students offered their suggestions, but none satisfied the group.

"When two people are angry with each other," the teacher explained, "the distance between their hearts increases. Therefore, the angrier they are, the louder they must shout to cover the growing distance between them.

"When two people truly love each other, they don't shout. They speak to each other softly. What happens when two people are especially close? They whisper. They may even understand each other without having to speak at all. There's no longer a gap between their hearts.

"Anger creates the greatest gulf between two hearts. An angry heart is a treacherous place from which to speak or act. Anger, Krishna tells Arjuna, is one of the three passages to a tormented existence, one of the three gateways of Tamas that destroy the self."[40]

The teacher turned to his students: "So whenever you disagree with each other, be careful never to create distance between your hearts. Remember, words have power. They can make a person laugh or cry; they can inspire or destroy. Like sharp arrows, our words—once released—can never be recalled, so take great care with them.

"Krishna defines discipline of speech as speaking words that don't disturb others and that are true, kind and helpful.[41] So whenever we have a pressing urge to speak, we can first ask ourselves: 'Will my words disturb others? Are they true? Are they kind? Are they helpful?' If our words don't pass these four 'gates', then it's better to exercise restraint by remaining silent.

"Use words to reduce the distance between your heart and the hearts of others, not to enlarge it. Otherwise, you may find one day that the distance between your hearts is so great that you can never find your way back."

–5–

An elderly master and his young apprentice, journeying on foot together to Mathura, came upon a wide, shallow river. The apprentice helped his teacher into the water, and they began to wade across carefully.

The teacher noticed a scorpion struggling in the water. He picked up the creature in his cupped palms to save it from drowning.

No sooner had the scorpion come out of the water that it promptly stung the teacher with its quivering, arched tail. An unbearable burning pain shot up the teacher's arm, and he immediately let go of the nasty arachnid.

Despite his agony, the teacher picked up the drowning scorpion from the water and began wading towards the bank; and again, the scorpion stung the old man.

The apprentice looked on aghast. "Teacher, put it down! Don't bother trying to save such a treacherous creature; it'll only sting you again. Just let it die!"

The teacher ignored his apprentice and took the scorpion to dry land. As he approached the bank, the scorpion stung the teacher a third time, before crawling into the undergrowth.

"Teacher, why didn't you just let it drown? That wretched creature nearly killed you," the apprentice cried.

"You're right. But this creature was simply following its nature. Just as a scorpion's nature is to sting, my nature is to show compassion and kindness to all beings. If the scorpion didn't abandon its nature, even when it risked losing its life, why should I abandon mine?"

When I first heard this story in a temple monastery in India, I reflected that we're sometimes faced with individuals and situations that feel toxic. These are our "scorpions". It's easy to react with anger, resentment, hatred and violence. It's easy to become venomous too. It takes true courage to respond with kindness, compassion, understanding and grace. If we're cultivating our divine or godly qualities, if this is part of our yoga practice, then even when faced with difficulty and pain, we can respond kindly.

If we can maintain our higher nature even during times of pain and misfortune, such as during a dark night of the soul, then the divine qualities we're culturing will have become an immovable, ineffaceable part of us. They can never be taken from us.

–6–

> I got what I wanted today, and I'll get what I want tomorrow. All this belongs to me, and in the future my wealth will increase further. I've killed one enemy, and I'll kill the others too. I'm the lord; I'm the enjoyer. I'm successful, powerful and happy. I'm wealthy and from a good family. Who else is there like me? I'll do some rituals and charitable giving, and then I'll celebrate.[42]

If we replace "kill" with "destroy", these might easily be the personal thoughts of a company CEO or politician today. They're Krishna's description of the ungodly mindset, written thousands of years ago.

Even outside the arena of competitive capitalism or politics, we may find ourselves thinking in similar terms: "I got what I wanted today, and I'll get what I want tomorrow."

It's tempting to believe we carry only the divine within us; but in the dark night of the soul, our dark side emerges. We're faced with parts of ourselves we may have never seen before, and which we don't wish to see or acknowledge.

"Divine" and "ungodly" refer simply to our higher and lower impulses, qualities that help us and qualities that harm us. We've all witnessed these two sides within ourselves. We may wish to conceal, ignore or banish our ungodly qualities. But it's in darkness that these qualities thrive. They prefer *not* to be seen. To ignore or banish them only makes them stronger.

As soon we shine a light on our lower impulses by acknowledging them, they lose much of their hold on us. By actively seeking refuge in the divine qualities, such as kindness, compassion and truth, the army of the dark retreats.

The ungodly qualities can't remain in the presence of the divine qualities. Hate can't tolerate the presence of love. Arrogance can't sit alongside humility. Falsehood can't live in the company of truth. One of the two must leave the room.

One morning, my teacher explained this principle in a way I could easily understand. Pointing to an empty jug nearby, he asked me how I would extract all the air it contained.

A young, inventive teenager, I imagined first sealing the mouth of the jug carefully. I would then need to somehow create a vacuum in the vessel, by drawing the air out through suction. It wouldn't be easy.

My teacher laughed affectionately. The easiest way, of course, is just to fill the jug with water, he explained. By filling the vessel with water, we automatically remove all the air. Likewise, the easiest way to empty our life of negative forces is to fill our life with the positive, vitalizing waters of the divine qualities, especially love and kindness.

If we fill our world with love and kindness, we leave no room for hatred and unkindness. If we fill our world with gratitude, we leave no room for want.

Some people try very hard to empty their world of all negativity. But emptiness (like a vacuum) is an artificial state. It's impossible for us, while we're alive, to have no thoughts or emotions at all; and if we focus continuously on removing toxic qualities, we may simply end up enlarging them. Therefore, the way to guard ourselves from unhelpful thoughts and states is to focus on creating vibrant, helpful ones.

I'm struck by this truth every time I think about everything I'm deeply thankful for. This generates immense vitality and abundance. When we focus on the things we're truly grateful for, we find that what we're grateful for keeps increasing in our life. The divine qualities are said to be unlimited states of being: the more we cultivate them, the more they grow, without limit.

Halfway through the *Bhagavad Gita*, Krishna tells Arjuna a secret: one who lives her life from her divine nature lives her life as an offering of love. Krishna calls such a person a *mahatma*, "one whose self is extraordinary".[43] All the divine qualities blossom naturally in a heart that overflows with love.

–7–

One way to collect "the wealth of the gods" is through *asana*, or yoga postures.[44] As well as being physical exercises, yoga poses are vehicles to cultivate self-awareness and develop the divine qualities, by awakening dormant aspects of our being.

There's a bridge between our posture and our consciousness. At the beginning of the *Bhagavad Gita*, Arjuna, overcome by grief, describes his physical symptoms: failing limbs, parched mouth, tremors, hairs standing on end, burning skin, and an inability to stand steadily.[45] Arjuna's posture mirrors his state of consciousness.

In yoga, *asanas* are dynamic poses that allow us to know and feel where our consciousness rests. Every *asana* is not only a physical posture, but also a posture of consciousness. It's therefore important to engage our breath and our awareness in our practice of *asana*. The deeper we enter into a yoga pose, the more it offers us.

There are 8.4 million possible *asanas*, according to one yoga text, as many as there are forms of life. Of these, 84 are preeminent, of which 32 are especially useful.[46] Beyond mere physical exercises, these *asanas* can manifest the divine qualities that lie dormant within us. For example, the Tree Pose (Vrikshasana) helps us develop the highest qualities of trees: strength, balance, flexibility, tolerance, generosity and grace.

The Warrior Pose (Virabhadrasana) inspires us to become a "yoga warrior" like Arjuna. We can summon the attributes of the warrior when we feel disconnected from our mission and purpose, when we feel conflicted internally, or when we feel lost or stuck, like Arjuna. This yoga posture reconnects us with the power of the self.

The Lotus Pose (Padmasana) brings out our "lotus

potential". Through the Lotus Pose (and the Half-Lotus Pose), we develop the divine qualities expressed by the lotus: rootedness, tranquillity, softness, openness and the ability to rise above life's tribulations.

One of the many Sanskrit words for "lotus" is *pankajam*, "that which is born out of the mud". Like the lotus, we can blossom not only despite the muck of everyday life, but *out of* it, including the dark night of the soul. Out of the ordinary muck of life we can manifest something truly extraordinary.

This transformation, represented by the lotus, is the essence of the "yoga of despair".

Notes

Part IV: "Let Discernment Be the Warrior's Sword"

1 This opening to Part IV is adapted from the teachings of Shri Shrimad Bhaktivedanta Narayana Maharaja in *The Essence of Bhagavad Gita* (2000), pp.14–15.

2 In *Bhagavad Gita*, 4.42, Krishna refers to *jnana-asina*, "the sword of knowledge", which belongs to the self. Krishna then directs Arjuna, "Take up this yoga and arise, O Bharata." In other words, this is the sword of yoga. Earlier, Krishna has explained to Arjuna that Samkhya employs the yoga of knowledge (3.3), and that there is no difference between Samkhya and yoga (5.4–5). For further references to *jnana-asina*, "the sword of knowledge", see *Bhagavata Purana*, 5.12.16, 11.13.33 and 11.28.17.

3 Krishna introduces Samkhya wisdom early in Chapter 2 of the *Bhagavad Gita*, but Arjuna doesn't understand how this relates to his crisis. Krishna therefore moves to Karma-yoga, and returns to the teachings of Samkhya later. The entire last third of the *Gita* contains different teachings that form part of Samkhya wisdom. But the Samkhya that Krishna teaches to Arjuna is different from traditional Samkhya, in that Krishna includes teachings about himself, the source of all beings. The *Gita* teaches a form of theistic Samkhya that stands in contrast to classical atheistic or non-theistic Samkhya philosophy.

4 Paraphrased.

5 In 2.10–30, Krishna explains the nature of the self. Krishna continues his Samkhya teachings in Chapter 13, where he distinguishes between "the field" and "the knower of the field". We so easily identify with what we see in the field of perception; but we are in fact the observer, beyond the ever-changing play of form in that field. In 15.7–11, Krishna returns to the subject of the individual soul present in this world within various forms of material embodiment. Those who possess "the eye of knowledge", Krishna explains, are able to perceive the existence of the soul within their own being.

6 *Bhagavad Gita*, 2.63. Krishna refers to *smriti-vibhrama*, "disturbed memory".

7 *Bhagavad Gita*, 18.73. The *Kena Upanishad* refers to *pratibodha-jnana*, literally, "awakened knowledge".

8 Krishna refers to the "eye of knowledge" in *Bhagavad Gita*, 13.34 and 15.10. Krishna says *pashyanti jnana-chakshushah*, those who possess the eye of knowledge can perceive the self.

9 Graham M. Schweig makes this point in *Bhagavad Gita: The Beloved Lord's Secret Love Song* (Kindle edition, 2010), locations 5916–5919.

10 The *Bhagavad Gita* (Chapters 14, 17 and 18) and *Bhagavata Purana* (Canto 11, Chapter 25) have detailed explanations of Sattva, Rajas and Tamas, and their effects. Krishna also describes the characteristics of one who has transcended these three qualities, having attained the highest spiritual realization.

11 In Chapter 16 of the *Bhagavad Gita*, Krishna distinguishes between the divine and ungodly natures.

12 *Bhagavad Gita*, 4.38. This verse is in a chapter on *jnana-yoga*, the yoga of knowledge, but it applies equally to Samkhya. Earlier, Krishna has explained that Samkhya employs the yoga of knowledge (3.3).

13 For example, in the *Bhagavad Gita* (13.7–11), Krishna defines knowledge in a way that is rather unexpected, as "humility, absence of deceit, non-violence, tolerance, simplicity…" By Krishna's definition, knowledge is a state of non-attachment to the changing fortunes of the world, as well as freedom from worldly want, rather than some form of intellectual process. The clear implication here is that knowledge is not about what we know; it's about our perception of reality, which will profoundly affect the way we live in the world.

14 The rishis, or sages, describe the soul—the unchanging self, amidst all change—as "self-luminous". For example, see *Bhagavata Purana*, 12.5.8 (*svayam-jyoti*, "self-luminous"); and Shrila Jiva Goswami, *Paramatma Sandarbha*, section 19 (*svayam-prakasha*, "self-luminous"), quoting Jamatri Muni.

15 *Katha Upanishad*, 1.3.3–4.

16 *Bhagavad Gita*, Chapter 13. The verse numbering in Chapter 13 varies slightly between different editions of the *Gita*, as some editions include an additional verse spoken by Arjuna at the beginning of the chapter. In traditional Samkhya terminology, the "field" (*kshetra*) is commonly referred to as *prakriti* and the "knower of the field" (*kshetra-jña*) as *purusha*.

17 Retelling inspired in part by the poem "The Bird in the Cage" by Sakshi
Gopal das. The 24 pillars of the cage symbolize the 24 primary elements in
Samkhya thought, which keep the soul encaged in this world. They also represent
the ribs of the human body in which the soul is held captive.

18 *Bhagavad Gita*, 2.14–15.

19 *Bhagavad Gita*, 2.15.

20 The *Kena Upanishad* refers to *pratibodha-jnana*, literally, "awakened
knowledge".

21 For example, see Shrila Jiva Goswami, *Paramatma Sandarbha*, section 19
(*cid-anandatmaka*, "of the nature of consciousness and bliss"), quoting Jamatri
Muni.

22 *Bhagavad Gita*, 3.17. Krishna describes a person who has realized the self as
atma-rati (finding pleasure in the self), *atma-tripta* (satisfied or fulfilled by the
self) and *atmany … santushta* (fully content within the self).

23 *Bhagavad Gita*, 14.17. "Wisdom" translates *jnanam* to indicate
transformative knowledge, as opposed to mere information. "Folly" translates
ajnanam, the absence of wisdom.

24 In his *Katha-lakshanam*, Shri Madhvacharya distinguishing between three
types of discussion: *vada*, *jalpa* and *vitanda*. The motive of the participants
in a *vada* discussion is to arrive at a deeper understanding of truth. *Jalpa* is a
discussion wherein one isn't interested in what is said by others, because one
simply wants to be heard. The primary motive is to impress or to win. In a
vitanda discussion, the primary aim is to undermine or shut the other participant
down, without any constructive intent. *Vada* discussion is in Sattva, while *jalpa*
and *vitanda* are governed by Rajas and Tamas, respectively. In the *Bhagavad Gita*,
Krishna exalts *vada* over other forms of discussion (10.32).

25 Krishna explains in the *Bhagavad Gita* that everything is of three types,
depending upon the *guna*, or quality, that predominates. This includes faith
(17.2–4), food (17.7–10), Vedic ritual (17.11–13), discipline (17.14–19), giving
(17.20–22), renunciation or letting go (18.7–12), knowledge (18.19–22), action
(18.23–25), the performer of action (18.26–28), intelligence (18.29–32), resolve
(18.33–35) and even happiness (18.36–39).

26 *Bhagavad Gita*, 18.25.

27 *Bhagavata Purana*, 5.26.2.

28 Ibid.

29 *Bhagavad Gita*, 14.6.

30 See *Bhagavad Gita*, 14.26–27.

31 See *Bhagavad Gita*, 14.21–25, which sets out the characteristics of one who has transcended the *gunas*. See also *Gita*, 2.55–72, 6.7–9 and 12.13–19, which describe the qualities of those who are enlightened.

32 Deepak Ramola, "12 Life Lessons From A Man Who Has Seen 12000 Deaths", published 15 May 2016.

33 *Bhagavad Gita*, 16.4. *Asuri-sampad*: literally, "the wealth of the ungodly".

34 "Absence of wisdom" translates *ajnanam*. Observation made by Vraja Kishor in "Evil Qualities", The Enquirer [blog], published 16 Jun. 2016.

35 *Bhagavad Gita*, 16.1–3. *Daivi-sampad*: literally, "the wealth of the gods".

36 Ibid. Likewise, *Narada-bhakti-sutra* affirms (Aphorism 78): "One should culture such virtues as non-violence, truth, purity, compassion and faith." See also *Bhagavad Gita*, 12.13–20, which sets out the qualities of one on the path of Bhakti, sacred love.

37 See Shrila Krishnadas Kaviraja Goswami, *Shri Chaitanya Charitamrita*, *Antya-lila*, 20.22–26.

38 *Mahabharata*, 12.115.11.

39 This teaching is found in *Shri Hari Bhakti Kalpa Latika*, 2.27: "They [who are devoted] do not see others' faults and lack of virtues, but their own."

40 *Bhagavad Gita*, 16.21–22. Krishna warns Arjuna about three gateways of Tamas: desire, anger and greed. The ceaseless river of desire in the heart leads to restlessness and continual dissatisfaction. When desire is frustrated, it turns into anger; when desire is satisfied, it turns into greed.

41 *Bhagavad Gita*, 17.15, which defines discipline of speech. That don't disturb others: translates *anudvega-karam*. True: translates *satyam*. Kind: translates *priya*, which can also mean "loving", "dear" and "pleasing". Helpful: translates *hitam*. Wise seers like Vyasa, Vidura and Bhishma spoke strong words to the blind emperor Dhritarashtra, and these words were always truthful, loving and beneficial; they weren't always agreeable or pleasing to the emperor, though. Pleasing in the sense of flattery, of being biased or selective, or of saying only what someone wishes to hear would contradict truth, so *priya* has to be taken in the sense of coming from a kind or loving place. Moreover, if *priya* is translated as pleasing, then "words that do not disturb others" would be rendered redundant.

42 *Bhagavad Gita*, 16.13–15

43 *Bhagavad Gita*, 9.13. *Mahatma* means, literally, "great self" or "extraordinary self".

44 This section on *asana* is inspired by Catherine Ghosh, "The Body as a Doorway to Consciousness", in Catherine Ghosh and Braja Sorensen, *Yoga in the Gita: Krishna and Patanjali: The Bhakti Dimension* (2016), Chapter 21.

45 *Bhagavad Gita*, 1.29–30.

46 *Gheranda Samhita*, 2.1–2.

PART

V

THE FOURTH AGREEMENT:
"LET SACRED LOVE BE YOUR ONLY GOAL"

Bhakti-Yoga,
The Yoga of Offering Love

V

To help Arjuna through his crisis, Krishna teaches him different, complementary yoga paths, each suited to a different kind of practitioner. But having heard these teachings, Arjuna is still not at peace. Krishna then offers Arjuna a more advanced definition of yoga as "the unwavering offering of love".[1] He advises Arjuna to make his entire life a work of devotion.

In the ancient, mystical Bhakti tradition of India, the yogi or yogini uses love and devotion to reawaken her natural connection with the Soul of the Universe. This practice is called Bhakti-yoga, the yoga of offering love. Krishna gives many Bhakti teachings to Arjuna, and they can be summarized as follows:

1. Engage your heart in your yoga practice.
2. Widen your circle.
3. Write your story with love and compassion.

Earlier, when Arjuna's mind was overcome by fear, lamentation and confusion, Krishna stressed the importance of disciplining the mind and senses. Yoga requires control over the restless mind, which can be a challenge, especially in the dark night of the soul. As Arjuna confesses, "The mind is unsteady, Krishna, and it is impetuous, powerful and obdurate. I think controlling the mind is as difficult as controlling the wind!"[2]

Krishna agrees, even if controlling the mind is possible with practice. More potent than the mind, however, is the heart. By engaging our heart in our yoga practice, Krishna explains, we can overcome even the greatest obstacles on our yoga path.

Generally, yoga is passed formally from teacher to student. But Arjuna and Krishna are close friends. Theirs is a relationship of love. Their deep friendship highlights the importance of a connected heart in yoga. Krishna confides that, inspired by Arjuna's love for him, he's encouraged to reveal the yoga teachings once more, sharing that "ultimate secret" formerly known to the ancients.[3]

This brings us to Krishna's second teaching on love: "*Widen your circle.*"

Krishna has taught Arjuna that a yogi sees all beings with equal vision, at the level of the soul, without judging or exploiting.[4] As Krishna explains, "One who sees everyone's happiness and suffering as if it were his own, O Arjuna, is considered to be the highest yogi."[5]

But how do we culture a love like this? Krishna's immediate response to Arjuna's crisis, his dark night of the soul, was to give him Samkhya, the sword of discernment. Without discernment, our love is conditional and founded on many misunderstandings and false identifications. This is because it is love within the limitations of our small human story. We could call it "small love".

By contrast, sacred love is love that is *discerning*—in other words, wise love. It's love that is released from the captivity of our small, imprisoning human story. Such love is unconditional, and it extends beyond our small circle of family and friends.

How do we widen our circle of love in this way? Krishna's answer is surprising, and represents one of his most confidential and esoteric teachings.

We often hear that we can't truly love others until we first learn to love ourselves. How can we give to others what we don't yet possess ourselves?

Krishna takes this one step further. He advises Arjuna to direct his love inward—*as far inward as he possibly can*—to the sacred source of his being, the Soul of the soul.[6] Rather than direct our love first to our body, which is just a vehicle, or to our mind, we can direct our love to Krishna, the Soul of the soul and the source of consciousness, seated in the temple of our very being.

YOGA AND THE DARK NIGHT OF THE SOUL

By targeting our love to the sacred centre, our love alchemically transforms from small love into sacred love. This is the essence of Bhakti-yoga.

Krishna reveals to Arjuna that he is not only the Soul of the soul, but also the Soul of the Universe, known by countless names across the ages. Everything rests upon him, as jewels are strung on a thread.[7] How wonderful that the Soul of the Universe, the self-organizing and self-correcting principle of life, should be present in our very own heart.

By directing our love and affection inward to Krishna, the Soul of the Universe, our love and affection automatically encompasses all beings. No longer is it limited to oneself and a small circle of friends and family members.

Krishna has told Arjuna that he is the Soul of the Universe. But Arjuna wants to see it with his own eyes.

Krishna therefore reveals to him his Universal Form, inconceivable and awe-inspiring. In this form, Arjuna sees the entirety of time and space, undivided and yet manifold, situated in one place.[8] If a thousand suns were to rise in the sky at once, such brilliance might resemble the brilliance of that great being. Faced with this form of Krishna's, Arjuna can see the birth and death of all beings; he can see everything that ever was, is, or will be. There's no beginning, middle or end to that form, which extends from the heavens to the earth and in all directions.

Through yoga perception, Arjuna is now able to understand Krishna's identity as the Soul of the Universe. Krishna is death who devours all things, and he is the origin of all things yet to be. He is the energy of those who possess energy, the wisdom of the wise, and the existence of all that exists. He is the hidden basis of all things.

In the esoteric Bhakti tradition, the yogi who has developed sacred love can directly perceive Krishna, the Soul of the Universe, in the temple of her heart.

This brings us to the final teaching of Bhakti: *Write your story with love and compassion.*

Ultimately, all forms of yoga are meant to help us cultivate love and compassion. If our yoga is taking us not closer to, but further away from, love and compassion, then it has lost its way. If our practice is hardening our heart, it is not yoga.

In Arjuna's dark night, his thoughts and decisions are at first guided by grief, pity and shame, his mind's "GPS" system.[9] Krishna teaches Arjuna how to be guided by sacred love instead.

This is possible when we form a *sankalpa*, or immovable resolve, to make our life an offering of love. We'll explore how to do this, following Arjuna's example. When performed correctly, a *sankalpa* has the power to reshape our destiny.

On the path of Bhakti, the yogi or yogini makes everything in her life an expression of loving service to Krishna, the Soul of the Universe.[10] This beautiful teaching—that everything can be an offering of love, a sacred act—enables us to write the most beautiful story we're capable of.

Sacred love is an unlimited state of being, and the practice of offering love can make every moment fulfilling. As Krishna confides, this yoga "is joyfully practised and is limitless".[11] The more we practise offering love and kindness, the more our love and kindness grows, without end. Our every effort and our every breath can be an act of love, a sacred engagement that is deeply satisfying for us, and deeply satisfying for everyone we touch in our life.

Admittedly, when we're caught in the throes of our own inner turmoil, it's easy to become discombobulated and to forget these teachings. Can we love when we're in pain? Can we open a passageway to sacred love amid our own crisis and despair?

Krishna reassures Arjuna that we can. In the yoga tradition, we enter the temple of sacred love by taking refuge in Krishna, the Lord of Yoga.[12] Krishna therefore tells Arjuna, finally, "Relinquishing all forms of dharma, take refuge with me only. I will release you from all misfortune: don't despair!"[13]

In our crisis and despair, when we've lost all our power, we can take shelter of Krishna, the Universal Teacher and source of all power: "I'm no longer a 'hero' in the story of my life. Today, I bend to your will. I'm open to whatever way life unfolds. I surrender my ego and dedicate myself to you. Please make me your instrument."

THIS SAME ANCIENT YOGA IS TODAY TAUGHT BY ME TO YOU
BECAUSE YOU HAVE OFFERED YOUR LOVE AND ARE ALSO
MY FRIEND. THIS IS INDEED THE ULTIMATE SECRET.[14]

—*Bhagavad Gita*, 4.3

FOURTEEN

Engage Your Heart
in Your Yoga Practice

—I—

Kat sat watching President Trump address the United States Congress—according to him, from his heart—and her frustrated commentary went something like this: "What a Muppet Show! Why's everyone celebrating this narcissistic power game? Oh my god, now they're cheering at the Dakota Pipeline, ripping up the beauty of our planet with an oil field. What ignorance! Yes, let's all cheer along making money from heartless destruction.[15]

"Oh, now they're applauding at professing to dispel violence and poverty. Easy to do sitting on billions, while radiating hatred and transmitting violent communication, completely unaware of their impact. Do they have any intelligence at all? Low life, vile, self-righteous and so stupid, ugh!"

And so it went on. Until she caught herself, and took a breath.

For a moment, she had allowed herself to get swept up into the divisiveness, the conflict, the separation, the hatred spewing out in America's dark night of the soul.

Kat is a PR and creativity consultant, and a friend of mine. She holds workshops at yoga studios aiming to inspire women to embody and express their true purpose.[16] Witnessing her own distasteful reaction to the overwhelming political circumstances, she remembered that the dark night of the soul is a calling to sacred love.

"So let this be our calling," she thought. "Every time we encounter divisive and unkind communication, let it be our calling to love; a reminder to connect even more deeply to our heart, to compassion, to kindness. Let it be our reminder to choose to listen to and be guided by our heart, to fulfil our true nature and purpose, to perpetuate peace, generosity and love."

The first step to engaging our heart in our yoga practice is to be more conscious of its state: "Is my heart becoming softer or harder? Is my heart opening and expanding, or is it shrinking and shutting down? Am I acting from a place of love and kindness, or from a place of competition and fear?"

For many today, the heart is more like a "dead" organ. Like the appendix, we're not quite sure what it's for. We may think it doesn't serve us well. Often, we prefer to use our heads— our *intellect*.

Over a lifetime, we invest enormously into improving our mind through years of education, reading, conferences, discussions and stimulating debates. But how much time and energy do we put into improving the capacity of our heart? We have no schools for the heart in our society.

Faced with life's tribulations and challenges, our heart can become harder or softer. The art of allowing life to make our heart softer is called yoga.

Whenever we practise any form of yoga (even yoga postures), we can remember that the aim of our practice is to open our heart, to increase our capacity to love. This then reframes everything we do in yoga.

With this focus, we naturally become more conscious of our state of heart. We can be more aware when people or events trigger us; and we can use that mindfulness in the service of love. When we're driven by lower qualities that diminish or oppose love, by the "wealth of the ungodly", we can avoid acting from that state. Instead, like Kat, we can shelter in the divine qualities.

–2–

As a young boy, I used to make my own pottery in school: tall, twisting vases, bowls with gorgeous glazes, and bright ceramic fish. When absorbed in creating, I would enter a different realm—it was as if time and the world with all its troubles no longer existed.

My favourite creation during one term was a shallow bowl. A deep sky-blue on the inside, it finished in a dark lapis lazuli at the rim.

I was the last pupil to leave. Walking home, I cradled the

creation in my arms, having carefully wrapped it in newspaper. As I made my way up Catherine Street, I felt something sharp pressing against my lower back.

"Give me your money or I'll stab you," a voice behind me commanded. It was Rufat, a local bully who preyed on younger children. I froze.

"I don't have any money," I whimpered, holding my ceramic bowl close.

Rufat began to laugh. He now revealed he had been pushing an open pen into my back, not a blade. The distress the deception had caused pleased him.

"What do you have there then?" he asked.

"Just something I made at school," I said.

This seemed to rile Rufat. With a heavy sweep of his arm, he flung the bowl out of my hands into the air. The vessel came crashing down on to the pavement. I could hear it shatter instantly.

Tears in my eyes, I opened the newspaper, revealing a collection of ceramic shards. Rufat's eyes gleamed with delight.

On my way home, I considered throwing the sky-blue shards into one of the bins on the sidewalk. But it didn't feel right. I had put so much loving attention into creating the piece that tossing it away seemed disrespectful, so I took the bundle home.

Julia was a friend who loved handicrafts and pottery. She would make beautiful mosaics out of pebbles and fragments of ceramic. I gave what was left of my bowl to her.

Many years passed, and Julia and I went to separate universities. Occasionally we met in Leicester during holidays.

Despite all the opportunities it offered, university was a bewildering time for me. It culminated in my first dark night of the soul. Everything I knew fell apart. I tried to conceal my confusion and darkness. I pushed on with my studies and tried to portray an appearance of normality; but I was in pain.

I sheltered in alcohol. Looking back, I feel lucky to have made it through such a difficult time. In my final year, the suffering seemed especially brutal; and the inability to explain its cause intensified my loneliness. I felt ashamed and powerless.

Julia had some inkling of what was going on. One sunny afternoon in July, she came to give me a gift. It was wrapped in newspaper.

I unwrapped the gift and my eyes fell upon a sky-blue bowl with a rim of deep lapis lazuli. Streaks of bright gold ran across the bowl, branching out wildly like lightning. The bowl had obviously been shattered and then lovingly repaired with gold lacquer. It looked more beautiful for having been broken.

I looked up at Julia. She smiled. It was the same bowl I had made more than ten years earlier. She had carefully glued all the broken ceramic pieces back together with gold.

"If something's broken, it can still be beautiful," Julia said.

There's an ancient Japanese form of art known as Kintsugi, "to repair with gold". Broken pottery is repaired with lacquer dusted or mixed with powdered gold, silver or platinum. The philosophy of this symbolic art form is to highlight (rather than conceal) the damage caused by life. It treats breakage and repair as a natural part of the history of an object. The intrinsic value of the object doesn't decrease because of "brokenness". Rather, it appreciates.

In our life, we build an identity and a story, rather like fragile ceramic ware. That creation is susceptible to the breaks, the knocks and the shattering of life. The dark night of the soul breaks us apart.

In a culture obsessed with image and perfection, we try to disguise the breakages. We want to forget the damage of life, certainly not highlight it. If something is broken we usually throw it away.

But ancient wisdom traditions have, for thousands of years, taught us how to embrace the flawed and the imperfect, highlighting the freedom and spaciousness this brings. There's great beauty in life's imperfections.

Kintsugi delivers the message that we can embrace our own brokenness, claiming it as a natural process of being alive. Rather than hold our shattered pieces with shame, fear or self-loathing, we're called to hold them with love and tenderness—as if gilded in gold.

Love is the gold lacquer that allows us to put together the pieces of our brokenness in the dark night of the soul. Love and kindness make us whole and beautiful, imbuing our brokenness with wisdom and revealing the strength inherent in vulnerability.

It's easy to focus on the disappointments of life. The flaws. The broken pieces. This can make us cynical, hardening our hearts. It can make us impervious to the suffering of others. This is the path of *vi-yoga*, the opposite of yoga. By using love and kindness as a precious lacquer in our life and the life of others, we engage our heart in our yoga practice.

−3−

The pharaoh's darkened, shrivelled mummified corpse lay in one of the many glass display cases of the museum, its head unwrapped. A plain white notice read:

King Ramses II
New Kingdom, 19th Dynasty (c. 1279–1213 BC)

The notice listed the many ailments of our pharaoh: dental abscesses, severe arthritis in his hip joints, arteriosclerosis.

I wondered whether Ramses II (also known as Osymandias), the most powerful pharaoh of the Egyptian Empire, could ever have fathomed he would become a public display piece in a museum. Onlookers peered at his unwrapped face with a mixture of curiosity, awe and repulsion.

As a young boy, I wanted to become an archaeologist. Dreaming of discovering ancient cities and forgotten treasures, I began studying the lost cities of the ancient world. One of these was Ramses II's capital of Pi-Ramses.

Ramses II moved his capital city from Thebes in the Nile valley to a new site on the easternmost branch of the Nile. The new showplace city of Pi-Ramses, built with untold human toil, was dominated by huge temples and the king's vast palace. This was one of the largest cities of ancient Egypt, seven times larger than the City of London.[17] Poems were written about its splendour.

Pi-Ramses was to fall upon hard times, however. Only two generations after Ramses II, the easternmost branch of the Nile began to silt up, leaving the city without water. The Twenty-first Dynasty of Egypt dismantled the entire capital and transported it to a new branch of the Nile, many miles away.

For the next three thousand years, the ancient site of Pi-Ramses was lost in Egypt's sandy silence. The massive feet of a broken statue of Ramses are all that remain above ground today.

Ramses II had wanted his legacy to survive the ravages of time. He had built on a scale unlike almost anything before, and had erected more statues of himself than any other pharaoh. Inscribed on the base of one of his statues was the following triumphant boast:

> King of Kings am I, Osymandias. If anyone would know how great I am and where I lie, let him surpass one of my works.[18]

The pharaoh's hollow boast now seemed to echo with the laughter of the Egyptian gods.

Archaeology has taught me that nearly all human endeavour is vanity. Our entire life is one long, convoluted expression of our own narcissism. Even our "good works" are often concealed narcissism. They are expressions of our underlying dark night of the soul, our lack of wisdom. Importantly, archaeology has also taught me that nothing, not even our greatest creation, withstands the erosion of time.

As I gazed at the shrivelled mummified corpse of Osymandias, King of Kings, I realized I was looking at my own reflection. Like the great pharaoh, we all hope to make our mark in this world, eager to be recognized and to become a King of Kings of sorts. And in the end, after a life of feverish striving, it's death that awaits each of us. Unless what we do is an expression of kindness and loving service, our efforts are little more than the meaningless toil of the dead.

Not only individuals, but whole societies, go through dark nights of the soul. According to the sacred texts of India, we're currently in a global dark night, known as Kali-yuga, an age of darkness and crisis.[19] As a society, we've lost our way; our sense of meaning is shattered.

The only way to heal is through love and compassion. Of course, "love" is a word with many meanings, and is often misused. In order to act from this deeply powerful place, we first need to find and restore its sacred meaning. Before beginning to share his most confidential teachings on love, Krishna indicates that the transition from small love to sacred love is the perfection of yoga.[20]

As physical exercise alone, yoga can't help us in our own dark night or in our societal dark night. But by making yoga a practice of the heart, we not only illuminate our own darkness, but light up the dark corners of our environment too.

The dark night of the soul can help us become deeply compassionate, both to ourselves and to others. Deep within, love is what is most sacred to us all. We're ready to love and be loved. Love is our natural inclination, the calling of the soul. Nothing less will satisfy or nurture us.

As my teacher explained, "We can experience so much of life while our most central need, the need to love and be loved, remains unfulfilled. Love's power is unimaginable. All else can be eliminated and forgotten if we come in touch with true love and affection. When one questions or challenges the principle of love, one has to accept defeat. Love is the most substantive principle."[21]

When we understand this, we engage our heart in our yoga practice, making unconditional love the aim of our practice.

ONE WHO SEES EVERYONE'S HAPPINESS AND SUFFERING
AS IF IT WERE HIS OWN, O ARJUNA, IS CONSIDERED
TO BE THE HIGHEST YOGI.

—*Bhagavad Gita*, 6.32

FIFTEEN

Widen Your Circle

—I—

Walk into any coffee shop, and you'll see what an incredibly sophisticated vocabulary we have for coffee: Americano, cappuccino, latte, espressino, café cubano, flat white, macchiato, café au lait, chai latte, frappuccino... The list seems endless. But oddly, we have only one or two words for love.

"Love" is a beautiful word. But that same little, delicate word can be used to mean any number of things, from what pleases our palate to sexual passion and from deep friendship to love for all beings, and more.

The Ancient Greeks had six words for different types of love.[22] I've counted more than twenty in the esoteric, heart-based Bhakti tradition of India. Its sacred texts distinguish between fleeting, conditional love based on our small human stories and undying, unconditional love at the level of the soul, beyond our temporary narratives. We might call the first type "small love" and the other "sacred love".

Even within the category of sacred love, the incredibly

detailed Bhakti teachings differentiate between various kinds of love, defined by their flavour and strength. These esoteric texts, written to illuminate the journey of the soul, describe the profound experiences of the greatest of devotional mystics. They articulate the steady development of sacred love, guiding the student in a way that fully satisfies the heart.

What are some of the differences between small love and sacred love?

The sacred texts sometimes speak of the *purity* of love. This implies that what passes as love in everyday life can be contaminated—by ego, by the desire to manipulate or control, by narcissism, jealousy, unkindness, false perception and selfish intent.

When we say, "I love you", we're usually more focused on the "I" than on the quality of love we're offering. This expression of the illusory ego is known as "small love".

Trapped within our own small, imagined stories, our expression of love is fickle and limited. If someone supports us in our story, they have our love and attention; but if someone undermines or subverts our story, we feel threatened and withhold our love. Put simply, small love can be highly *conditional*.

In small love, we often believe our love depends first on finding the *right* person to love. Packaging ourselves as a commodity, we try to enhance our own value by making ourselves more attractive. We then look for someone who represents a good exchange in the relationship marketplace.

In small love, we also don't truly see the person we claim to love at the level of the soul. We see only a secondary character in our own little story. We perceive others in relation to our own illusory ego and its needs. Ultimately, it's a love based on illusion; and therefore it generally lasts only as long as the relationship serves both parties in some way.

Hence, we find that two people can declare their undying love for each other one day, and their intense hatred for each other another day. Ardent friends become ardent enemies. This is the conditional and temporary nature of small love.

Moreover, small love is typically limited to just a small circle of friends and relatives. While some people extend their love to their community or their country, rarely do we find a kind of love that extends to all souls, without discrimination. We struggle to love those we can't relate to, or those who hurt or betray us. We may even have difficulty holding love in our heart for ourselves. This can be the most demanding of all.

By contrast, sacred love operates beyond the stories we enact and the play of form in this world. Embracing all souls, sacred love is not an accidental venture, a love we "fall" into. Rather, it's a capacity that is awakened and strengthened. Someone whose heart is filled with sacred love expresses their love in all their relationships.

Sacred love therefore doesn't depend upon finding the *right* person to love, nor does it oscillate between love and hate. *All* souls, not least ourselves, are rightful recipients of love.

In Sanskrit, sacred love is called Bhakti. Bhakti-yoga is the yoga practice of culturing such unconditional love, by directing it to the Soul of all souls.

The word Bhakti first appears in the *Bhagavad Gita* in a chapter on "realized knowledge", or wisdom.[23] This disassociates Bhakti both from mere intellectualism and from mere sentimentality. Sacred love doesn't indulge our illusions, nor does it blind us. Rather, it's deeply illuminating, connecting us with what is true. It's the living heart of wisdom.

Sacred love, or Bhakti, is the only kind of love that can quench the thirst of the soul. This love, when awakened, flows freely from the soul and leads to immense happiness and fulfilment. The yogi who has attained sacred love experiences ecstasy.

We might think, "This kind of selfless, unconditional love that extends to everyone is the way saints love. I'm not a saint. I can't possibly love that way." But remember, Arjuna was not a wandering saint, but a warrior. Krishna's teachings on sacred love are therefore meant for *everyone*. We can all find soul fulfilment through a love like this.

Krishna reveals that Bhakti-yoga is his most confidential teaching, his secret of all secrets.[24] In Bhakti-yoga, the yogi or yogini intensifies her love by purifying and deepening it. Love and compassion in their truest sense are unlimited states of being: the more we practise them, the more they grow.

At first our love might be tainted by ego, attachment and the desire to control. But gradually, through practice, our love can become purer and shine more brightly, leaving it unbounded, healing and deeply fulfilling.

−2−

Gautama was a young student at the ashram of his teacher, a rishi expert in Bhakti lore. Located on the bank of a river, the ashram was circled by a forest of mango trees and forest creepers, where peacocks danced in the open spaces.

One day the teacher needed to go on a journey. He asked Gautama to tend his beautiful Parijata tree, a variety of fragrant jasmine. Legend has it that the Parijata is one of five celestial trees.[25] Its flowers are said to help one remember past lives and incarnations.

The Parijata tree, which stood at the farthest end of the garden, was heavily laden with blooms. Gautama's teacher, who used these flowers for his daily worship of Krishna, emphasized the importance of caring for them.

The rishi set off and Gautama began tending the celestial flowers. He collected fresh water from the river and sprinkled it carefully on the tree's buds. There were thousands of them and it took him a long time.

That evening, after the sun had set, countless star-like flowers opened out, permeating the air with an intoxicating, heavenly fragrance. The delightful Parijata flowers were white like milk, with a beautiful orange-red centre. Gautama's heart soared with delight.

The next day, Gautama returned to the tree. His heart sank. The Parijata flowers he had tended with such care had all dropped from the tree—every one of them. He walked over a carpet of fallen flowers, his heart filled with sadness.

Maybe he hadn't given them enough loving care. Again, Gautama cleaned and watered all the buds. This time he also spent his day wiping the tree's leaves tenderly with a damp cloth.

As expected, the tree exploded into life at dusk. And again the following morning, all the flowers had fallen.

The young Gautama was concerned. Perhaps someone was plucking flowers or disturbing the tree at night. He decided to keep vigil.

Sure enough, thousands of Parijata flowers opened out at dusk. The light breeze was laden with the scent of longing and celestial tales. But at sunrise Gautama watched with tears in his eyes as all the Parijata flowers in full bloom fell from the tree, one by one.

∾

Several days later, the rishi returned from his journey and Gautama revealed everything to him.

The sage smiled knowingly. He had intentionally asked Gautama to care for the Parijata flowers, so that he could impart the three yoga teachings of Parijata to him. Sitting on the veranda with Gautama, the rishi shared an ancient tale.[26]

"There was once a king who had a beautiful daughter named Parijata," the rishi began. "This sensitive girl fell in love with Surya, the sun god, as he rode his fiery chariot from the east to the west in the sky.

"'Leave your kingdom and be mine,' the sun god propositioned passionately.

"Parijata shed her royal robes and followed her beloved. But the sun god soon tired of her and grew cold. Abandoning her, he fled back to the sky, leaving the young princess to die of a broken heart.

"The king, filled with sorrow, cremated the princess's body. From her ashes arose a single tree with the purest of white flowers, each containing a blazing orange heart. Since the tree can't bear the sight of the sun, her flowers open only after the sun has left the sky; and upon the touch of the sun's first rays at dawn, all her flowers immediately fall to the ground and die.

"Parijata teaches us about love, loss and heart-break," Gautama's teacher continued. "The love of this world is ephemeral. If the sun could witness the true beauty of Parijata, he would never have left her. But Parijata reveals her celestial beauty at night—the one place the sun is unable to go. So as the sun crosses the sky, all he ever sees is a pitiable tree and a carpet of wilting flowers.

"Our true beauty is hidden too. The beauty of the soul can't be seen with the external eye or the light of the sun. For those who haven't yet learned to see with the eyes of sacred love, the soul remains unseen.

"This is the first teaching of Parijata," the teacher concluded. "For this reason, the Parijata is sometimes known as the 'tree of sorrow'."

"What's the second teachings of Parijata," Gautama pleaded.

"Come back tomorrow and I'll teach you," the rishi replied.

Gautama had a restless night, as he thought about Parijata's unrequited love. The sun was destined to never see Parijata's beauty. Gautama wondered how much beauty in life was hidden from him too.

What was the second teaching of the beautiful Parijata? Gautama longed to know. The next day he returned to his teacher's ashram.

"The aim of Bhakti-yoga is to expand our love, by deepening and widening it," the rishi began. "There are two ways of doing this. The first is to direct our love to every individual in our life. This is like watering individual buds and leaves of the Parijata plant. It's a well-meaning approach, but not one without limitations. As there are buds and leaves we won't be able to see or reach, we'll tend those buds and leaves close to us, and neglect those outside our reach.

"Instead of focusing on individual buds and leaves, we can focus on the tree's root, which is the source of the entire tree. If we water the Parijata's root with love, we automatically nourish the entire tree. The water of our love and affection will flow to every part of the plant.[27] This is a wiser approach.

"In Bhakti-yoga we widen our circle of love by directing it to the source. The sages and mystics explain that the Soul of all souls is the root of the tree of life.[28]

"We're each a spark of the divine. Our own individual consciousness is a ray of the supreme consciousness. Our existence depends on this supreme consciousness, as the leaves and flowers of a plant depend on its root.

"Krishna, our dearest friend and inner guide, is present within our soul. Just as the root of a tree, hidden beneath the ground, is invisible to the eye, so Krishna, the root of existence, is hidden from our outward-looking senses. Krishna is seen only by the inward vision of the yogi whose heart is overflowing with sacred love.[29]

"By offering love to Krishna, the supreme source, the Soul of every soul, our love automatically extends to all souls, without prejudice or limitation. By touching the sacred source of life through yoga, we make our circle of love the widest it can be. We see all beings as family. We have a space in our heart for everyone—even those we haven't met. No one is a stranger.

"If someone doesn't have love in their heart for all beings, then they haven't developed love for Krishna, the Soul of all souls. Likewise, if our devotion to Krishna doesn't automatically lead us to love others, then that devotion is false. If it doesn't engender kindness and compassion in the heart, then it isn't Bhakti. True yogis see the happiness and suffering of others as their very own.[30]

"Widening our circle of love by directing it to the sacred centre, the root of the tree of life, is the second lesson of Parijata."

The teacher took the boy to his Parijata plant. At the base of the tree, leaning against one of its roots, was a small, charming figure of Krishna. Gautama wondered how he hadn't noticed it before. He must have been so preoccupied watering the buds and leaves in the branches above.

Gautama was now eager to know the third teaching of Parijata.

❧

The next day, before dawn, Gautama made his way to his teacher's ashram, which was illuminated by a full moon and countless stars. The rishi, his eyes closed, was deeply absorbed in meditation under the Parijata tree, facing his deity of Krishna. Gautama sat next to him in silence. He felt an indescribable peace in the presence of his teacher.

As dawn approached, flowers began to fall one by one from the Parijata tree. They rained down upon the charming deity of Krishna in an offering of love. What beauty! Heaps of fallen blossoms collected on the dew-drenched grass. It was an enchanting sight that took Gautama's breath away.

Gautama watched as the rishi came out of his meditation.

"The Parijata represents the transition from small love to sacred love," the rishi explained. "Our nature is to love. The soul is constructed and destined to love, and yet the small love and affection of this world is ultimately a source of sorrow.

"We can choose which quality of love we hold in our heart. We can transform our small love into sacred love, through the alchemical practice of Bhakti-yoga."

The rishi now collected a handful of delicate, fragrant flowers from the ground. Due to their vermillion orange core, the ancients considered the flowers symbolic of fire, the purifying flame of awareness. This flame burns away the impediments of the mind to reveal the petals of pure love.

Gautama looked at his teacher intently. The rishi was dressed in saffron cloth, dyed using the same fiery orange hearts of these Parijata flowers.

"In the daytime, the Parijata flowers are closed," the rishi continued. "They don't reveal their true celestial beauty and fragrance. Likewise, the small love of this world, mixed with self-interest and a thousand longings, doesn't reflect the true unearthly beauty of the soul. How can it? But during the night, which represents the inner practice of the yogi, these flowers of devotion release their full fragrance and beauty.

"Parijata experienced the sorrow of this world and the futility of small love. Instead of offering her heart to this mortal world, she now saves her flowers for the worship of Krishna, the root of the tree of life.

"The origin of the tree of life is known by countless names. 'Krishna' means 'All-attractive'. Another of his names is Shoka-nashana, 'Destroyer of sorrow'.[31] Krishna removes the suffering of those who take shelter of him through yoga and gives them sacred love. He transforms our small love into sacred love. This is the third and most confidential yoga teaching of Parijata."

The rishi gave a handful of flowers to Gautama. Together they made an offering to Krishna at the base of the tree.[32]

"Be careful what you wish for," the rishi warned. "Parijata fulfils whatever one desires under her shade.[33] As you offer these flowers to Krishna, the lord of your heart, ask only for sacred love."

In a captivating melody, the rishi began singing an ancient Sanskrit prayer composed by Arjuna's grandfather, Bhishma: "I seek refuge in Krishna, who sits on a golden seat in the shade of a Parijata tree. His complexion is that of a dark raincloud, he has long broad eyes, and his face is captivating like the moon…"[34]

Hearing the rishi's heartfelt song, Gautama longed to attain pure devotion to Krishna, the Soul of the Universe. He felt happier than he had ever been. And as he sat in the shade of this Parijata tree, he knew his wish had already come true.

–3–

Sitting in lotus position facing the ocean, I withdrew into meditation, focusing on the sacred name of Krishna. As dawn arrived, the sun and moon gazed at each other across a saffron sky.

Desiring to direct my love to Krishna, the Soul of all souls, I realized I needed to know more about him. Krishna is the root of the very consciousness that is attempting to find him. He's *behind* the eyes that are looking outward. How then can we come to know Krishna? How do I, as a practitioner of yoga, experience Krishna in *my* everyday life?

My own experience led me to understand Krishna first as the inner guide within the temple of my heart. Just as Arjuna turned to Krishna for guidance, we too can always turn to

Krishna, the Universal Teacher in our heart, and ask for the guidance we need.

Sometimes Krishna will manifest externally as a particular teacher in our life. Sometimes Krishna will also teach us through the challenges we face each day. In ancient India, the yogis and mystics understood that anything that inspires us and awakens our higher potential, the god-like and goddess-like qualities within us, is a manifestation of Krishna, our inner guide.[35]

In the *Gita*, Arjuna asks Krishna, "How am I to know you, O yogi, and constantly fix my mind upon you? In what various forms of existence can I conceive of you, O you who possess all potency?"[36]

In reply, Krishna tells Arjuna all the places in which he, as the original yoga teacher, is to be found. We experience Krishna in the taste of water, the radiance of the sun and moon, the sound in space, the pure fragrance of the earth, the brilliance in fire, the ocean, time, consciousness, the wind, the life of all beings, and much more.[37] Krishna is the beginning, the middle and the end of all things. Of all forms of knowledge, he is knowledge of the soul. He is death, who devours everyone, and he is the origin of all things still to be.[38]

"But what is the need for you to understand this in detail, Arjuna?" Krishna adds. "With a single part of myself, I pervade and sustain this whole universe."[39]

One of Krishna's names is Vishvam, "The Universe". Krishna reveals his identity to Arjuna as the hidden basis of all things.

Large, heaving waves tumbled upon the sandy shore, one after the other, with great force. As I sat in my meditation, I felt the presence of Krishna, the Soul of the Universe, all around me, in the mantra I was quietly repeating, in the life force of my own being, in the beauty and the abounding power all around me.

It's Krishna's presence in all of nature that causes us to be so profoundly stirred by it. Meditating on this, I felt myself in awe of a divine presence surrounding me and running through me.

–4–

Anita got straight to the point: "Is Krishna a fictional character?" There was silence in the room. Fifty faces turned towards me.

Anita is a yoga teacher from London. Her Indian parents had emigrated to the United Kingdom in the 1970s. She was attending one of my seminars on the *Bhagavad Gita* at a popular yoga venue in London.

"No," I replied. "The rishis and yogis have direct perception of the Soul of the Universe in their meditation, which many have documented in the sacred yoga texts. But Krishna manifests according to the vision of the yoga practitioner.[40]

His ability to show himself differently to different souls is celebrated by one of his many names, which translates as 'He who takes infinite forms'.[41]

"If we treat Krishna as a symbol, metaphor or literary device, our experience of him will be limited to a symbol or metaphor. We'll be able to obtain some relevance from his words, but we'll remain closed off to all other aspects of him. But if we treat Krishna as the Soul of the Universe, as literally the power that rules the universe, that's how Krishna will reveal himself in our life.

"The empiricists, who trust only what they can perceive through the external physical senses, will marvel at the beauty and wonder of the universe and its guiding laws, including time. This is Krishna's energy. To the empiricists, Krishna manifests himself in that way, not more.

"Then there are the seekers of spiritual knowledge. They'll perceive Krishna as the hidden basis of all things, the fountainhead of all possibility from which everything manifests and into which everything returns. They'll know Krishna as the self-organizing and self-correcting principle of life, the Soul of the Universe, unseen and unknowable through ordinary sense perception.

"According to their perception, Krishna is an all-pervasive field of existence, without form, known in the ancient sacred texts as 'Brahman'.[42] This Brahman is the realm of pure potentiality, supporting all existence and non-existence.

"Then there is the vision of the mystics. Through meditation, the mystics perceive Krishna within their very own heart as the Universal Teacher. This is not merely an idea or belief; such yogis and yoginis have direct *perception* of Krishna through such inward-looking contemplation.

"All three are looking at the same thing, but what they see is different, depending upon their perspective and preference."

"How do *you* see Krishna?" Anita asked. "As the empiricist, the seeker of spiritual knowledge, or the mystic?"

"I'm on the path of Bhakti-yoga, so I see Krishna as the personification of beauty and the captivating Lord of love," I replied. "In Bhakti-yoga, we offer our heart to Krishna. This is the most mystical of traditions. Bhakti is nurtured through a very personal and intimate relationship with the Divine, just like the relationship of love between Arjuna and Krishna.

"Remember, Krishna reveals to Arjuna his limitless Universal Form, but Arjuna isn't attracted to this form. He wants a personal relationship of love with Krishna. To develop such an intimate union with the Soul of the Universe through sacred love is the aim of Bhakti-yoga, the yoga of offering love.

"The ancient mystical texts say Krishna can't be seen with the material eye or understood with the material mind.[43] His very form is composed of love, and therefore he remains invisible to a heart hardened by violence and devoid of love.

"Those who practise the yoga of offering love are able to see the beautiful form of Krishna in the core of their heart, through the eyes of love. That form becomes visible to them, reflected on the mirror of their pure heart.[44]

"But take great care! Be warned! Once someone glimpses Krishna, even for a moment, she loses all attraction for the ordinary things of this world. They appear to her as valueless as broken pieces of glass."

I had revealed more than I had intended. These esoteric teachings of the yoga of the heart are normally kept confidential.[45] For millennia, they've been explored by sadhus, or shamans of the heart, and passed down in sacred lineages.

But Anita was eager to know more.

"Tomorrow I'll tell you about Shri Radha, the Goddess of Sacred Love," I said. "In my own lineage, we worship her above Krishna."[46]

TO THOSE ALWAYS SITUATED IN YOGA,
WHO OFFER SERVICE WITH LOVE,
I GIVE THAT YOGA OF DISCERNMENT
BY WHICH THEY COME TO ME.

—*Bhagavad Gita*, 10.10

SIXTEEN

Write Your Story
with Love and Compassion

—I—

I stood barefoot on the red-ochre granite steps of Vishram Ghat in Mathura, which descended into the flowing waters of the River Yamuna. The wet steps glistened like glazed pottery, as the rising sun pierced through the morning fog.

In the dark night of the soul, our life story is shattered. This opens an opportunity to rewrite our story, this time consciously, using the highest design principle: love and compassion. What if we could make our entire life an expression of love and service? What if we could write our story out of sacred love, rather than out of fear, ego, neediness and attachment?

Writing our story with love is an art; and like the mastery of any art, it requires practice. It requires an understanding of the ancient technique of creating an infallible intent, called a *sankalpa*, as well as of how to nourish and protect sacred love. I learned this in India one autumn day.

Amid several thousand pilgrims, I stood at Vishram Ghat with my teacher. It was the first day of a one-month pilgrimage. We had come to this sacred place to perform a *sankalpa*. The Sanskrit *sankalpa* means "definite intention", "resolve" or "vow". It's a powerful technique in yoga.

Krishna explains to Arjuna that those with resolve have their intelligence fixed on one point, while the intelligence of those without resolve has many branches and diversifies without limit.[47] Krishna is speaking here about the importance of *sankalpa*, the ancient practice of fixing one's resolve.

A *sankalpa* takes our deepest desire and manifests it in the world. It gives it a form. What that form looks like depends upon the command given to the mental force by the one making the *sankalpa*.

A *sankalpa* isn't the simple idea that I make a wish and then do a little spiritual practice to bring it about. When performed correctly, a *sankalpa* is more potent than matter. It allows us to achieve the impossible. It has the power to reshape our destiny.

Our *sankalpa* becomes our inspiration, illuminating our entire being and stirring our soul into activity. It's best not to waste the power of a *sankalpa* on anything trifling or trivial. The *Bhagavad Gita* advises us not to settle for a *sankalpa* that relates to our small human stories.

Even the removal of unhelpful habits in our life is not weighty enough to be our *sankalpa*. While essential, it isn't the purpose of our life. When we choose our *sankalpa* and it lights up our soul, our unhelpful habits will fall away automatically.

Krishna tells Arjuna that one whose *sankalpa* is free from

selfish desire, and whose actions are thereby purified by the fire of knowledge, is truly learned.[48] When a person lets go of all selfish *sankalpas*, she is advanced in yoga.[49]

The dark night of the soul is a perfect opportunity to find our *sankalpa*, our true north on this journey through life. A *sankalpa* is formed of the deepest desire fuelling our practice. Even Krishna, the Lord of Yoga, has a *sankalpa*.

Arjuna's problem at Kurukshetra is that he stands to fight without a *sankalpa*. If you remember, he no longer knows where he's going, and in his crisis on the battlefield, he finds himself lost and without strength or direction.

If we don't have a *sankalpa*, then when life presents challenges and difficulties we'll simply want to run away, like Arjuna. Krishna helps him find his *sankalpa* at the level of the soul, and in doing so, speaks the *Bhagavad Gita* for generations to follow. The *Gita* guides the reader to the deepest fulfilment of one's soul purpose.

No one can select our *sankalpa* for us. Only we can do that. And once we've decided upon our *sankalpa*, it shouldn't be changed until it becomes a reality in our life.

Importantly, only one *sankalpa* is to lead the way at any one time, so don't accept a new *sankalpa* until the previous *sankalpa* has been fulfilled.

There are four steps to the process of *sankalpa*: receive, articulate, resolve and remember.

൶

Step One: Receive

A *sankalpa* is not constructed by the mind. It's *revealed* in our heart, from the depths of the soul.

The first step is therefore a process of *receiving*. Krishna, the Universal Teacher, gifts our *sankalpa* to us, and we receive it. We can ask Krishna to reveal our *sankalpa* to us so that it comes into our awareness in a clear, precise, unmistakable way.

Our *sankalpa* will most easily enter a heart that has let go of the worldly story we live and that has taken refuge in Krishna.

Take your time to discover your *sankalpa*. Don't select a *sankalpa* that doesn't spring from the deepest yearning of the soul. Don't pick a *sankalpa* on the basis of popular opinion either. Tell yourself, "I'll find my *sankalpa*." It can take a full year to discover it, so don't rush.

When your *sankalpa* is revealed to you, accept it with humility and reverence. This is an important part of receiving it. A *sankalpa* is worthy of worship, because it's the yearning of the soul.

The nature of the soul is to offer love. A *sankalpa* that is truly an expression of the soul will be connected in some way to an offering of love, or to the soul's journey towards sacred love.

Our *sankalpa* will be revealed more easily and distinctly when we have a clarity through yoga practice or through illuminating company. Like a clear diamond or crystal, consciousness reflects the qualities of its surroundings. Therefore, it's easiest to receive our *sankalpa* when we're in the company of a teacher or someone who inspires the best in us and whose heart is filled with sacred love.

When we first come to understand our *sankalpa*, it may fill us with surprise, maybe even fear, initially. This is because our *sankalpa* may ask of us something that seems difficult, even impossible. But know that within every *sankalpa* lies the full potential of its fulfilment, just as a little acorn contains the invisible compressed potential of an entire oak tree.

∽

Step Two: Articulate

The second step is to articulate our *sankalpa* clearly and precisely in words. Our *sankalpa* cannot be vague, confused or ill-defined. We won't have truly understood our *sankalpa* until we can articulate it clearly.

Find the shortest, clearest, most concise and positive way to express your *sankalpa*, beginning with "I will…". Try to use five or six words, or even less. There is no need for several paragraphs; keep it simple, clear and filled with the essence of your truth.

Words are very powerful. They have immense creative

potency. Therefore select your words carefully. The closer you are to your true *sankalpa*, the louder the statement will speak to you, generating energy in your heart.

A *sankalpa* is not to be revealed to anyone. This helps retain its potency. When we keep something a secret, it grows in intensity and power. My teacher once counselled me, "Keep your *sankalpa* concealed from the world like fragrant camphor sealed in a container. If you keep opening the lid, the camphor will evaporate and disappear. In the same way, if you share your *sankalpa* with others, it will quickly evaporate."

Krishna himself has a *sankalpa*, and this is his most closely guarded secret—a truth he doesn't disclose, not even to Arjuna.

᠅

Step Three: Resolve

Discovering your *sankalpa* isn't enough. To harness its true potential, you'll need to fully own your *sankalpa*, embracing it wholeheartedly.

In this step we transform our deep *desire* into an *intent*, which we then release into the world. We're sparks of consciousness, fragments of divine energy, caught up in this illusory world. Our own power is tiny and belongs to Krishna, the source of all potency. Our ability to act with any potency, therefore, is intrinsically connected to the Soul of all souls. In recognizing this, the release of our *sankalpa* takes the form of a prayer.

The strength of our resolve is likely to wane over time. But Krishna is known as *amogha-sankalpa*, one whose resolve is infallible.[50] By connecting with the divine, our *sankalpa* can become unfailing too. It can become our means to overcome any obstacle on our spiritual path.

One way to sanctify or consecrate this third step is with a sacred ritual, such as offering a lamp or a candle. The flame represents our *sankalpa*, which we offer to the Soul of the Universe.

When ritualizing a *sankalpa* at Vishram Ghat in Mathura, we would take water from the Yamuna in the palms of our hands and offer it back to the sacred river. This symbolizes that we've received the gift of our *sankalpa* and are offering it back to Krishna with humility and love. Accepting the precious gift of our *sankalpa* from the Divine within us, and then offering that *sankalpa* in the service of the Divine, we approach our *sankalpa* in the most powerful way: as an expression of loving service.

Offering fragrant flowers can be a part of the *sankalpa* ritual too, as well as the repetition of mantras, or sacred syllables. Choose an offering, prayer or ritual that has special meaning to you. You can visit a sacred place to make your *sankalpa*, or you can travel there with your mind and heart, consecrating your intention from there.

When performing this third step of birthing your *sankalpa*, it's most important to connect with the *emotions* behind your *sankalpa*, feeling the "fire" of your *sankalpa* in the depths of your being.

✧

Step Four: Remember

By giving us a clear, focused direction, our *sankalpa* will help us in our daily decision-making. We can ask ourselves whether something moves us closer or further away from the fulfilment of our *sankalpa*. Listening to our heart will reveal what next steps we should take in the service of our *sankalpa*.

To allow our *sankalpa* to guide us, we'll need to remember it, keeping it alive within our heart. One way to remember our *sankalpa* is by repeating it to ourselves with love and attention, making it a daily meditation. This reaffirms and intensifies it.

We can meditate on our *sankalpa* at any time during the day or night. It's especially helpful to remember our *sankalpa* at times when we're most receptive to it. I make it my first thought upon waking and my last thought before sleep overtakes me. Other helpful times include the beginning and end of our yoga practice; the beginning and end of meditation; before and after meals; in our dreams; upon visiting or worshipping at any shrine or temple; before making any important decision or beginning any important task; and upon completing a difficult task.

When repeating a *sankalpa*, it's important to do so with the *heart*. It should be as if all our mental and emotional energy, all our faith, all our devotion and dedication are being concentrated into the form of our *sankalpa*.

It may help to visualize the fulfilment of your *sankalpa*— what does such a state look or feel like? Maintain a positive attitude towards your chosen *sankalpa*, and move forward without a hint of doubt or self-questioning.

There may be times when there will seem to be a huge gap between our *sankalpa* and its fulfilment. At such times, it helps to repeat the *sankalpa* as a prayer in a heartfelt way, with tears in our eyes, for tears are the highest form of prayer.

At the beginning of the *Bhagavad Gita*, Arjuna is lost and confused. But by the end of Krishna's yoga teachings, Arjuna has found his *sankalpa* and is now willing to face the battlefield. As he declares, his confusion has vanished, and he's ready to engage with life, this time with awareness of his true identity beyond the play of form of this world.

"My confusion is destroyed, and by your grace I have regained memory, O Infallible One. I'm firmly resolved, with doubts dispelled, and I'm ready to act according to your words," Arjuna affirms.[51] These are his final words in the *Gita*.

What kind of *sankalpa* has Arjuna made? His confusion destroyed and his memory regained, we can know that his *sankalpa* doesn't concern the illusory ego and its narratives. When we're free from our stories, we discover our true *sankalpa*, or soul purpose; and with a fixed *sankalpa*, all our doubts are dissolved. We're then ready to act on the field of life with unearthly potency, even in the face of the greatest adversity.

Arjuna acknowledges here that this has occurred by the grace of Krishna, the Universal Teacher. "By your grace," he says to Krishna. Discovering our *sankalpa* is the result primarily of *grace*.

The function of a *sankalpa* is to obtain infallible resolve— where our intent becomes more powerful than the universe itself. With such one-pointed resolve held in our hearts, feelings of confusion and being stuck vanish. Our *sankalpa* gives us one-pointed focus, shedding the weight of extraneous efforts, distractions, negativity and unhelpful chatter of the mind, and in the absence of doubt, even the greatest challenges we face begin to shrink.

Usually, our problems take immense significance in our mind. But they're "right-sized" by our *sankalpa*. Like a lamp, our *sankalpa* dissolves the fearful darkness and illuminates our path. It's not that we no longer experience any difficulties.

Rather, those challenges become less significant, and our *sankalpa* gives us the strength we need to overcome them.

Arjuna doesn't openly state what his *sankalpa* is, as a *sankalpa* is to be kept secret. But there are clues. Krishna has just revealed to Arjuna the teachings of Bhakti-yoga, his "most secret of all secrets", and Arjuna now states, "I'm ready to act according to your words."

We know, therefore, that Arjuna's *sankalpa* is about making his life an offering of love. The warrior is now ready to engage with life, no longer as an expression of false ego, but of sacred love. In redirecting our energy, a *sankalpa* is the best way to rewrite our story. If our *sankalpa* is an expression of sacred love, then we can rewrite our entire story out of sacred love.

In dismantling our previous conceptions of self, the dark night of the soul offers an opportunity to receive our true purpose, our *sankalpa*. To find our *sankalpa* is one of the most valuable gifts of the dark night of the soul.

—2—

Without food, all life dries up, extinguishes and dies. Likewise, if we don't know how to nourish and feed our love, it will wither and die.

So what food does love need? I asked this question to my teacher.

"To love means to serve," my teacher replied. "Love grows

through attentive, loving service, as well as through humility. This is its food."

Love isn't simply a feeling. The real nature of love is sacrifice for the object of love, my teacher explained. Therefore, love is expressed and nourished by loving service, which opens our heart and increases our capacity to love.

We're all servants already. Mostly, we spend our time serving our uncontrolled mind, with whom we identify and to whom we have handed the reins of our chariot on the field of life. If we direct our capacity to serve to the Soul of the Universe, seated within our own heart, then we nurture a love that extends towards all beings.

It's better to be a servant of love than a master of self-interest. Exactly the same activity, such as writing this book, can be an expression of loving service or an expression of ego. The same activity can take us forward on our yoga path, or backwards.

Importantly, loving service is a way to create our life where we're not obsessively putting ourselves in the centre, an especially fruitful challenge during times of personal crisis. By focusing on serving, we move away from the small human story we're trapped in that causes us so much suffering.

When we give selflessly of ourselves and cast aside all measure of gain, we gain beyond all measure. Indeed, true love doesn't serve any purpose except itself. As my teacher explained:

Love has nothing to take but everything to give. ...

We want to be completely selfless in our dealings, and for this we have the example of the tree, which gives its bark, roots, fruits, leaves, wood and shade. The tree offers everything to others with no expectation of remuneration. Why can't we human beings be so selfless?[52]

We can make everything we do an expression of love and affection. This is known as "continuous practice". Rather than being something we reserve for the yoga mat only, yoga now becomes our life practice.

One of the most surprising questions Arjuna asks Krishna in the *Bhagavad Gita* is, "What is knowledge?"[53] Arjuna has a sense that real knowledge is not about storing ideas and information in our mind. After all, Arjuna has learned so much from wise elders and sages; but on the battlefield of Kurukshetra he finds himself utterly lost and confused. So, what does it mean *to know?*

In reply, Krishna gives Arjuna an incredibly beautiful list of divine qualities: "Humility, absence of deceit, non-violence, tolerance, simplicity…" This, Krishna declares, is knowledge; all else is the absence of knowledge.[54]

All else is the absence of knowledge. If the information we hold doesn't create *transformation* within, if it doesn't elevate us, it's simply another manifestation of folly, or the absence of knowledge.

The first quality Krishna places in his list is humility. We can know so much, but if we don't have humility, Krishna is saying, we've not learned anything at all.

Yoga begins with humility. When the heart is filled with pride, with a mood of superiority, we're unable to serve anyone except ourselves. Humility is therefore the highest wisdom.

When a tree is heavy with ripened fruit, when it has something to offer the world, its branches bow down to the earth. Clouds hang low when filled with fresh rain. Ears of rice bend to the ground as they ripen.

The word "humility" comes from the Latin *humus*, meaning "ground". When we understand humility, we conquer the false ego.

Sacred love grows on the soil of humility. Without humility, sacred love can't manifest in the heart, just as a plant can't grow without nutrient-rich soil.

Humility is freedom from the false identity of our story. If our humility is natural and genuine, then we'll begin to see ourselves as servants. When we see ourselves as the smallest of the small, we can make room for the whole world.

My teacher explained once, "When even a little Bhakti has entered someone's heart, then humility will certainly be there. Where there is no humility, we can understand that there is no Bhakti."[55]

The highest humility, my teacher continued, is found in Shri Radha, the Goddess of Sacred Love: "She is the pinnacle of humility. In whomever she detects even a trace of Bhakti, she considers that person worthy of her reverence. She offers prayers to that person, thinking, 'I should try to become like them.'"[56]

But in fact, it's her mood of humility and her endless compassion that we should hope to embody. As the source of all loving service, we can look up to her in our own practice.

We can envisage each day as being a beautiful, fragrant flower that we offer to Shri Radha, the Goddess of Sacred Love. In our morning meditation, before beginning our day, we can place that flower at her feet: "Today, I offer this day to you, Shri Radha. Please guide me so that I can be an instrument in your service."

At the end of a day of service, as we go to sleep, we'll long for the next day to arrive, so we can offer an even more beautiful flower to the Goddess of Sacred Love.

−3−

To write my story out of love and compassion, I would need to understand not only what feeds love, but also what *harms* love.

While there are so many things that obstruct love, they have one thing in common: they're all expressions of disrespect.

The Sanskrit word for disrespect is *aparadha*, which means, "without Radha".[57] In other words, disrespect is that which causes Shri Radha, the Goddess of Love, to leave that place. Love can't bear to remain where there is any form of disrespect.

So how do we respect others? We can begin by learning to look at others at the level of the soul, beyond the stories we live out.

When we define others through the lens of our little stories, we engage in a form of disrespect. We fail to truly see the other person before us.

The stories we manufacture and live out in our life are self-serving: they're designed to put us at the centre. Our imaginary self, the lead character in our story, then begins to take on immense significance. We look at others through our own small narrative and try to co-opt them into our own service. We determine our friends and enemies by their relationship to our ego.

This is the basis of the entire conflict at Kurukshetra. At the beginning of the *Bhagavad Gita*, the blind emperor Dhritarashtra is caught up in this paradigm of "I" and "mine".

Krishna's first teaching to Arjuna is therefore about the soul. By the end of the *Gita*, as students of yoga, we'll hopefully have loosened the grip of Dhritarashtra's paradigm of fear, ego and illusion, moving our vision beyond that, to see all beings at the level of the soul. We'll hopefully enter a space of self-reflection before setting people apart as enemy or friend.[58]

This opens the door to love and affection for all beings, not simply those who support our flawed human narrative.

Ultimately, we alone are our own best friend or worst enemy, not anyone else, as Krishna explains: "Indeed, the self alone is the self's friend, and the self alone is the self's enemy."[59] Understanding this is the first step to being able to respect all beings, and to loving them.

The best possible time to develop this vision is in the dark night of the soul. With our story torn apart forcefully, against our will, we can practise relating to others from a higher perspective.

One of the secrets to cultivating kindness and respect in our life is to start by being kinder and more compassionate to ourselves. We can do this by treating our own story less seriously and seeing the beautiful foolishness of our own life. If we're continually judging and punishing ourselves through the lens of our illusory ego, how can we expect not to judge and punish others through that lens also?

By releasing the grip our story has over us and becoming aware of our existence as a soul alongside all others, we learn self-kindness and are able to see and honour others. Self-kindness fosters kindness to others. Non-violence therefore begins at home, with ourselves. That's why the *Mahabharata*, the larger epic in which the *Gita* is situated, affirms, "Non-violence is the best of friends."[60]

–4–

What is Krishna's most closely guarded secret?[61] What is *his sankalpa*?

I was so eager to know, and it took me many years to discover. Every autumn, the monks from the monastery with whom I had lived for nearly ten years go on a barefoot pilgrimage throughout Braj, and while in India, I always joined them.

Braj, the sacred land of Krishna, encompasses forty-eight forests, with countless lakes and smaller ponds. I'm always drawn to its many secret places, such as "The Lake of Sacred Tears", "The Forest of Loving Desire" and "The Pond of the Goddess of Love".[62]

Like many regions of India, Braj has in recent years suffered deforestation and over-development. But it remains a timeless place of pilgrimage. A sacred land, Braj is compared to a lotus flower situated above the turbulent waters of the phenomenal world. For the spiritual aspirant and the mystic, Braj represents a doorway to the highest level of transcendence, a land composed of sacred love.

In one ancient text it's said that the trees in Braj are wish-fulfilling trees and the land is made of wish-fulfilling gems, the water is nectar, all speech is song, all movement is dance, and the flute is the dearest friend.[63] *That* Braj is the goal of the pilgrims' wanderings. We can enter this enchanted land with the help of a sadhu, or spiritual guide, and with a mood of loving service.

It was Kartika, the month of Shri Radha, the Goddess of Sacred Love. We made our way to Shri Radha-kunda, her divine pond. The waters of this pond are said to be non-different from Shri Radha herself. One who bathes in them with an open heart develops unconditional love.[64]

Shri Radha is the supreme goddess. She is Krishna's eternal paramour, and he is completely controlled by her selfless love.[65] The highest love is found in her. All of Krishna's power, all his happiness, all his handsomeness and sweetness, all his expertise and other virtues are under the dominion of Shri Radha.[66] Therefore, in my lineage we worship Shri Radha above Krishna. Our life is dedicated to her.

Krishna is the root of all happiness, yet he continues to exist only because of Shri Radha's beauty and excellences. Overcome by her grace and his love for her, he dances in madness and declares with pride that it is she who teaches him to dance.[67]

Within their forests, whatever meets with Shri Radha and Krishna changes its nature. Fire becomes cold, and fresh water feels hot. Transfixed by their beauty, animate beings appear inanimate. The splendour of Shri Radha and Krishna puts brilliant objects in the shadow, while non-luminous articles become radiant. The Yamuna River flows upstream and the rocks melt.

While some in the Bhakti tradition worship Shri Radha to attain the favour of Krishna, we worship Krishna to attain the favour of Shri Radha. She is our main object of worship, and our relationship with Krishna is through her.[68] As my teacher used to say, "If anyone asks me who is Krishna, I will only say that he is the life and soul of my master, Shri Radha."[69]

Shri Radha's fair complexion is said to resemble saffron that has been ground upon a slab of pure gold. Her dress is the colour of the rising sun. The shining brilliance of her face defeats the effulgence of millions of autumnal full moons.[70] The flower garlands she dons on all parts of her body are none other than her excellent qualities. The dot that dazzles on her fair forehead is made of good fortune, and her heart overflows with the most astonishing transformations of sacred love. She enchants Krishna completely. My teacher explained that day, that Krishna himself worships Shri Radha. She is the Soul of his soul, superior to him in every way.

When Krishna is speaking the *Bhagavad Gita* to Arjuna, he's doing so as part of his own practice of loving service to Shri Radha. Krishna also has a fixed *sankalpa*, which he keeps a closely guarded secret, and that is to serve Shri Radha. The deeper teaching is that even the Soul of the Universe is controlled by sacred love.

How wonderful that Krishna, the Lord of Yoga and the Soul of the Universe, is bound by sacred love. He too has a story; not a small ego-centric story filled with anguish and false perceptions, but an eternal, spiritual love story beyond the play of form of this fleeting world.

Divinity is neither male nor female—but always both.

To play a small part in their divine love story is the highest attainment in yoga.[71]

Shri Radha is the greatest yogini. The aim in my lineage is to gain her blessings, by which she manifests sacred love within our hearts. That sacred love is non-different from her own essence and being. Dedicating our life to Shri Radha's service is the key to writing our story out of love and compassion.

This is Krishna's most confidential yoga teaching of all, the bright illumination of the dark night of the soul, the most sublime rerouting of our despair. This is the secret he most wants to tell.

WHERE THERE IS KRISHNA, THE LORD OF YOGA,
AND WHERE THERE IS ARJUNA, HOLDER OF THE BOW,
THERE IS GOOD FORTUNE, UNUSUAL TRIUMPH, STRENGTH,
AND ABIDING WISE CONDUCT. THAT IS MY CONCLUSION.

—*Bhagavad Gita*, 18.78

Notes
Part V: "Let Sacred Love Be Your Only Goal"

1 *Bhagavad Gita*, 13.10: *bhaktir avyabhicharini*, "the unwavering offering of love". Krishna advises Arjuna to pursue no other form of yoga.

2 *Bhagavad Gita*, 6.34.

3 *Bhagavad Gita*, 4.3.

4 For example, *Bhagavad Gita*, 5.18.

5 *Bhagavad Gita*, 6.32. See also *Bhagavata Purana*, 6.10.9 and *Mahabharata*, 5.36.16.

6 *Bhagavad Gita*, 10.11: Krishna is *atma-bhava-stha*, "situated in the existence of the soul". See also *Bhagavata Purana*, 10.14.55: Krishna is *atmanam akhilatmanam*, "the Soul of all souls".

7 *Bhagavad Gita*, 7.7.

8 This form is known as Vishva-rupa, which means, literally, having all things as its form. It contains the entire universe across all time, including past and future.

9 Debashis Chatterjee, *Timeless Leadership: 18 Leadership Sutras from The Bhagavad Gita* (2012), p. 18. Chatterjee acknowledges Prasad Kaipa for the humorous acronym.

10 *Bhagavad Gita*, 9.27: "Whatever you do, whatever you accept, whatever you sacrifice, whatever you give away, whatever discipline you undertake—make that an offering to me, O Son of Kunti."

11 *Bhagavad Gita*, 9.2.

12 Krishna is Yogeshvara, the "Lord of Yoga": *Bhagavad Gita*, 11.4, 11.9, 18.75 and 18.78. Arjuna also addresses Krishna as "O Yogi" (*Bhagavad Gita*, 10.17).

13 *Bhagavad Gita*, 18.66. In following Karma-yoga and other practices described in the first six chapters of the *Gita*, one relies on one's own efforts to transform oneself. However, Krishna, seated within the heart of all beings,

directly frees one who is devoted to him. This is apparent from *Gita*, 7.14, 10.11, 12.6–7 and 18.66.

14   This is the first time in the *Bhagavad Gita* that the word *bhakta*, from the noun *bhakti*, appears. This verse, which is found in the context of Krishna's Karma-yoga teachings, highlights the role of sacred love in nurturing all forms of yoga.

15   Adapted with permission from Kat Byles, "A Trump Calling to Go Deeper into Your Heart" [blog], published 2 Mar. 2017.

16   To learn more, go to www.katbyles.com.

17   According to estimates from ground-penetrating radar, Pi-Ramses was spread over about seven square miles. The City of London, colloquially known as the "Square Mile" (after its approximate size), is the area of London originally within the ancient city walls, and is today the world's leading international finance centre.

18   Diodorus Siculus, *Library of History* (1961). This is paraphrased in Percy Bysshe Shelley's poem "Ozymandias", first published in 1818.

19   Shri Madhvacharya explains that Duryodhana represents Kali-yuga, the societal dark night of the soul. See Shri Madhvacharya, *Mahabharata-tatparya-nirnaya*, 2.146. The battle of Kurukshetra occurs just before the onset of Kali-yuga at *yuga-sandhi*, the point of transition of one age to another. Hence, Krishna's yoga teachings in the *Bhagavad Gita* are meant specially to help us in Kali-yuga, the present age of darkness and despair.

20   *Bhagavad Gita*, 6.32 and 6.47. As we'll see in the next chapter, sacred love extends to all beings, as a result of directing that love to the sacred source of all beings, the Soul of all souls.

21   Shri Shrimad Bhaktivedanta Narayana Maharaja, *Beyond Liberation* (2003), p. 14. Adapted from commentaries.

22   The Ancient Greeks' six words for love were (1) *eros*, or sexual passion, (2) *ludus*, or playful love, (3) *philia*, or deep friendship, (4) *pragma*, or longstanding love, (5) *philautia*, or love of the self, and (6) *agape*, or love for everyone.

23 *Bhagavad Gita*, 7.17. This is the first time the word *bhakti* appears as a noun. Catherine Ghosh makes this insightful observation in "Remaining Loving When All Our Triggers Go Off", in Catherine Ghosh and Braja Sorensen, *Yoga in the Gita: Krishna and Patanjali: The Bhakti Dimension* (2016), Chapter 5.

24 *Bhagavad Gita*, 18.64: *sarva-guhyatama*, "the greatest secret of all".

25 Indra, chief of the celestials, thought the Parijata far too beautiful for the earth. He therefore seized this tree and gave it to his wife, Indrani. Known to have the most beautiful eyes, Indrani is the goddess of wrath and jealousy. She planted the Parijata in her heavenly garden. There it grew as one of Indra's five celestial trees, until Krishna brought it to earth.

26 Sometimes attributed to the *Vishnu Purana* or *Vayu Purana*. For example, see Nanditha Krishna and M. Amirthalingam, *Sacred Plants of India* (Kindle edition; 2009), locations 3997–4000.

27 This teaching is also found in the *Bhagavata Purana*, 4.31.14.

28 One name of Krishna, or Vishnu, listed in *Vishnu-sahasranama* is Vriksha, "The Tree". Krishna is the tree of life that nourishes and supports all beings.

29 The yogi connects with Krishna in the heart through yoga, by developing yoga perception that is inward-facing (*antar-mukha*), rather than outward-facing (*bahir-mukha*).

30 *Bhagavad Gita*, 6.32.

31 *Vishnu-sahasranama* lists one of Krishna's names as Shoka-nashana, "Destroyer of Sorrow". Krishna is also known as Arti-hara, "The Remover of Distress". For example, *Bhagavata Purana*, 10.73.8: *prapanna arti-hara*, "Remover of the distress of those who have taken shelter".

32 Traditionally, flowers used in the ritual worship of Krishna are picked directly from a plant, but the Parijata flower is an exception. It is the only flower used for worship that is collected from the ground.

33 The *Padma Purana* (4.10.1–4) states that the Parijata is a *kalpa-vriksha*, a tree that fulfils wishes.

34 *Vishnu-sahasranama*, Dhyana, verses 6–7. After the battle of Kurukshetra, the Pandavas headed by Yudhishtira approached Bhishma on his deathbed, to seek advice and wisdom. Bhishma, the grandfather of Arjuna and the Pandavas, lying on a bed of arrows, uttered this prayer with great feeling.

35 Names of Vishnu, or Krishna, listed in *Vishnu-sahasranama* include Guru ("Teacher"), Gurutamah ("Greatest teacher"), Neyah ("Guide") and Guhah ("He who dwells in the cave of the heart").

36 *Bhagavad Gita*, 10.17. O you who possess all potency: translates Bhagavan, following Parashara Muni in *Vishnu Purana*, 6.5.74. Bhagavan is the source of all beauty, strength, fame, wealth, knowledge and renunciation. As these attributes have the power to influence or make an impression, they may be described, individually or collectively, as "potency". They are sometimes referred to in English as Bhagavan's "six opulences".

37 See *Bhagavad Gita*, 7.8–12.

38 See *Bhagavad Gita*, 10.20–40.

39 *Bhagavad Gita*, 10.42.

40 *Bhagavad Gita*, 4.11.

41 Names of Vishnu, or Krishna, in *Vishnu-sahasranama* include Naikarupah, "He who takes infinite forms".

42 Krishna tells Arjuna that he is the foundation on which the unchanging impersonal Brahman exists (*Bhagavad Gita*, 14.27).

43 For example, *Shvetashvatara Upanishad*, 4.20 and *Kena Upanishad*, 1.3–8. Krishna is known as Adhokshaja because he is beyond the purview of the material senses and mind.

44 *Shri Brahma-samhita*, 5.38. Names of Vishnu, or Krishna, in *Vishnu-sahasranama* include Yogah ("He who is realized through yoga") and Yoga-vidam-neta ("The guide of those who know yoga"). Krishna tells Arjuna that those who focus their minds on his personal form are considered by him to be the most absorbed in yoga (*Bhagavad Gita*, 12.2).

45 See *Bhagavad Gita*, 18.67–71. Sharing Krishna's most confidential yoga teachings with those who are ready to hear them, Krishna tells Arjuna, pleases him most of all and is the highest act of loving service. But Krishna also warns Arjuna that these teachings should never be shared with anyone who is without discipline, who is bereft of love, who doesn't wish to hear them, or who holds envy in their heart.

46 In the Bhakti lineage of Shrila Rupa Goswami, we worship both the masculine and feminine aspects of divinity (which are, in truth, non-different from each other), but with emphasis on the divine feminine. This is because Shri Radha is the embodiment of the highest devotion, and completely controls Krishna through her love. She is *parama-devata*, the "supreme object of worship" (Shrila Krishnadas Kaviraja Goswami, *Shri Chaitanya Charitamrita, Adi-lila*, 4.90). Shri Radha is our main worshipful deity, and our relationship with Krishna is through her (see Shrila Raghunatha Dasa Goswami, "Gandharva-prarthanashtakam", 2; Shri Shrimad B. R. Shridhar Goswami Maharaja, "With Pride He Announced: 'It Is the Best Day'" [lecture], Navadwip, 9 Sep. 1983; and Shri Shrimad Bhaktivedanta Narayana Maharaja, "*Vilap-kusmanjali*: Verse Seven" [lecture], Mathura, 20 Oct. 1991).

47 *Bhagavad Gita*, 2.41.

48 *Bhagavad Gita*, 4.19.

49 *Bhagavad Gita*, 6.4. See also *Gita*, 6.24.

50 For example, *Bhagavad Purana*, 2.9.28.

51 *Bhagavad Gita*, 18.73.

52 Shrila B. V. Narayan Goswami, lecture, Odessa (Ukraine), 22 Sep. 2002. See also *Bhagavata Purana*, 10.22.33–35.

53 *Bhagavad Gita*, 13.1.

54 *Bhagavad Gita*, 13.8–12.

55 Lecture published in Shri Shrimad Bhaktivedanta Narayana Maharaja, *Bhakti-rasayana* (2006), pp. 84–5.

56   Ibid., p. 85.

57   *Apagata radha yasmat iti aparadha*, "*Aparadha* is that by which Shri Radha is lost to us". The Bhakti tradition eschews disrespect to all that is sacred, including other living beings, known as *jiva-aparadha*.

58   Chapter 12 of the *Bhagavad Gita*, entitled "Bhakti-yoga", describes a yogi as "one who is the same toward both enemy and friend" (12.18: *samah shatrau cha mitre cha*). Such a yogi, Krishna says, is dearly loved by him. See also *Bhagavad Gita*, 6.9, which describes the preeminent yogi whose discernment remains the same when considering friends, allies, enemies, the disinterested, neutrals, the hateful, relatives, the virtuous and the wicked.

59   *Bhagavad Gita*, 6.5.

60   *Mahabharata*, 13.117.38 (*ahimsa paramam mitram*).

61   Krishna gives an indication of his *sankalpa* to Arjuna in the *Adi Purana*, but not in the *Bhagavad Gita*. See Shrila Krishnadas Kaviraja Goswami, *Shri Chaitanya Charitamrita*, Adi-lila, 4.216, quoting the *Adi Purana*.

62   Prema-sarovara, Kamyavana and Shri Radha-kunda, respectively.

63   *Shri Brahma-samhita*, 5.56.

64   Shrila Rupa Goswami, *Shri Upadeshamrita*, 11.

65   For example, *Bhagavata Purana*, 10.32.22 and "Shri Radha-Kripa-Kataksha-Stava-Raja" (spoken by Shiva to Gauri in the *Urdhvamnaya-tantra*), verse 3. To understand and taste the sacred of love of Shri Radha, Krishna comes to this world as Shri Chaitanya Mahaprabhu, a Bhakti practitioner in search of the summit of mystical devotional ecstasy. See Shrila Krishnadas Kaviraja Goswami, *Shri Chaitanya Charitamrita*, Adi-lila, Chapter 4.

66   Shrila Vishvanatha Chakravarti Thakura, *Shri Vraja-riti-chintamani*, 1.62.

67   Shrila Krishnadas Kaviraja Goswami, *Shri Chaitanya Charitamrita*, Adi-lila, 4.124.

68 Shrila Krishnadas Kaviraja Goswami, *Shri Chaitanya Charitamrita, Adi-lila*, 4.90: *parama-devata*, "the supreme object of worship". See also *Shri Chaitanya Charitamrita, Adi-lila*, 4.95.

69 For example, see Shri Shrimad Bhaktivedanta Narayana Maharaja, "*Vilap-kusmanjali*: Verse Seven" [lecture], Mathura, 20 Oct. 1991.

70 See "Shri Radhikashtakam" by Shrila Rupa Goswami, "Shri Radha-Kripa-Kat(aksha-Stava-Raja" and other Sanskrit prayers and poems.

71 *Padma Purana* (*Uttara-khanda*), 272.166–7, quoted by Shrila Rupa Goswami in *Bhakti-rasamrita-sindhu*, 1.2.301–2. These verses describe the highest attainment in yoga of the great rishis of ancient times dwelling in the Dandaka Forest. Also, see *Bhagavata Purana*, 10.82.39 and 10.87.23; Shrila Rupa Goswami, *Shri Upadeshamrita*, 10; Shrila Rupa Goswami, *Bhakti-rasamrita-sindhu*, 2.5.38; Shrila Prabodhananda Saraswati, *Shri Radha-rasa-sudha-nidhi*, 33, 78, 148 and 240; and Shrila Krishnadas Kaviraja Goswami, *Shri Chaitanya Charitamrita, Madhya-lila*, 8.98, 8.196 and 23.53.

BIBLIOGRAPHY

BHAKTIVEDANTA SWAMI PRABHUPADA, A. C., *Bhagavad-gita As It Is* (New York: Macmillan, 1972).

BYLES, KAT, "A Trump Calling to Go Deeper into Your Heart" [blog], published 2 Mar. 2017. <http://www.katbyles.com/2017/03/a-trump-calling-to-go-deeper-into-your-heart>. Accessed 30 Mar. 2017.

CHATTERJEE, DEBASHIS, *Timeless Leadership: 18 Leadership Sutras from The Bhagavad Gita* (Kindle edition; Singapore: John Wiley & Sons, 2012).

CHURCHILL, WINSTON, speech in the House of Commons, 17 May 1916. <http://hansard.millbanksystems.com/commons/1916/may/17/royal-assent#column_1578>. Accessed 12 Mar. 2012.

COPE, STEPHEN, "Everything Is Already OK" in Stephen Cope, ed., *Will Yoga and Meditation Really Change My Life?* (North Adams, Mass.: Storey Publishing, 2003).

DASGUPTA, SURENDRANATH, *Philosophical Essays* (Delhi: Motilal Banarsidass, 1982; first ed. Calcutta: 1941).

DiCara, Vic (Vraja Kishor), "Evil Qualities", The Enquirer [blog], published 16 Jun. 2016. <https://vicd108. wordpress.com/2016/06/16/evil-qualities/>. Accessed 13 Sep. 2016.

Gheranda, *Gheranda Samhita* (Gaudiya Grantha Mandira [website], published 11 Jul. 2016). <http://www. granthamandira.net>. Accessed 2 Jun. 2017.

Ghosh, Catherine, "Are You Hiding Depression Behind Your Yoga?" Elephant Journal [website], published 2 May 2011. <http://www.elephantjournal.com/2011/05/ are-you-hiding-depression-behind-your-yoga-catherine-ghosh>. Accessed 16 May 2015.

—— "Remaining Loving When All Our Triggers Go Off", in Catherine Ghosh and Braja Sorensen, *Yoga in the Gita: Krishna and Patanjali: The Bhakti Dimension* (Kindle edition; United States: Golden Dragonfly Press, 2016), Chapter 5.

—— "The Body as a Doorway to Consciousness", in Catherine Ghosh and Braja Sorensen, *Yoga in the Gita: Krishna and Patanjali: The Bhakti Dimension* (Kindle edition; United States: Golden Dragonfly Press, 2016), Chapter 21.

—— "Yoga in The Gita: Dynamic Participation in Your Daily Life", Elephant Journal [website], published 11 Mar. 2012. <https://www.elephantjournal.com/2012/03/ yoga-in-the-gita-id-rather-die>. Accessed 20 Mar. 2014.

—— "Yoga in The Gita: Love Changes Our Perception",

Elephant Journal [website], published 25 Mar. 2012. <http://www.elephantjournal.com/2012/03/yoga-in-the-gita-love-changes-our-perception/>. Accessed 20 Mar. 2014.

Haas, Simon, *The Book of Dharma: Making Enlightened Choices* (Leicester, United Kingdom: Veda Wisdom Books, 2013).

Hardy, Richard P., *John of the Cross: Man and Mystic* (Washington, D.C.: ICS Publications, 2004).

Jiva Goswami, Shrila, *Bhakti-sandarbha* (Gaudiya Grantha Mandira [website], published 26 May 2003). <http://www.granthamandira.net>. Accessed 30 Apr. 2017.

—— *Paramatma-sandarbha* (Gaudiya Grantha Mandira [website], published 26 May 2003). <http://www.granthamandira.net>. Accessed 30 Apr. 2017.

Jobs, Steve, Stanford University commencement speech, 12 Jun. 2005. <http://news.stanford.edu/2005/06/14/jobs-061505/>. Accessed 10 Oct. 2017.

John of the Cross, St, *Dark Night of the Soul* [*Noche oscura del alma*] (trans. by E. Allison Peers; from the critical edition of Silverio de Santa Teresa; Dover Publications, 2003).

Kaviraja Goswami, Shrila Krishnadas, *Shri Chaitanya Charitamrita* (trans. and commentary by Shrila A. C. Bhaktivedanta Swami Prabhupada; Bhaktivedanta VedaBase 2003, Bhaktivedanta Archives, Bhaktivedanta Book Trust).

KRISHNA, NANDITHA and M. AMIRTHALINGAM, *Sacred Plants of India* (Kindle edition; Penguin Books, 2009).

MADHVACHARYA, SHRIMAD ANANDA TIRTHA, *Katha-lakshanam* (Madhva Library). <http://www.tatvavada.org/eng/etexts/sarvamula/kl_dng.pdf>. Accessed 30 Apr. 2017.

—— *Mahabharata-tatparya-nirnaya* (trans. by B. Gururajah Rao; Bangalore: 1941).

MAHARAJ, NISARGADATTA and ROBERT POWELL, *The Nectar of Immortality: Sri Nisargadatta Maharaj's Discourses on the Eternal*, ed. by Robert Powell (Delhi: Motilal Banarsidass, 2004).

MOORE, THOMAS, *Dark Nights of the Soul: A Guide to Finding Your Way Through Life's Ordeals* (Kindle edition: Little, Brown Book Group, 2011).

NARADA, MAHARSHI, *Shri Narada-bhakti-sutra* (Gaudiya Grantha Mandira [website], published 26 May 2003; collated by Toke Lindegaard Knudsen). <http://www.granthamandira.net>. Accessed 30 Apr. 2017.

NARAYANA MAHARAJA, SHRI SHRIMAD BHAKTIVEDANTA, *Beyond Liberation* (New Delhi: Gaudiya Vedanta Publications, 2003).

—— *Bhakti-rasayana* (Vrindavan, India: Gaudiya Vedanta Publications, 2006).

—— *Shri Brahma-samhita* (with commentaries of Shrila Jiva

Goswami, Shrila Bhaktivinoda Thakura and Shri
Shrimad Bhaktivedanta Narayana Maharaja) (Vrindavan,
India: Gaudiya Vedanta Publications, 2003).

—— *Shrimad Bhagavad-gita* (with *bhavanuvada* of the
commentary of Shrila Vishvanatha Chakravarti Thakura
and commentary by Shri Shrimad Bhaktivedanta Narayana
Maharaja) (Vrindavan, India: Shri Gaudiya Vedanta
Samiti, 2000).

—— *Shri Prabandhavali* (Vrindavan, India: Gaudiya Vedanta
Publications, 2003).

—— *The Essence of Bhagavad Gita* (New Delhi: Gaudiya Vedanta
Publications, 2000).

—— "*Vilap-kusmanjali*: Verse Seven" [lecture], Mathura,
20 Oct. 1991. <http://bit.ly/2tfQcrP>. Accessed
27 Jun. 2017.

ORLOFF, JUDITH, "7 Habits of Surrendered People", Dr Judith
Orloff's Blog [blog]. <http://bit.ly/1Gap2Re>.
Published 26 Feb. 2014. Accessed 9 Dec. 2014.

PATANJALI, *Yoga Sutra* (Gaudiya Grantha Mandira [website],
published 19 Jul. 2003). <http://www.granthamandira.
net>. Accessed 30 Apr. 2017.

PRABODHANANDA SARASWATI, SHRILA, *Shri Radha-rasa-sudha-
nidhi*, ed. and trans. into Hindi by Shri Haridas Shastri
(Vrindavan, India: Shri Gadadhara Gaurahari Press,

2007; digitized on 25 Feb. 2017). <https://archive.org/
details/radha_rasa_sudha_nidhi>.

Proust, Marcel, *In Search of Lost Time*, Vol. 2, *Within a Budding
Grove*, trans. by C. K. S. Moncreiff and T. Kilmartin
(London: Chatto and Windus, 1992).

Raghunatha Dasa Goswami, Shrila, "Gandharva-
prarthanashtakam" in Shri Shrimad Bhaktivedanta
Narayana Maharaja, *Shri Gaudiya Giti-guccha* (Vrindavan,
India: Gaudiya Vedanta Publications, 2003).

Ramola, Deepak, "12 Life Lessons From A Man Who Has
Seen 12000 Deaths", published 15 May 2016. <http://
projectfuel.in/blog/2016/05/15/12-life-lessons-from-a-
man-who-has-seen-12000-deaths/>. Accessed 29 Aug.
2016.

Rea, Shiva, "Welcome Summer with Shiva Rea's Solstice
Prostration Practice", Yoga Journal [website], published
17 Jun. 2016. <https://www.yogajournal.com/practice/
shiva-reas-prostration-practice-for-summer-solstice-and-
international-yoga-day>. Accessed 9 Aug. 2017.

Rupa Goswami, Shrila, *Bhakti-rasamrita-sindhu* (Gaudiya
Grantha Mandira [website], published 20 Dec.
2003; based on Haridas Das's edition [Navadwip, India:
Haribol Kutir, 1946; third edition, 1979]). <http://www.
granthamandira.net>. Accessed 21 Nov. 2017.

—— "Shri Radhikashtakam" in Shri Shrimad Bhaktivedanta

Narayana Maharaja, *Shri Gaudiya Giti-guccha* (Vrindavan, India: Gaudiya Vedanta Publications, 2003).

—— *Shri Upadeshamrita* (with commentaries by Shri Radha-Ramana Goswami, Shrila Bhaktivinoda Thakura and Shrila Bhaktisiddhanta Sarasvati Goswami Thakura), from Hindi trans. of Shri Shrimad Bhaktivedanta Narayana Maharaja (Vrindavan, India: Gaudiya Vedanta Publications, 2003).

SAKSHI GOPAL DAS, "The Bird in the Cage". <https://parividha.bandcamp.com/album/the-bird-in-the-cage>. Accessed 22 May 2016.

SANATANA GOSWAMI, SHRILA, and SHRILA GOPALA BHATTA GOSWAMI, *Shri Hari-bhakti-vilasa* (with "Dig-darshini-tika" by Shrila Sanatana Goswami), Sanskrit to Bengali trans. by Maha-nama-vrata Brahmachari (Kolkata: Mahesh Library, 1993).

SCHWEIG, GRAHAM M., *Bhagavad Gita: The Beloved Lord's Secret Love Song* (Kindle edition; HarperCollins, 2010).

SHAKESPEARE, WILLIAM, *The Oxford Shakespeare: The Complete Works*, second edition, by Stanley Wells, Gary Taylor, John Jowett and William Montgomery (Oxford: Oxford University Press, 2005).

SHANKARACHARYA, SHRI, *Gita-mahatmyam* (Bhaktivedanta VedaBase 2003, Bhaktivedanta Archives, Bhaktivedanta Book Trust).

SHELLEY, PERCY BYSSHE, "Ozymandias" (first published in 1818), Representative Poetry Online [website], University of Toronto Libraries. <http://rpo.library.utoronto.ca/poems/ozymandias>. Accessed 30 Apr. 2017.

SHRIDHAR GOSWAMI MAHARAJA, SHRI SHRIMAD B. R., "With Pride He Announced: 'It Is the Best Day'" [lecture], Navadwip, 9 Sep. 1983.

Shri Hari Bhakti Kalpa Latika, author unknown (Bhaktivedanta VedaBase 2003, Bhaktivedanta Archives, Bhaktivedanta Book Trust).

"Shri Radha-Kripa-Kataksha-Stava-Raja" in Shri Shrimad Bhaktivedanta Narayana Maharaja, *Shri Gaudiya Giti-guccha* (Vrindavan, India: Gaudiya Vedanta Publications, 2003).

SICULUS, DIODORUS, *Library of History* (trans. by C. H. Oldfather, Loeb Classical Library, vol. 303 [Cambridge, Mass.: Harvard University Press, 1961]: I, 47).

SIMPSON, JOHN (ed.) and EDMUND WEINER (ed.), *The Oxford English Dictionary*, 20 vols (second edition; Clarendon Press, 1989).

VALMIKI, MAHARSHI, *Valmiki Ramayana* (Gaudiya Grantha Mandira [website], published 19 Dec. 2016; based on text entered by Muneo Tokunaga et al., revised by John Smith, Cambridge). <http://www.granthamandira.net>. Accessed 30 Apr. 2017.

Veda-Vyasa, Krishna Dvaipayana, *Brahma-sutra* (Gaudiya Grantha Mandira [website], published 16 Sep. 2005; ed. by Andrés Rodríguez Cumplido and the Grupo de Estudios Clásicos y Semíticos at Universidad Pontificia Bolivariana, Medellín, Colombia). <http://www.granthamandira.net>. Accessed 30 Apr. 2017.

—— *Brihadaranyakopanishad* (Gorakhapur, India: Gita Press).

—— *Chandogyopanishad* (Gorakhapur, India: Gita Press).

—— *Kathopanishad* (Gorakhapur, India: Gita Press).

—— *Kenopanishad* (Gorakhapur, India: Gita Press).

—— *Mahabharata* (Internet Sacred Text Archive [website], from electronic files created by Prof. Muneo Tokunaga of Kyoto; ed. by John D. Smith). <http://www.sacred-texts.com/hin/mbs/>. Accessed 21 May 2016.

—— *Mundakopanishad* (Gorakhapur, India: Gita Press).

—— *Rig Veda Samhita*, ed. R. L. Kashyap and S. Sadagopan (Bangalore: Sri Aurobindo Kapali Sastry Institute of Vedic Culture, 1998).

—— *Shrimad-Bhagavata Maha-puranam* (Gorakhapur, India: Gita Press).

—— *Shvetashvataropanishad* (Gorakhapur, India: Gita Press).

—— *Skanda Purana* (Gorakhapur, India: Gita Press, 1951).

—— *Vishnu Purana* (Gaudiya Grantha Mandira [website], published 11 Dec. 2016; based on Bombay: Venkatesvara Steam Press, 1910). <http://www.granthamandira.net>. Accessed 29 Nov. 2017.

VISHVANATHA CHAKRAVARTI THAKURA, SHRILA, *Shri Vraja-riti-chintamani* (Gaudiya Grantha Mandira [website], published 25 May 2003). <http://www.granthamandira. net>. Accessed 2 Jul. 2017.

WARE, BRONNIE, *The Top Five Regrets of the Dying: A Life Transformed by the Dearly Departing* (Bloomington, Indiana: Balboa Press, 2011).

WILDE, OSCAR, *Soul of Man under Socialism* (1891); published in Oscar Wilde, *Collected Works of Oscar Wilde* (Ware, Hertfordshire: Wordsworth Editions, 1997).

WILSON, EDWARD O., *Consilience: The Unity of Knowledge* (New York: Vintage Books, 1999).

YAMUNACHARYA, SHRI, *Gitartha Samgraha* (Gaudiya Grantha Mandira [website], published 26 May 2003). <http:// www.granthamandira.net>. Accessed 2 Jul. 2017.

THANK YOU...

Pedro Catena for the elegant design and layout of this book; Sudevi Geary for copyediting the manuscript on the bank of the Ganges River in India; Kat Byles for her creative guidance and feedback; James Ellis-Brown for overseeing the final production and printing at Veda Wisdom Books and for all his generous help over many years; Vaijayanti Mala and Ariadna Landman for kindly looking over the manuscript and offering valuable feedback; Catherine Ghosh for her inspiring writings on the *Bhagavad Gita* and Bhakti tradition; Vasanta Das, Dylan Hendrix, Rob Elings and Britt Janssen for their friendship, inspiration and infectious energy; Jagad Mohini Dasi in Escazú, Costa Rica, for opening her home for me to share the teachings of the *Gita*; Edgar Ortiz for kindly inviting me to give seminars on the *Gita* at his beautiful yoga studio, Yoga Mandir; Jeffrey Sweeney and Charles Towle for their friendship, advice and kindness over the past ten years; my wife, Mohini, for her extraordinary qualities and for being a light of inspiration in my life; and all the friends who supported this project along the way. On this sacred journey of the soul, thank you to all.

ABOUT THE AUTHOR

Born in 1975, Simon Haas first became interested in the study of ancient wisdom traditions thirty years ago. As a young boy, Simon studied the sacred writings of India and spent ten years living in temples and monasteries in India. He apprenticed for sixteen years with an elderly master practitioner in the Bhakti tradition, within an unbroken line of teachers that dates back thousands of years.

Simon graduated with honours from the University of Cambridge. Currently, he focuses on making the teachings of ancient India widely accessible to contemporary readers and audiences. He lectures and gives seminars and workshops internationally on the philosophy of yoga and the ancient teachings of India.

Simon is author of the bestseller *The Book of Dharma: Making Enlightened Choices.*

www.simonhaas.com
simon@simonhaas.com